COSTLY MONUMENTS

Barbara Leah Harman

COSTLY MONUMENTS

Representations of the Self
in George Herbert's Poetry

Harvard University Press
Cambridge, Massachusetts, and London, England   1982

Publication of this book has been aided by a grant
from the Andrew W. Mellon Foundation

Library of Congress Cataloging in Publication Data

Harman, Barbara Leah.
    Costly monuments.

    Includes bibliographical references and index.
        1.   Herbert, George, 1593–1633—Criticism and interpreta-
tion.   2.   Self in literature.   I.   Herbert, George,
1593–1633.   II.   Title.
PR3508.H37 1982   821'.3   82-926
ISBN 0-674-17465-8   AACR2

To the memory of
Max and Anna Stern

PREFACE

Writing about George Herbert's poetry, and about the state of literary criticism in the 1950s, Rosemond Tuve expressed a concern that deserves our attention today. She feared what she called "a grasshopper plague of explainers-of-poems"—a plague of critics, really, who would generate readings with hardly a sense of what those readings were for. Of course Tuve was writing a local, polemical essay whose purpose was to undermine the New Criticism, but her words are not less powerful for that. In the face of what can only be described as an extensive critical literature on Herbert, one is left to wonder whether her fear has not become a reality.

In the following pages I hope to suggest that Herbert criticism presents us not with a plague of explainers but rather with a group of remarkable critics whose contradictory readings of Herbert are really a function of their divergent critical beliefs. Herbert's commentators write criticism but they also—wittingly or unwittingly—write theory, and their readings are best understood when both are studied together. My purpose in the Introduction to this book is therefore to uncover the relationship between critical practice and critical belief in the work of some of Herbert's most important critics. I have necessarily concentrated on a handful of these because to have presented more would have strained the reader's patience. But the sample seems to me a telling one. Whether critics do or do not examine their interests, whether they acknowledge or fail to acknowledge their theoretical beliefs, the history of Herbert criticism is nonetheless a history both of those interests and of those beliefs.

To say so, of course, is to point to the dependence of my own work on the critical principles that inform it, and to acknowledge, at the same time, the limits that are its consequence. No critic happily acknowledges these, but such acknowledgments are necessary. This book is not, as its readers will discover, an argument for the unity of *The Temple*, an extended analysis of Herbert's Anglicanism, or even a reading of all of the poems in "The Church." It is rather, as I shall explain more fully toward the end of my introductory chapter, an effort to understand the way a particular problem takes shape, and is worked out, in a central group of Herbert's poems. That problem I take to be the problem of representing the self, and I shall argue in the following pages that the impulse toward self-representation is a powerful one in Herbert's work, and that it is also an impulse thwarted, and redesigned to suit what thwarts it, in enormously complex ways.

My introductory chapter is thus an effort both to make sense of the variety of Herbert criticism and to situate myself within it. But it is also an effort to demonstrate that the questions with which I am concerned—how does the self represent itself in language? what is the value of self-representation? what are its costs?—have always been central to Herbert studies, even when its practitioners have fervently disagreed about the way such questions should be answered.

ACKNOWLEDGMENTS

I have compiled a long list of debts during the years I have been at work on this book: to Allen Grossman, my secret interlocutor in these pages, whose extraordinary questions I am often answering and whose voice I hear throughout; to Sharon Cameron, my friend of many years, whose early essays taught me what it meant to imagine myself a critic; and to Ellen Bassuk, whose insight made it possible for me to teach myself how to write. George Herbert has gathered to him a formidable group of critics, and my intellectual debts to them are recorded in the pages of this book. But I wish to single out, for their ongoing generosity, Stanley Fish, my dear friend and unofficial mentor, with whom I have long tangled to my profit; and Helen Vendler, for whose consideration and intelligence I continue to be grateful. I also wish to thank Stephen Greenblatt, Edward Said, and Patricia Meyer Spacks—whose books have instructed and inspired me, and who have supported this project in so many ways.

Portions of two chapters were first presented as papers to the Cambridge Humanities Seminar, whose members provided me with helpful criticism. I am especially grateful to Michael McKeon whose notes and comments on a particularly troublesome chapter saved me from traveling too long on the wrong path. Versions of several portions of the book have appeared in print: "George Herbert's 'Affliction (I)': The Limits of Representation," *ELH* 44 (Summer 1977), published by the Johns Hopkins University Press; "Fictions of Coherence: George Herbert's 'The Collar,' " *PMLA* 94 (October 1978); and "Herbert, Coleridge and the Vexed Work of Narration," *MLN* 93 (December 1978) published by the Johns Hopkins University Press. The National Endowment for the Humanities, the Mary Ingraham Bunting Institute of Radcliffe College, and Wellesley College granted me (respectively) the funds, working space, and leave time that made the completion of this book possible. Hsaio-ti Falcone, of the Wellesley College Computer Center, and Louise Heim, who prepared the manuscript, instructed me in the complexities of word processing: without their help I would still be sitting at my typewriter.

I also wish to thank my colleagues at the Bunting Institute—especially Maurianne Adams, Mary Anderson, Naomi Harman Chazan, and Nancy K. Miller—for reaffirming my belief in community. And I am grateful to Liz Frank, Sylvia Harman, Marcia Ian, Patricia Joffee, Gail Reimer, Beth Sack, and Carolyn Williams for their enduring interest and friendship. I am also grateful to my father, Sidney Harman, who provided valuable support at times when I particularly needed it.

My final debt of gratitude is to William E. Cain who has read this book in all of its many incarnations, and whose patience, encouragement, and affection have sustained me.

CONTENTS

COSTLY MONUMENTS

INTRODUCTION:
THE CRITICAL CONTROVERSY

When George Herbert Palmer published in 1905 his multivolume edition of *The English Works of George Herbert*, he could hardly have anticipated the outpouring of critical interest that would characterize Herbert studies in this century. In fact, Palmer published his edition precisely *because* he could imagine no audience for it, and in his "Preface" to the *Works*—from which my own title comes—he openly declared: "There are few to whom this book will seem worth while. It embodies long labor, spent on a minor poet, and will probably never be read entire by any one. But that is a reason for its existence. Lavishness is in its aim. The book is a box of spikenard, poured in unappeasable love over one who has attended my life . . . I could not die in peace, if I did not raise a costly monument to his beneficent memory."[1] Palmer's vision of his critical task is, in many ways, extraordinary. To begin with, he understands his project as a compensatory one: the edition is not a testimony to the importance of its subject; it is an effort to restore that subject to visibility, to make the poet, quite literally as it turns out, appear. Indeed, Palmer's response to the fear that his book might "never be read entire by any one" was to endow it with a "lavish" physical life. It is not merely a piece of writing, it is also an expensive (and restorative) ointment ("a box of spikenard"); and it is not merely a work of criticism but also a rich (or "costly") monument. Indeed, the project's very lavishness becomes the means by which the editor gives his poet material life and rescues him from oblivion. The book takes its place as an object in a world both of objects and of living persons: it can be read or not read (like most pieces of writing), but it can also be poured out, continuously and unappeasably, like the costly oil poured out by Mary Magdalene on Jesus' feet; and it can serve, even to those who do not read it, as testimony to the material existence of the poet it commemorates.

But if the project is a compensatory one (monuments stand for invisible or absent persons; if we were in no danger of forgetting them we would not need so carefully to mark their places), there is virtually no suggestion elsewhere in Palmer's work that what stands behind his endeavor is a theory of representation, a belief that his book will stand in place of, and as a substitute for, its missing and undervalued original. Indeed, Palmer's monument does not stand *for*, that is *in the place of*, the poet at all. Instead, it reconstitutes the poet and makes him available to us in what can only be understood as the *living* monument—at once material and fluid—of his work.

For Palmer's method is not a method of representation but of presentation in which the person of the author appears to us in his work as clearly and as vividly as, Palmer might say, we appear to ourselves. When he suggests that his "association of Essays, Prefaces and Groups of poems" may permit the author (he calls him "my poet") "that opportunity for self-portraiture which a prose writer usually obtains in a Life and Letters" (p. xv), Palmer both uses the language of representation and suggests, simultaneously, that portraits *give us persons*. The poems depict stages of a biographical life and, like the editor's analysis of the author's "body, temperament, intellect and religion," they "make him live" (p. 83). Palmer's belief is that, in "grouping the poems in something like a living order," we merely permit the author to appear in his own person. "The series," Palmer declares, "becomes connectedly interesting, almost dramatic." By dramatic, Palmer means that it shows the author acting out his life. "A highly individual personality," he declares, "emerges" (p. 119).

What Palmer really means, then, when he calls his work a costly monument to Herbert's memory, is not that the book portrays its subject (in a world where there are only portrayals), nor that it stands for him in his absence as an admittedly poor second, but rather that, in all of its rich texture, in all of its materiality, it gives us the "veritable experience" of Herbert's world (p. 109). "All art," Palmer declares, "is personal and anthropomorphic" (p. 102). The book is not a representation of life, it is life unmediated by representation: life itself.

I begin with Palmer because he is Herbert's first twentieth-century critic, but also because his edition makes clear the extent to which critical work is a function of critical belief. Palmer, I am sure, would hardly think himself a theorist, and, in the ordinary sense of things, he is not. But his work—like the works of all the critics I shall discuss in this chapter—derives from a set of convictions about the role of the critic and the status of literary discourse, and these convictions are the moving force behind the analysis of Herbert that Palmer gives. In fact, Palmer's *true* reading of the poems is his rearrangement of them, for in his mind the poems speak for themselves. Like the stones in Herbert's altar they seem to declare that "no workmans tool hath touch'd them,"[2] that their editor only gives them an order they already have.

Of course the fact remains that Palmer *is* the presenter of Herbert's "body" and "temperament" as he is also the presenter—and notorious rearranger—of Herbert's poems. But interestingly enough he sees himself only as the instrument by which the poet may be seen. His construction of the life and works is portrayed as a restoration: he puts things "together again" (p. 83) and thereby suggests that he neither takes a position with respect to the materials nor makes a contribution to them. This effacing of the critic's self before the author's is not, of course, at all unusual in literary criticism, but it is both fascinating and troubling in Palmer's work precisely because he bears the name of the author to whom he introduces us:

> When I lay in my cradle, a devotee of Herbert gave me the old poet's name, so securing him for my godfather . . . As I grew, the wisdom hidden in the strange lines was gradually disclosed, and in daily experience,
>
> > *His words did finde me out, and parallels bring,*
> > *And in another make me understood.*
>
> For fifty years, with suitable fluctuations of intimacy, he has been my bounteous comrade.   (p. xi)

George Herbert Palmer's relationship to the "old poet" is that of godson to godfather, and the relationship is an intimate one—so close, in fact, that the poet's words find the godson out and "disclose" their wisdom to him. Palmer even declares that, before he "could well read," he knew the poet's meanings. If he believes in the possibility of unmediated relationships between readers and authors and works, that is in part because—mistaking self-knowledge for knowledge of others—he identifies so completely with his namesake. Palmer's costly monument embodies not only the author but the author's editor, not only the other, but also the self.

The critical procedures and consequences of Palmer's work are, of course, precisely those which the New Criticism existed to overturn. When William Empson theorized, in the eighth chapter of *Seven Types of Ambiguity* (1930), about his own methods and about the relationship of the literary text to its critics and readers, he emphasized the fact that he was not interested either in presenting or in re-presenting the consciousness of the authors about whom he wrote.[3] In fact he suggested, as the New Criticism would generally, that poems are often ambiguous even when poets try not to be, and that poetry cannot be equated with the consciousness of the author who produces it.[4] The movement of attention away from the author and its reinvestment in his "critical principles . . . and [those] of the public he is writing for" (p. 241) seems a small

movement indeed; it displaces the author himself only to rein-
state his "principles." But in generalizing the author (his beliefs and those of his audience are presumably collective and
not particular), Empson means to deprive authors of their
control over poetic meaning, and he begins to refer, in this
chapter, not to authors but to the "mode of action of poetry"
(p. 243), not to readers but to the way "a properly-qualified
mind works" (p. 248) when it is reading the poem.

This double effacement of the writer's and the critic's self is
effacement in the service of the text, and the text is now understood to be an independent entity subject to analysis.
Moreover, the independent status of readers and authors and
texts is reaffirmed in the process of analysis: readers must
"have the power first of reacting to a poem sensitively and def-
initely . . . and then, having fixed the reaction, properly
stained, on a slide, they must be able to turn the microscope
on to it with a certain indifference and without smudging it
with their fingers" (p. 247). Empson's description of the critic-
as-scientist implies an understanding of the poem as speci-
men, as object of analysis. And this understanding is rein-
forced by his belief that criticism's value derives, at least in
part, from its capacity to teach the critic about his own independence both from the text and from the world at large. The
critic's task is the explication of the text, but the text is understood to be outside of and separate from the critic, much as it
is outside of and separate from the consciousness of the author. The critic must be "indifferent." He must not "smudge"
the slide with his fingers. (Nor must it, could the analogy be
turned around, smudge him.) Moreover Empson's defense of
analysis "appeals to the self-esteem of the readers of the analysis, and assume[s] that they possess a quality that is at present much respected. They . . . possess a fair amount of equilibrium or fairly strong defences" and this gives them the "power
of dealing with anything that may turn out to be true" (p. 247).
Empson's point is that the reader who is capable of seeing the
poem as an independent object will be reassured by that capacity—he will know that the fruits of his labor are authentic
ones, and he will also have learned, in the process, about his
own capacity to bear the truth. The method of read-

ing Empson recommends will, he claims, improve his reader's confidence that the world outside of him really is outside of him, and because he will learn at the same time that the world's otherness is no threat to him, he will only have increased his sense of power in relation to it, of mastery over it:

> Such an advance in the machinery of description makes a reader feel stronger about his appreciations, more reliably able to distinguish the private or accidental from the critically important or repeatable, more confident of the reality (that is, the transferability) of his experiences . . . What is needed for literary satisfaction is not, "this is beautiful because of such and such a theory," but "this is all right; I am feeling correctly about this; I know the kind of way in which it is meant to be affecting me."   (p. 254)

Empson's criticism is really, as he suggests here, a method (or "machinery") of description, and what it describes are the reader's "appreciations"—explaining them in such a way as to make him feel stronger about them for knowing what produces them, for knowing how they work. And this in turn improves his confidence both in his own reality ("I am feeling correctly about this") and in the reality of his experiences—improving his belief that the text is, and its effects are, not private or accidental but repeatable, generalizable, and therefore real.

One of the assumptions of Empson's theory is that locked in the grip of self and world, texts are locked in a grip that simplifies. Their release from interfering minds and limiting contexts permits us, he suggests, to see them in all of their originality and complexity. Only the mind that fears such complexity will worry over finding it, and Empson's critic is in no real danger here (he has, it will be remembered, strong defenses). The critic freed for explication is able to describe the difficult and singular "mode of action" of a poem, and this is, of course, the task to which Empson puts himself in the examples of ambiguity to whose explication his book is devoted.

In Herbert's case, Empson turns to an explication of "The Sacrifice" and suggests that the poem is not the work of simple piety one might expect it to be (one in which "the theological system is accepted so completely that the poet is only its mouthpiece" [p. 226]) but is, rather, a poem of "so high a degree of ambiguity" (p. 227) that it is truly "unique" (p. 226). Empson points, for example, to the refrain of Jesus in the last verse—"Only let others say, when I am dead, / Never was grief like mine" (ll. 251–252)—and suggests:

> He may wish that his own grief may never be exceeded among the humanity he pities, "After the death of Christ, may there never be a grief like Christ's"; he may, incidentally, wish that they may *say* this, that he may be sure of recognition, and of a church that will be a sounding-board to his agony; or he may mean *mine* as a quotation from the *others*, "Only let there *be* a retribution, only let my torturers say never was grief like theirs, in the day when my agony shall be exceeded." (Better were it for that man if he had never been born.)   (pp. 228–229)

The poem's vision of Jesus as he whose grief exceeds all other grief and who nevertheless prays that mankind may never suffer as he has, is matched in this analysis by a vision of Jesus as he who invokes his powers of retribution and wishes upon his torturers a grief that surpasses even his own. The passage reflects, moreover, a division even in the attribution of its words—these may be Christ's words, they may be the words men speak about Christ ("Only let others say"), and they may be words men speak about themselves.

Readings like this one lead Empson to conclude that though Herbert is often thought to be "a cricket in the sunshine," it is also the case that one is often "shocked on discovering the habits of such creatures; they are more savage than they seem" (p. 229). And he concludes his essay with the assertion that "Herbert deals in this poem, on the scale and by the methods necessary to it, with the most complicated and deeply-rooted notion of the human mind" (p. 233).

Empson's reading of "The Sacrifice" is a daring, indeed a liberating, one and though much of the analysis seemed wrong-headed to Empson's readers, even his sternest critics found in it things to praise. Empson's most vocal critic was, of course, Rosemond Tuve, who responded to Empson's analysis in her 1950 essay on "The Sacrifice" in the *Kenyon Review*, and later, in an expanded form, in *A Reading of George Herbert* (1952). But Tuve's difficulties with Empson's reading are more complicated than they first appear. The point of most obvious disagreement has to do with Tuve's belief that a poem is "irremediably implicated in its past,"[5] so that what Empson calls features of the poem's originality are really features of its conventionality (a subject to which I shall shortly return). But this problem has its origin in a prior disagreement. For it is Empson's objectivity about and distance from the literary text (the poem-in-itself) that Tuve finds so disturbing. The critic sundered from the text—and from the universe of discourse to which the text belongs—claims in her view a false and unobtainable objectivity. And the text's independence from the reader fosters not a useful attention to the text but an elevation of the critical process itself. "Actually," Tuve declares, "there is no such thing as 'the phrase in itself'. The locution marks a modern critical error, and philology should have taught us all to be wary of it. 'The son stealing from his father's orchard is a symbol of incest', says Empson . . . But to whom? Perhaps it is the answer to this last question which every critic has a responsibility to make clear" (p. 31). Tuve's real point here is that it is precisely the claim that texts are independent of both the critic's present and their own past that occasions this focusing on the critical process: "The same old modern swindle, process substituted for essence, has caught us again. 'How beautiful', we say. A beautiful point, a beautiful analysis, a beautiful instance of modern ideas glimpsed before their time" (p. 20). In the absence of other interests and constraints the critic's methods colonize the poem—so that despite, or indeed because of, his claims to objectivity and distance, the critic becomes the (unacknowledged) authority on meaning.

Tuve's point is a central one. Critical objectivity is impossible. Phrases, and poems, always mean *to* someone, and the critic's assertion of an almost scientific objectivity (no smudging with one's fingers) combined with his refusal to acknowledge, in this case, that he "merely wishes to discover what a poem can mean to him" (p. 31), amounts to a refusal to "acknowledge his paternity" (p. 32).[6] Empson, Tuve claims, is really an authority on meaning-to-himself, but he claims to be the opposite: precisely that critic whose meanings are to be trusted because they refer neither to the consciousness of the author nor to the consciousness of the critic.

Tuve's position is significant at least in part because, although we know her as a historical critic, she does not claim for herself a false or impossible objectivity. Nor, it should immediately be noted, does she claim the opposite. Instead, Tuve sees the possibility of inhabiting (in the case of modern poetry) or of recovering (in the case of seventeenth-century poetry) the world inhabited by literary texts. Her ideal reader is not, like Empson's, sundered from the text and its contexts. He is, rather, a reader whose ignorance has been repaired and who comes to the text knowing "what every literate man once knew" (p. 42). But Tuve is not interested simply in creating or recreating a class of informed readers. Instead, she means to dismantle precisely those barriers between reader and text erected by the New Criticism—and she accomplishes this by *blurring* the very distinction between outside and inside upon which the New Criticism was founded. Since "the areas of human ignorance shift and change quite as much as do human needs or human knowledge" (p. 21), it is impossible to say, at any moment, what is outside and what is in, and it is surely the case that "much that is 'outside' a poem to us was well inside it to our forefathers . . ." (p. 27). But the difficulty is not simply that the boundaries between inside and outside are difficult or impossible clearly to mark—for if this were the case we might, with greater labor and dedication, succeed in clarifying the terms for critical work. Instead, Tuve's real point is that they *should not be marked*, because to mark would be to participate in the division and fragmentation of the universe. Insides and outsides, phrases and contexts, poems and historical worlds—once we acknowledge their separation from one another we accede to that sense of isolation and disconnection which threatens to define for us life in modern times.

Instead, Tuve imagines the world of "resemblances," "connexions," and "complexes of meaning" (p. 63) to which poems belong, and to which readers may gain or regain access. In fact, Tuve agrees with Aristotle that the "capacity to see resemblances" is a true "sign of genius" and she suggests that when we call Herbert an original poet we should do so because "his connexions . . . reawaken into new life whole complexes of meaning" (p. 63), "generate new energies out of their intercourse with each other," and stir "all the old depths into motion" (p. 80). What she values is not the newness and originality which must, of necessity, separate poet from reader, but rather that "acceptance of universal meaningfulness" and of the "systematic correspondences between meanings" which underlies not only Herbert's poetry but "all writing or other arts in the symbolic mode" as well as the " 'aesthetic' province" and "the great religions" themselves. "It is a mode of approach to truth which," she declares, "Western culture has slighted for some centuries, with bitter results . . ." The history of all modern poetry with any claim to be called great is the history of our attempt to recapture this way of viewing the world" (pp. 104–105).

In other words, Tuve's antagonism to Empson's reading is an antagonism to his critical method, a function of her belief that our modern situation is a "desperate" one because it substitutes investigation and comparison for "aesthetic activity," anthropology for literature, scientific analysis for "belief" (p. 105). "If our poetry dies," she declares, "and our understanding of the great symbols with it, it will be because we gave them not our belief but only our respectful critical attention" (p. 106).

The disagreement between Empson and Tuve includes, but is not limited to, a disagreement about the ontological status of the poem (is it free-standing or implicated in its past?). And it is really, perhaps centrally, a disagreement about the sort of world each critic would like to inhabit. Empson's world is—at least in Tuve's view—a broken one. It begins by separating writers from poems, poems from critics, critics from historical worlds, and it ends by fragmenting experience itself: poems become ambiguous, writers' minds divided. Tuve's world, on the other hand, is a seamless one—or it could be if critics would "repair" (p. 42) the ignorance that afflicts them.[7] Critical work is healing work but in its absence, Tuve fears,

> there must follow a grasshopper plague of explainers-of-poems, for the child who has never met mystery in the shape of the inexplicable Trinity or symbols in the Alpha and Omega of the church window becomes the adult who does not know there are any mysteries until he is beaten on the head by the tragedy of his own destiny. The idea that there are no mysteries has not served the twentieth century very well. Seeing no riddle to be read, men cut the whole world into a vast image of the shadow cast by their own selves. Poetry cannot be got whole into that image.   (p. 108)

If the world Tuve imagines is a seamless one, it necessarily follows that all of the divisions about which we have spoken are resolved into common ground by her method. Poems are *of necessity* not original creations (how could they be?) but are, rather, embodiments of the contexts, conventions, and traditions to which they belong. They are not creations out of nothing but fashionings, or refashionings, of old materials; they do not invent knowledge anew but rather reawaken it. And if the separateness and originality of the poem and its writer are relinquished in this view, so is the separateness and originality of the critic: "It would be a happy thing if the criticism of poetry could escape what seems to be the universal aftermath of throwing out 'absolute' standards of value—the setting up of ourselves as the Absolute. A large position to relinquish, but insecure. If we could bring ourselves to this act of self-conquest, it is possible that we should gain back a past" (p. 98). The critic becomes, as Tuve says elsewhere, a truly "sensible" man (p. 109), a "humble part of all he sees" (p. 107), and he does this by becoming, as it were, a feature of the landscape he describes. Tuve continues: "What kills good poems through the eye is a reader's blind determination to see nothing in the round world but himself ... In poetry which uses symbols, uninformed reading amounts to a kind of mumbo-jumbo, and poetry becomes a fetish rather than a mode of insight into the depths of life; modern criticism is indeed not innocent of this fetish-worship" (p. 109). It is also, Tuve might have added, not innocent of this *self*-worship, for as Tuve has been suggesting all along, the fetishizing of the poem-in-itself is not only a function of the way we separate it from its origins, but also of the way, separated from them, the critic and his methods inevitably occupy the territory these exclusions have cleared away.

Tuve's vision of the critic's self as the "humble part of all he sees" (or of the reader as the self who "already knows" [p. 61]) is also, and inevitably, a vision of the poet's self as similarly humble. Indeed, exactly like the critic, the poet's self becomes, in Tuve's view, a part of the Christian landscape of meanings to which her work always refers us. This poet/self "uncovers rather than creates . . . meanings" (p. 104), and serves as more than "the mere conveyance of a particular individual's emotion at a given time, that thin subject with which modern readers have come to be content, but which Herbert throws to one side . . ." (p. 117). Tuve's contempt for the modern interest in the poet's "self"—divided or otherwise—is of a piece with her contempt for his originality, and both attest to the belief, everywhere expressed in her writing, that such interests are a form of fetishism and imprisonment. They lock us into a fiction of the poem's independence, and submit us to the reality of the critic's domination; they lock us into a meager present, and our poems into a reified past:

> It is in so far as they are figurative that poems most defeat time, and carry the weight of meanings which illuminate us here and now . . . Without this the poem stays locked, an historical curiosity, in the time that gave it birth. But although this is what makes any good poem contemporaneous with the reader, it is paradoxically not very likely to happen until he has freed himself of his own "here" and his own "now" and entered into the full purport of alien images, like an inhabitant, as to the manner born. (p. 111)

The abandonment of the critic's present leads, "paradoxi-cally," to his recovery of it, because when he frees himself "of his own here and now" he gains, for his losses, entry into a world once alien but now familiar. He becomes not a visitor but "an inhabitant" of a superior world; and he lives in it as if born to it.

In an important study published two years after Tuve's *Reading*, Joseph Summers, in *George Herbert: His Religion and Art*, would essentially affirm the positions I have here attrib-uted to Tuve—declaring, for example, that "interpretation can be 'relevant' only when based on an understanding of the work within its cultural context."[8] And although Summers did not declare membership in that symbolic (and aristocratic) universe so central to Tuve's critical vision, he was neverthe-less committed (as she was) to a serious treatment of Herbert's Christianity—"without either apologies to the gods of inevita-ble progress, an air of bravura, or an attempt at literary psy-choanalysis" (p. 27)—and to an equally serious description of the ordering processes at work in Herbert's poems. But Sum-mers claimed that the "poetic and critical revolution" which gave us the Donne revival, and the revival of Metaphysical po-etry generally, was really a revolution based on skepticism (p. 24). Despite "Eliot's conception of 'unified sensibility,' the divided mind was held at a premium, and the 'tortured indi-vidual' was as highly esteemed as ever in English criticism" (p. 25). It is easy to see Empson's 1930 reading as part of this critical trend, though Summers also points out that the New Critical fascination with division and fragmentation produced, for the most part, a view of Herbert as "an inferior John Donne," a poet of " 'narrower experience' " and " 'comfort-able limits' " (p. 25).[9] It was not until the period after the Sec-ond World War that an alternative set of values made possible not so much a rereading of Herbert as a re-evaluation of him. As Summers suggests, "the best of recent criticism places a growing emphasis on order rather than tension and conflict as a literary value, and it recognizes that the wholeness of a poem does not necessarily demand a sharply fragmented texture" (pp. 26–27).[10]

The commitment to order is everywhere evident in Summers' reading and it surfaces, first, in his balanced view of Herbert's religious life—the life of "the middle way" (p. 73):

> Herbert might be considered a "mystic" of the *via positiva:* . . . valuing union with God, but expecting it fully only with death; expressing joy for the moments of the presence of God and lamentations for the days of His absence; believing that the proper service of God consists in works as well as acts of devotion; conscious of sin but striving to conform to the will of God; seeing in the world and human life images which show God's creation and His love.   (p. 69)

The range of Herbert's experience is not, in this view, either narrow or limited; nor, of course, are the experiences presented here those of a tortured individual. Joyful and sorrowful, committed to a service of both works and acts, conscious of corruption and yet capable of working toward his own reformation, Summers' Herbert is not comfortable but instead complex—and not divided but instead balanced. Moreover this middle position on religious matters is significant because "proper worship," Summers argues, "resulted in an ethical and spiritual ordering of the worshipper's life" (p. 76). In other words, a balanced and orderly view of religion—of the relationship, for example, between devotional works and devotional acts, or between personal corruption and holiness—would lead one to the balanced and orderly conduct of religious life which would itself be productive of personal order. Of course the ethical and spiritual ordering which is the outcome of proper worship is itself the outcome of that prior sense of order to which Summers openly declares an allegiance in the early pages of his book. This commitment to order and the "ordering process" (p. 74) organizes and balances Summers' view of Herbert's Anglicanism, and of his ethical and spiritual life as well. But it also organizes his understanding of the self in Herbert's poems, and his view, finally, of the nature and status of the work of art.

Initially, Summers' view of the self, like his view of Herbert's Anglicanism, is characterized by that sense of balance which distinguishes so many of his descriptions. But while his view is productive of some final sense of order, it does not lead us toward a coherent or enduring vision of the self. Summers declares that "most of the older writers conceived neither that personal experience was the only sanction for reality nor that personality must be 'refined out of existence'" (p. 95)— thereby separating himself both from biographical criticism of the sort exemplified by Palmer and from that effacement of the author's self characteristic of the New Criticism. And when Summers comes to describe his own sense of Herbert's struggles with the problem of self he too appears to take a middle position: "The self-centred pride which wished to take 'the way that takes the town' must be firmly rejected; but equally firm must be the rejection of a sense of unworthiness so strong that it prevented all action" (p. 45). But the rejection of a sense of unworthiness is important in Summers' view not because it rescues the self from oblivion, but because an excessive sense of unworthiness "stemmed from a continuing preoccupation with 'self' which, carried to its logical conclusion, implied a distrust of God's grace—that grace which could create 'of earth and clay' a sacred vessel. Herbert's acceptance of Bemerton and his ordination as priest were marks of the submission of self in both those senses" (p. 45). In other words, Summers rescues the self precisely because to fail to do so would be to reconstitute self-importance on the other side of the issue. This passage, with its emphasis on double submission—the relinquishment of self-centered pride, and also of that sense of unworthiness which merely perpetuates the self's preoccupation with itself—suggests that Summers' "balanced view" is weighted rather heavily in the direction of what Tuve called the immolation of the individual will. In fact, as Summers later suggests, reiterating his opposition to the sort of criticism practiced by Palmer and to the view of self represented by it,

> Any attempt . . . to find either in individual poems or in the sequence of the poems a direct revelation of autobiography will fail, for the primary purpose of the poems

was not what we understand by self-expression. There is, of course, no question of sincerity. The poems are a "picture" of meticulously observed spiritual experience. But the self to Herbert was not the valuable thing which it became to a later age ... "Personality" and personal experiences were of interest to the poet exactly in so far as they could be profitably used in the objective creations which were his poems.   (pp. 84–85)

Like the passage before it, this passage emphasizes the importance of self-submission, though Summers here suggests that, because the self "was not the valuable thing which it became to a later age," self-relinquishment is not so much a problem as it is a resource. The issue is less one of relinquishing the self with difficulty and more one of using the self as raw material for creation. Here, as in the previous passage, submission is submission *in the service of* something else, so that what we lose on the one hand we gain on the other: the loss of self is compensated by the production of "the objective creations which were [Herbert's] poems."

What lies behind this view is the commitment to order with which, in our discussion of Summers, we began. Indeed, Summers' view of the self, or of self-expression, or of personality (what Tuve calls "that thin subject with which modern readers have come to be content") is essentially an unhappy one: the self appears to be the origin of disorder and alienation, of corruption and division, though there is no question about its capacity to be transformed. The creation of "a work of decency and order ... was the privilege and duty of every Christian" (p. 84) and it is Summers' sense that the relinquishment of the self in the service of those "objective creations which were his poems" would bring about exactly that transformation—of disorder into order, of the idiosyncratic and alien into the collective and shared, of the private into the corporate—which a vision of decency and order would require. In a sense, the sacrifice of self on behalf of these creations is also a sacrifice which generates community of feeling—as Summers reminds us, Herbert "desired that his poems should be burned if [Nicholas] Ferrar did not think they could be turned to the advantage of any dejected poor soul" (p. 84)—so that the loss of the individual self is intimately tied to its reconstitution as a member of the collectivity. Summers is not interested in preserving the idea of self in Herbert's poems, despite his insistence that the self has work—the work of literary creation—to do. Instead, his writings suggest, like Tuve's, that the self is a "thin subject" readily relinquished on behalf of poetic creation, where poetic creation is not a *representation* of self but rather a *substitute for it*—a substitute, moreover, that betters the thing it replaces precisely because the relinquished self is let go not on behalf of that which serves the self but on behalf of the sort of creation that serves others and fosters community. In fact Summers' now-familiar notion that Herbert's poems are "hieroglyphs"—that their forms "image" the subject they undertake to explain (p. 135)—is intimately connected to the communal vision that I have been describing: first because hieroglyphs do not exist as "a total mystery or as an isolated beauty, but as a beauty and mystery which were decipherable and related to all creation" (p. 145); and second because his sense of the poems as constructions is part and parcel of his belief that the poet-as-maker contributes to the world by *making order* in it: "Herbert's distinction lies in his successful development of the conceptions that the entire poem could be organized around a hieroglyph and that the poem itself could be constructed as a formal hieroglyph . . . The hieroglyph represented to Herbert a fusion of the spiritual and the material, of the rational and sensuous, in the essential terms of formal relationships" (p. 145).

But the emphasis in Summers' view on the materiality of Herbert's poem is, again, not a reflection of his belief in the power of the self to embody itself. It is, rather, a reflection of his understanding that the poems exist at the expense of self, and that they imitate not the self's order but rather God's: "The composition of the poems, imitative as they were of that ordering which he had experienced and which he hoped to experience again, was the act of the craftsman who shapes the imperfect materials of his own suffering as well as joy into a pattern symbolic of the divine order" (p. 94). When Summers suggests, then, that "the emphasis [in Herbert's poems] is on construction rather than pilgrimage" (p. 89), he gives voice to a belief everywhere evident in his work: that it is the business of the poet to make "formal relationships" (p. 145) out of informal ones, to transform wanderers into composers.

Summers' view is important in its own right, but it becomes especially interesting when seen in relation to Stanley Fish's controversial work on Herbert published in 1972 in *Self-Consuming Artifacts: The Experience of Seventeenth-Century Literature*. Fish calls Herbert's poems "self-consuming artifacts" because he sees them as a "graduated series of 'undoings' ": "the undoing of the perceptual framework in which we live and move and have our (separate) beings . . . the undoing of the self as an independent entity . . . [the] undoing of the poem as the product of a mind distinct from the mind of God" (pp. 157–158).[11] He might easily have asserted, contra Summers, that the emphasis in Herbert's poems is *on pilgrimage rather than construction*—because what interests him is the *process* by which the "undoings" he describes are accomplished, and because it is in the nature of such undoings that the poems in which they occur become not "hieroglyphs" but "vehicles of their own abandonment" (p. 158). If it is true, as Fish suggests, that "to read many of Herbert's poems is to experience the dissolution of the lines of demarcation we are accustomed to think of as real" (p. 164), then those lines which permit us to pick out the text—what we once might have called that "intransigently visible manifestation" (p. 189)—undergo dissolution as well. If Summers' work stresses the materiality of the text, Fish's work points—thematically and theoretically—to its dissolution.

Fish's reading of Herbert is, moreover, both a function and a reflection of his theoretical interests and concerns—expressed on occasion in the course of his chapter on Herbert in *Self-Consuming Artifacts* and developed more fully in an appendix to the book entitled "Literature in the Reader: Affective Stylistics." Unlike his predecessors, Fish does not countenance the effacement of the reader's self before the literary text—either on behalf of a quasi-scientific objectivity (Empson) or on behalf of a vision of community in which readers share both a group of texts and an understanding of them (Tuve and Summers).[12] Instead, Fish rescues the reader both from the critical oblivion to which New Critical doctrine would consign him, and from the critical community into whose collective body Tuve and Summers would absorb him. Fish legitimizes—indeed he privileges—the critic/reader, describing his method of analysis as one "which takes the reader, as an actively mediating presence, fully into account" (p. 384).

It is the intention of Fish's method to shift attention away from words on the page and to locate it, instead, in readers. And it is the intention of his method to alter our understanding of the ontological status of texts. For the legitimation of the reader is the legitimation of someone defined by the *activity* he undertakes—an activity which, in certain respects, has no boundaries because it never needs to "come to the point" (p. 410). A critical discourse centered upon reading is by nature less stable than one centered upon a belief in the determinacy of the artifacts it examines, and this is precisely the point Fish wishes to make. By focusing "on the reader rather than on the artifact" (p. 400), and by declaring that it is the business of the critic to analyze *"the developing responses of the reader in relation to the words as they succeed one another in time"* (p. 387), Fish means to dispel our illusions about the objectivity of the literary text. If meaning is not something to be found *in* texts but is, rather, *"an event"* (p. 389) in the reader's experience, then it becomes possible to *embrace* the assertion—uttered as a warning by Wimsatt and Beardsley—that, as a consequence of an interest in readers' responses, "the poem itself, as an object of specifically critical judgment, tends to disappear."[13]

The disappearance of the literary text is, however, not only a theoretical fact—a description of the text's ontology—it is also a thematic fact—a description of what the poetic speaker learns about his text in Herbert's poems. He learns, first, that it is impossible to rely on the perceptual framework in which (necessarily) he functions, that the lines of demarcation which permit him to distinguish this from that are mobile instead of stationary. He also learns that the most unreliable line of demarcation is the one between the self and God, a discovery which leads him to the understanding that his belief in "the self as an independent entity" is really an illusion. And he learns, moreover, that as there is no self independent of God,

there is no "poem as the product of a mind distinct from
God," a discovery which leads him to abandon the idea that he
is the author of his poems or that they are a representation of
his integrity. The speaker, Fish declares, is "forced to give up
more and more of the resources (and claims) of his art until in
the end he is reduced to silence, and disappears" (p. 191).
Moreover, Fish suggests, when "Herbert writes himself out of
his poems (weaves himself out of the sense)," the unweaving
is a "letting go" in which "both [the poems] and the consciousness whose independence they were supposedly asserting give themselves up to God . . ." (p. 190). The end result of
Fish's sequence of dissolutions—this into that, the self into
God, the poem into His word—is the disappearance as material entities both of the self and of the literary text.

In Fish's view aesthetic and personal lessons coincide, moreover, with theological and cultural ones: if "the action taking
place" in many of Herbert's poems is really the discovery
"that God's word is all," a discovery Fish calls "*self*-destruc-
tive" (pp. 156–157), that action is "a point of doctrine" and a
"seventeenth-century commonplace" as well (p. 156). Tuve
and Summers would of course agree with Fish about the relationship between poems and their cultures, though both
would have said that the relationship was a happy one for
poets and readers alike: it did not so much endanger the self as
restore it to its humble (but proper) place in the collectivity. In
the work of all three critics the disappearance of the self is tied
to the self's implication in a founding culture, but in Tuve and
Summers that culture is seen as an enabling one—it promotes
shared values, democracy, and the life of the community—
while in Fish the culture is seen as a disabling one—it disables
speech and selfhood, and it "renders superfluous the mode of
discourse and knowing of which [the poems] themselves are
examples" (p. 158).

In many respects Helen Vendler's *The Poetry of George Herbert*
(1975) serves as a corrective not only to Fish's dark vision of
the double fate of poems and selves, but also to the view,
shared with Fish by Tuve and Summers, that a "poem is irremediably implicated in its past" (Tuve, p. 23). In Vendler's
view Herbert's poems are not "limited in meaning to any dog-

matic content"[14]—though she does not suggest that the self triumphs over "religious means" (p. 79) by ignoring or exempting itself from them. Vendler argues, in fact, that Herbert "seems to have existed in a permanent reversible equilibrium between the two extremes of tradition and originality, diffidence and protest, the filial and the egotistic" (p. 56). And while she often refers to the individual in laudatory terms— pointing, for example, to the "winning sweetness of the speaking self" (p. 72)—she also suggests that the self alone, in Herbert's "The Windows" for example, can be "watrish, bleak, & thin" (l. 10) unless "doctrine joins with life, colors join with light, [and] both combine and mingle" (p. 82). But Vendler does argue that what is important in Herbert is his "originality in transforming his sources, in reinventing his topic" (p. 55) and she thus differs from her predecessors in at least two significant ways: first, in suggesting that sources are indeed subject to transformation; and second, in suggesting that transformations of the sort she describes are in fact achievements. In Summers and Tuve this is simply not the case: sources, traditions, and cultural auspices all have the status of defining and limiting origins, and it is, moreover, important that they do: in a world of shared symbols, beliefs and values, the self that cannot be differentiated can never be alone. When Vendler claims that persons (or poets) rewrite traditions she suggests, as Empson did, that they have the capacity to separate themselves from the culture—that they have value apart from it, and power over it. If, in Summers and Tuve, the self's inextricable relationship to the past transforms individuals into a collectivity, or if it causes, as Fish would say, the dissolution and disappearance of the self, then the self's capacity for separation, and its corresponding ability to rewrite or transform tradition, is a sign, in Vendler, of the power and persistence of the individual self, and of the triumph of that originality which is its hallmark.

Vendler's purpose, then, is to provide her readers with "an explanation in personal terms, an additional scrutiny of poetic (not religious) means" (p. 79), and her attention to the interests and claims of the poetic self derives from a larger commitment to all selves whose "fidelity to truth" is remarkable. In

Vendler's view the traits of a good poet are the same as those of a good person, for both ask themselves "Is this what I feel? Is this what I mean? Am I permitting myself illusions?" (p. 7). Herbert's attention to these questions, his "resolute unwillingness to take the world for granted," and his corresponding commitment to "plumb every appearance for its significant and original reality" (p. 6) are responsible, in his poetry, for a phenomenon Vendler calls "the reinvented poem"—the poem whose most distinctive feature is its "provisional quality," its persistent and "self-critical" rethinking (p. 25) of its own *donnés*, its "constant reinvention of [its] way" (p. 27): "[Herbert's] poems are ready at any moment to change direction or to modify attitudes. Even between the title and the first line, Herbert may rethink his position. There are lines in which the nominal experiences or subjects have suffered a sea-change, so that the poem we think we are reading turns into something quite other" (p. 25).

Unlike Fish's self-consuming artifact, whose alterations are all "undoings," Vendler's reinvented poem is a "reinvention . . . [that] unfolds toward its final form" (p. 30)—so that to reinvent is not to "weave [oneself] out of the sense" (Fish, p. 198), but rather to *recreate* the sense and thereby to refine both the sense and the self it continues to present. And to reinvent is not to undo the self, but, persistently, to revise and perfect it. Such "aesthetic victor[ies]" (p. 233) are, moreover, spiritual victories as well. A good ending transforms a religious commonplace ("the received idea, the cliché, the devotional triteness") into a religious truth, but it also "yield[s], finally, a picture of the self wholly itself, individual, unique and original" (p. 285). Vendler's work charts a path of retreat out of the desperate situation Fish describes, identifying speaker and poem so completely that a good ending redeems not only the reading experience, but the speaker himself. When poetic speakers "make intimacy from dogma" (p. 206) or when "lyric truths" subvert and reshape "homiletic effort" (p. 173), then good poems, and good persons, triumph together.[15]

When Barbara Lewalski declares, in the foreword to *Protestant Poetics and the Seventeenth-Century Religious Lyric* (1979), that her "argument proceeds by extrapolating from contemporary

Protestant materials a substantial and complex poetics of the
religious lyric" and "by considering what and how each [indi-
vidual seventeenth-century poet] drew from the common
stream," she argues, once again, that poets are defined by—
Vendler would complain that this limits them to—the dominant view of the culture in which they live and from which,
like a "common stream," they draw.[16] But Lewalski's view is
also a "revisionist" one: she proposes a specifically Protestant
poetic to counter the Augustinian renunciation of art described by Stanley Fish and others, and she proposes a specifically Protestant view of typology and meditation to counter
the Ignatian and Salesian models set forth in Louis Martz's *The
Poetry of Meditation* (1970). First, she declares, we must take account of the Bible's priority and centrality, for in this "milieu,"
"the Christian poet is led to relate his work not to ineffable
and intuited divine revelation, but rather to its written formulation in scripture. The Bible affords him a literary model
which he can imitate in such literary matters as genre, language, and symbolism, confident that in this model at least the
difficult problems of art and truth are perfectly resolved"
(pp. 6–7). Lewalski's emphasis in this passage is on the Bible as
"written formulation"—as art and writing—and also on its
function as a model for Protestant poets. Reformation belief in
"the one sense of scripture" led, she argues, to a heightened
attention "to the tropes and figures of scripture as the very vehicle of the Holy Ghost" (p. 77), and this provided sanction for
the use of figures and tropes in poetic texts. Indeed, the Holy
Ghost was himself "a magnificent poet" and the evidence for
this is "the glorious excess of figurative language, the proliferation of metaphor and figure that pervades the texture of
God's literal Word" (p. 85). Furthermore, the Bible was a
"compendium" of genres and kinds and (in the Book of
Psalms, for example) a compendium of forms as well:

> meditations, soliloquies, complaints, laments for tribula-
> tions, prayers for benefits, petitions against adversaries,
> psalms of instruction, consolations, rejoicings, praises of
> God for his glory and goodness, thanksgivings to God for
> benefits received, triumphs celebrating God's victories

over his enemies, artful acrostic poems, ballads, pastoral ec-
logues, pastoral songs, satires, elegies, love songs, an epithala-
mium, dramatic poems, tragical odes, heroic odes. (pp.
50–51)

Lewalski's view of the centrality of the Reformation Bible,
combined with her view that, in the seventeenth century, the
Bible was seen as both a literary text and a compendium of
such texts, leads her to argue that, in the Bible, Protestant
poets found sanction for their own activity: "Far from eschew-
ing aesthetics for a rhetoric of silence, or a deliberate anti-
aesthetic strategy, these poets committed themselves to forg-
ing and employing a Protestant poetics grounded upon scripture, for the making of Protestant devotional lyrics" (p. 7).

The Protestant poet's relationship to the Bible is not, moreover, limited to his use of it as a model for his own (literary)
activity. The Reformation emphasis upon "the application of
all scripture to the self," and the corresponding invitation to
"perceive the events and personages of Old and New Testament salvation history not merely as exemplary to them but as
actually recapitulated in their lives" (p. 131), meant that individuals *personalized* Scripture: they saw themselves as "the
stage for the enactment of the typological" drama (p. 141).
Moreover, in Protestant meditation, a similar process of per-
sonalization occurs. In Ignatian or Salesian meditation "the
meditator typically seeks to apply himself to the subject [of
the meditation], so that he participates in it; he imagines a
scene vividly, as if it were taking place in his presence." But
"the typical Protestant procedure is very nearly the reverse:
instead of the application of the self to the subject, it calls for
the application of the subject to the self—indeed for the subject's location in the self" (p. 149). What Lewalski means by
this is that the individual Christian meditator must think of
himself—of his own body—as the scene of action, as the location for the scriptural events upon which he meditates. And he
must also understand that scriptural events and texts *apply to*
him, *mean* him, and that he must therefore focus "upon his
own response to them and upon their significance for his salvation" (p. 171).

Protestant Poetics suggests, then, that the Reformation emphasis on the centrality of the Bible and on the belief that all Scripture must be applied to the self, combined to provide a double sanction for the poet and the poet's text. The Bible authorized the production (by imitation) of other literary works, and it also privileged the person—here the person of the poet—by making him not only the *agent* of inscriptions but also the *ground* of inscriptions. He was the one who generated texts in imitation of the founding text, and he was the one in whose body the scriptural story was enacted (p. 150)—the one to whom it "applied" (p. 149).

I shall return, shortly, to a discussion of these views of the poet's relationship to Scripture, but I wish first to emphasize the fact that, in Lewalski's reading, seventeenth-century history, theology, and culture are *hospitable to* and *sponsoring of* individuals and individual texts. In Herbert criticism as a whole the commitment to an analysis of poems in their cultural contexts has often coincided with the *devaluation* of persons—as though the turn toward history and culture were necessarily a turn away from individual human persons. It has also coincided, on occasion, with the devaluation of the literary text—which becomes, in Rosemond Tuve's work, part of a larger symbolic network, and which cannot, in Stanley Fish's analysis, sustain the "illusion" of its independence. Lewalski's work privileges both human persons and human texts, but it does not do so either by exempting them from doctrinal constraints (Empson) or by assigning to them the power, and the privilege, of overcoming constraints (Vendler). What Lewalski's writing suggests is that the dichotomy between individuals and cultures is a false dichotomy; but her work also perpetuates a notion with which, in the work of Tuve and Summers, we are already quite familiar. Like these predecessors, Lewalski assumes that culture determines the possibilities for selfhood and textuality—though in her case, because the description of culture has changed, the possibilities for selfhood have also undergone transformation. When Lewalski establishes the priority and centrality of the Bible in the Reformation she also assumes that poets are *necessarily* led to "associate [themselves] straightforwardly" with it (p. 4). The Bible is not only central,

its centrality makes it a model, and models must be copied—
so that the relation of persons to Scripture is assumed to be a
harmonious one and, in the end, a relation of identity. The
idea of the Bible as a "compendium," and the discovery of the
multiplicity of genres and kinds in the Psalms, authorizes, explains, and "encourage[s] just such a collection of lyric poetry
as we find in Herbert's 'The Temple' " (p. 51): "Luther declared that the Psalms record the emotional history of all the
faithful . . . Among English Protestants also we find this notion
and this language everywhere" (pp. 42–43). And as the Bible is
"source and model" (p. 13) for poetry, so doctrine generally is
a "detailed chart" or "map" for seventeenth-century English
Protestants (p. 14). Doctrine sets down and elaborates the
terms for personal life and the elaboration is at the same time
a prescription.

Lewalski's presentation of the theological contexts in which
Protestant poets function makes an important contribution to
our knowledge, but the absence in her work of an argument
for literary influence—for the way in which poems take
"sources" for "models"—is extremely problematic. When
Lewalski suggests, for example, that the "Song of Songs is so
named because it surpasses, and supplies the quintessence of,
all the biblical lyrics" (p. 71), or that biblical genres and kinds
are "totalities whose completeness and whose truth is in part
manifested by exhausting the possibilities of expression"
(p. 70), she means to provide evidence of the Bible's power as
a literary model, but her words argue *against* a theory of harmonious imitation. After all, the model she describes is characterized by its *pre-emptive* power: it "exhausts" rather than
furnishes possibilities for "expression," and it does so precisely because it is a "totality," because it does supply the
"quintessence." If the Bible is a sponsor and ally, it is also, it
seems, an opponent over against which, around and through
which, poetic speakers are forced to move. Indeed the complexity of the relationship between personal and scriptural
stories can hardly be overemphasized, and Lewalski's material
is often more suggestive of this than her analysis would
openly admit. She describes the poet as agent and generator of
stories: his productivity is sanctioned by the prior existence of

scriptural agents and tales. But she also describes him as the one to whom Scripture must be "applied": he is the "stage for the enactment of the typological movement from type to anti-type" (p. 141) or he becomes the "embodiment of the subject" upon which he meditates (p. 150). But the contradiction between these two roles—agent of inscriptions; container, object, or ground of inscriptions—makes the point. The Bible may sanction literary productivity, but what it also sponsors (in this view) is a writer whose agency is immediately subverted by the discovery that he is not only the writer but the written-upon. Lewalski takes both points as evidence of the fact that Protestant poets personalize Scripture—they take *up* writing and they take writing *to* themselves—but she might easily have seen them as evidence of the fact that the Bible provides a model for activity only to subvert activity, that it transforms subjects into objects, embodiers into embodiments.

Now if this is the case, then the complexity of the model itself means that there are more possibilities for action and reaction than Lewalski's uniform assertions would have us believe. Indeed one of the problems with theories of influence is that the "source" materials they bring forth must themselves be interpreted before they can be declared to be the origin of anything else, and the interpretation and elaboration of the model is as fraught with difficulties as the interpretation of the materials which are said to derive from it. Lewalski means to revise our medieval, Anglo-Catholic, Augustinian views and she is, in many ways, successful in doing this (there should no longer be any question about the importance of reading seventeenth-century poets in light of their specifically Reformation sources); but the materials she brings before us are clearly in need of further interpretation themselves. Moreover, the complexity of the "model" and the corresponding difficulty of establishing it as an unambiguous "source" is related to an issue of equal, if not greater, importance. There is no direct argument, either in Lewalski or in Summers or in Tuve, for the power of models completely to determine the scope of the works that derive from them. Lewalski claims that doctrine is a "detailed chart" and a "map" for seventeenth-century Protestants, but, as we have already seen, the charts and maps are often complex and contradictory, and their "details" are often difficult to read. Furthermore—and this is the point I wish to stress—even in the absence of contradiction, the absolute hegemony of models would still need to be established. In Rosemond Tuve's work the force of the sponsoring culture is declared to be complete, but Tuve is engaged in the creation of an ideal universe whose very ideality consists in the fact that it excludes division and conflict. There is no inside to distinguish from an outside, no speaker to distinguish from a context, no critic to distinguish from a text: all are absorbed into a world of universal and systematic meaningfulness, a world whose members become, when they learn to speak the language, a class of made aristocrats who inhabit their new country as if "to the manner born." The attention, in Tuve and Summers, to inherited and shared meanings, and the dismissive attitude expressed in their work toward that origin of idiosyncratic meaning—the self—combine to make an investigation of the writer's position with respect to cultural materials impossible.

I do not want to argue that we should stop attending to cultural models. I only want to suggest that we must consider the *multiple* ways in which models have force, and the extent to which they cover—and fail to cover—the field. For in the face of historical criticism, one is often inclined to assert, as Empson did in his rejoinder to Rosemond Tuve (*Kenyon Review*, 1950) that "surely Herbert did not feel himself shackled by tradition to this extreme degree; and if the scholar is allowed to cut down the meaning of every poem to that of a previous poem there will be a considerable change in the literary scene." "I am reminded," Empson continues, "of an Emperor of China, who returned a poem to its author with a somewhat embarrassed air and said 'But surely there is no such poem?', meaning that he could not recall the classical poem which it must be presumed to imitate."[17]

Empson's point is an important one. If cultures define in every respect the literatures to which they give rise, then writers can neither contribute to, nor alter, nor shape traditions. Nor can they oppose them, struggle with them, make space within them, reject them. In the presence of a text whose meaning deviates from that of a previous (that is, sponsoring) text, one would simply be left to declare, "Surely there is no such poem," or "Surely there is no such writer," or "Surely there is no such self."

In many respects Empson is Vendler's true forebear: he champions the poem as an original work, and champions the writer as its individual agent. No mere transcriber of, or slave to, a tradition, the author, he assures us, writes works which do not so much participate in, as deviate from, their sources—and this deviation is itself a sign of value. Vendler's work takes its Empson seriously—concentrating on the ways in which poetic speakers transform the intractable materials of doctrine and specify toward originality both traditional materials and the selves who voice them. But if Tuve and Summers and Lewalski err in viewing doctrine as prescription, Vendler errs in overestimating (and overvaluing) the individual's power to refine and discard prescriptions. The poem in which "homiletic effort is subverted by the lyric truths that keep reshaping it" is declared to be a successful poem, and the one in which doctrinal materials appear to have displaced personal ones is declared to be a poem "of less than adequate insight or inspiration" (p. 197). Vendler's interest in and commitment to the individual self offers a corrective to the view that cultures determine selves, but it does so by privileging the self and devaluing the culture in ways which merely reverse the terms in which we have so far been interested. Instead of describing seventeenth-century theology as a powerful force in the shaping of persons, literary texts, and ideas, Vendler describes it as a collection of clichés and devotional commonplaces with which Herbert must somehow deal. And instead of empowering culture, she then empowers the self, which is charged with the rigorous and demanding task of rewriting, redefining, and specifying the culture toward an original conception. Vendler reverses, in other words, the relationship of persons to cultures with which many Herbert critics are concerned—assigning to selves precisely the power to model and determine culture which, in Lewalski, culture is given to model and determine the self.

I want to assert, along with Vendler (and Empson), that writers do indeed rewrite cultural materials—or that they write their way into them, around them, and through them. But I also want to argue that the process works in the opposite direction as well: cultural ideas exert a force on persons—sometimes an extremely visible one, sometimes a less apparent and less easily describable one—and they shape the self's power to write itself up, out of, or, as Herbert says in "Jordan (II)," "into the sense" (l. 14). What we need, therefore, is not a description of the way persons determine cultures, or culture determines persons, but rather an analysis of the dialectical relationship between the two.

Fish's chapter on Herbert in *Self-Consuming Artifacts* promises, at first, to offer just such an analysis. The chapter is subtitled "The Dialectic of the Self in Herbert's Poetry" and the dialectic Fish has in mind is the one between "an egocentric vision which believes in, and is sustained by, the distinctions it creates, and the relentless pressure of a *resolving* and *dissolving* insight" (p. 157). The "egocentric vision" believes in the existence of independent material entities—the place, the self, the poem, the mode of discourse—and Fish points both to the entities and to their materiality himself. In his discussion of "The Altar" he openly declares that the "most notable and noticeable feature of the poem is, of course, its shape" which "call[s] attention to itself as something quite carefully made; and at the same time [calls] attention . . . to the skill and ingenuity of the maker, who is presumably the poet" (p. 207). In fact Fish often invokes the relationship between writing and embodiment: he refers to speech as "the vehicle of self"; he describes the writing of poetry as "egregiously *self*-assertive"; and he claims that poems would "seem to be irreducibly there, an intransigently visible manifestation of the self" (p. 189). But it is the purpose of his analysis to narrow to nothing, and finally to deny, the distinctions to which—but only for the sake of argument—he begins by pointing. When pressed to describe what is really going on in Herbert's poems Fish does not offer a dialectical description at all: rather, he claims that "to read Herbert's poems is to experience the dissolution of the distinctions by which all . . . things are" (p. 158).

Moreover, the argument for dissolution is at once an argu-

ment for the hegemony of a seventeenth-century doctrine—
"thy word is all"—and an argument for a twentieth-century
theory—affective stylistics. The connection between the two is
a crucial one (Fish might say an obvious and necessary one),
but while the import of the theory and that of the doctrine are
similar, they do not, in fact, function in the same way. The
doctrine, for example, dissolves lines of demarcation (between
this and that, between the self and God) and this leads to a
dissolution in which the speaker can distinguish neither himself nor his poem from "the deity whose omnipresence he has
acknowledged (thy word is *all*)" (p. 157). But while the theory
also denies the objectivity (really the objecthood, the materiality) of literary texts, the text doesn't dissolve because the
lines of demarcation between it and other objects have eroded.
It dissolves because its formal features, and therefore its status
as a material object, are declared to be illusory and are flatly
denied. The doctrine and the theory have, in other words, a
significant point of contact—their shared belief that "the poem
itself, as an object of specifically critical judgment, tends to
disappear"—but in Herbert's poems the doctrine is one to
whose truth we must be led through argument and debate. In
Fish's theory, however, *all* poems are self-consuming artifacts:
they don't disappear at the end of a dialectical process in
which their materiality is discovered to be an illusion; they
disappear as soon as the reader is persuaded that poems are
not words on a page but rather events in the reader's experience. And if this knowledge has been acquired in advance of
the reading experience then no dialectic need be called in to
produce it.

And yet it is precisely at those moments when the dialectical
process fails to convince us of the doctrine's truth that Fish
calls upon his theory to make the point. He imagines "an unsympathetic reader who would object that the conclusion of 'A
True Hymne' [in which God writes '*Loved*'] is only a trick. It
is, after all, Herbert, not God, who writes 'Loved.' " And because he does, the reader might say, neither Herbert as writer,
nor the poem as his production, can be said to disappear into
God's word. Fish replies:

On one level, of course, this is an unanswerable objection, but on another, it is beside the point. The crucial question is, where exactly does a poem live, on the page or in its experience? If one answers "on the page" the fact of heavenly intervention has no more authority than any other formal feature in the poem, and in these terms "Inspiration" is unprovable; but it is provable if one turns from the form of the poem to the form of the reader's experience; for if, in that experience, a sense of God as maker displaces our awareness of Herbert, then it is not too much to say that the poem is no longer his, or ours.   (p. 202)

Fish here declares for reading as over against writing, and by so doing answers the question of his unsympathetic reader (of course Herbert wrote "*Loved*") by declaring it not so much unanswerable as uninteresting. The scene of action and interest is the *reader's experience*, in which "God as maker" usurps the authorial role.

There is, on one count, no arguing with Fish here: in poems whose very business it is to deliberate questions of authorship, it hardly makes sense to deny that the questions are serious ones merely by pointing to the author's name on the title page. But Fish's view is also a problematic one because he makes his doctrinal point—the poem is a discovery that God's word is all—by making a theoretical one—when one turns from the page to the reader's experience, then all poems cease to be *objects* of ownership and no poems are any longer "ours."

This slipping from doctrine to theory is significant because, as I have already suggested, while the doctrine engages in a dialectical struggle with "an egocentric vision which believes in, and is sustained by, the distinctions it creates," the theoretical base of Fish's work strongly suggests that *there is no dialectic* either of the text or of the self.[18] The objectivity of persons and of poems is an illusion, and the nonmaterial status of both is a *prior* ontological fact. It is perhaps for this reason that in the four categories into which Fish divides Herbert's poems the outcome of all activity is the same: places, selves, poems, modes of discourse, all suffer dissolution. And the end result of dissolution is the silencing of voices, the relinquishing of authorship, the letting go both of persons and of texts.

What Fish's work cannot, thus, account for is the difference *between* poems—even the difference between poems in his own (different) categories. In one important group of Herbert's lyrics (Fish includes in this group "The Temper," "Evensong," and "Church Monuments"), our experience is indeed an experience of "the dissolution of the lines of demarcation we are accustomed to think of as real" (p. 164). But when Fish moves to his next category and discusses poems in which "the self as an independent entity" (p. 158) is at stake, dissolution is often not an ongoing issue at all but rather a late phenomenon which, when it points to the collapse of the self, does so only after having sustained the "illusion" for the greater part of the poem. What Fish's reading cannot do—especially when it slides from doctrine to theory—is to account for the way in which the self as an independent entity not only *dissolves* but *persists*. Poems like "The Holdfast," "Miserie," "The Pearl," and "The Collar" are indeed dialectical, but they are so precisely because they both threaten and preserve the experiences about which they speak. What is striking about the poems Fish describes in his second and third categories (poems whose subjects are the undoing of the self as an independent entity, and of the poem as product of a mind distinct from God) is *not* only that they end in the silencing of the speaker's voice and the relinquishing of his authorship (what Fish calls, after Herbert, " 'making . . . no thine and mine' " and " 'mak[ing] *the action fine*' (by making it not mine)" [p. 158]), but that they are at pains to elaborate, to embody, and to conserve the very self whose silencing they also record.

As I have already suggested, Fish's reader-centered theory is often brought in to dissolve the text when doctrinal dissolution has not completed the task. But Fish also suggests that certain poems are simply failures and they are thus named when they do not, as it turns out, succeed at self-consumption. In his discussion of "Jordan (I)," for example, Fish declares: "But if the 'immolation of the individual will' is the *desideratum* here as elsewhere, the poem fails, since its effect is to call our admiring attention to the very individual will of the speaker"

(p. 195). The question of course is this: *does* the poem fail? Or
is there, finally, no way to accomplish the "immolation" to
which (speaking, here, in Rosemond Tuve's words) Fish
points? Is there no way to make selves, and to make texts, disappear?

There is, of course, a way. There are, indeed, numerous
ways, and some of them have already been described in these
pages: by inscribing the text into a cultural framework from
which, then, it cannot be distinguished; by asking how the
culture disables textuality and selfhood; by viewing the text as
an "event" or an "experience" and thus denying its materiality
and that of the self who makes it. The difficulty posed by these
methods, however, is that they cannot account for the *persistence* of selves, nor, I would argue, for the materiality of texts. If
the effect of "Jordan (I)" is to "call . . . attention to the very individual will of the speaker" perhaps we ought to attend to
that effect instead of dismissing the poem as a failure. For if we
need to understand the dialectical relationship of persons to
cultures, then we also need to ask how, or in what ways, the
relationship between them comes to be *embodied*. For writing is
always an act of embodiment; it is the means by which selves
and their experiences come to be represented, and the representations writing gives us are therefore "telling." They do not
tell us everything; they tell us what can be put in writing, what
can be made manifest, and this, it seems to me, is one of the
things we look to writing to learn.

My view is, in this sense, a materialist view, for it asks:
What does writing make visible to me in the work I am reading? What experiences does it represent? What does it exclude
or declare not representable? If discursivity (as Michel Foucault has called it) or textuality (as Edward Said and others
have called it) is what characterizes writing, then we do not
simply want to ask how the culture disables speech and selfhood but also how, and in what ways, it enables them.[19] The
questions, of course, belong together and the mistake is not in
asking the former but in not asking the latter. If there is, then,
an assumption which, more than any other, underlies what I
am saying here, it is this: as long as there is writing something
has found its way into representation, and as long as there is

writing both selves and texts are before us. The questions we must therefore ask are these: How does the self represent itself in writing? What enables representation? Are there ways in which the representation of self is compromised or disabled? And, if so, what are the consequences of this disablement? How, in other words, is the self formed, deformed, shaped, "fashioned"?[20] In Herbert's poems, I shall argue, self-representation is a central, and also a vexed, enterprise, and one of the clearest signs of this fact is the rather frequent appearance, in the poems I shall discuss in Part One, of a speaker who bears a disturbed relationship to his own account: who offers a story and then denies his identity with it in the end ("The Collar"); who tells a story without realizing until the conclusion that he is its subject ("Miserie"); who claims he has no tale to tell and then disclaims the disclaimer ("The Reprisall"); who proceeds with a lengthy account of experience only to conclude that it is inappropriate, or ineffective, or destructive to tell tales ("Affliction [I]"). In these poems—let us call them "collapsing poems"—speakers both protect and dismantle their own narratives, and because they do they raise questions about the values we attach to stories, about the costs we are willing to support in order to maintain them, and about the difficulties we undergo when stories fail to represent us in traditional ways.

If collapsing poems construct a space in which the human story can be told, they also relinquish, in the dramatic gestures with which they conclude, the very space they are at pains to create. In Part Two I shall explore the ways in which the representation of experience still occurs even when the construction of coherent narrative accounts is no longer an option. In the poems I consider here dissolution is, as Fish argues, truly the order of the day—but dissolution characterizes some, not all, of the poems in *The Temple*, and in these, moreover, speakers perform dissolution in public *as an act of embodiment*: they understand that coherent representations of experience are problematic, but they *represent* the self in the very process of dismantling those representations.

Herbert's poems also consider the ways in which personal stories can be rewritten as biblical stories (see my Conclusion), a process which permits persons to align themselves with accounts for whose existence there is greater sanction. In typological poems biblical stories rewrite privileged personal stories—first as Old Testament accounts, then as New Testament accounts, and finally as episodes in sacramental history—and these successive rewritings inscribe the speaker's story within an ever widening field. That field is the Bible itself, understood first as narrative and then as historical account, and the speaker's identification with it provides access to representation in ways unavailable to the speakers of collapsing poems. If interpretation is subversive there—it undermines invulnerable images of the self—here interpretation is constructive—it undermines invulnerable images but it subjects the self to rewriting before our eyes. In this final section I shall consider the ways in which the abandonment of personal stories and their alignment with biblical texts both solves and complicates the problem of self-representation which these pages exist to explore.

In certain respects, then, this book mediates between the opposing views of its predecessors: like Empson and Vendler I wish to demonstrate the ways in which persons make space for themselves and their works within the context of tradition, but like Tuve, Summers, and Lewalski I also believe that doctrines, traditions, and cultural commonplaces are contexts in which literary works must be read. Lewalski suggests, in opposition to Fish, that cultural and doctrinal beliefs are sponsoring of, not threatening to, the self, and once again the truth seems to lie between the two positions: they are neither completely enabling nor fully disabling. The questions we must ask are how, and under what circumstances, and at what expense, and for how long, and in what ways, do persons and cultures negotiate the representation of the self?

I have, in one sense, left my first critic, and George Herbert's first twentieth-century critic, behind. But Palmer's work is interesting to me precisely because he also sees writing—both his own writing and Herbert's—as a kind of embodiment.[21] He calls his work "a costly monument" because he means it to mark the absence of his author in so grand a way that no one will be able to miss him. And though he feared that even this effort would not succeed in bringing George Herbert before us, he nevertheless invested both his "long labor" and his name in the project. Palmer's work becomes problematic, of course, when his monuments stop being monuments and start being persons, so that what looks like an act of representation quickly becomes an act of incarnation in which the made quality of the text before us—its character as discourse, as textuality—vanishes, and the text is transformed into that "living record" about which Palmer was so fond of speaking. But I have taken Palmer's words for my title because, in other respects, they speak to the nature of the literary work as I am trying to describe it here. Texts are monuments because they make appear what does not otherwise appear—or, at least, what does not endure as appearance. I am not suggesting, as Palmer does, that they make persons appear, that they give us (as Vendler would sometimes have it) the inner, speaking self. I am suggesting, rather, that they present experience to us in whatever form experience *be presentable* and that they therefore encourage us to investigate both what we can and cannot see, what is put before us and what is not. Palmer imagined that his monument—like Herbert's poems—brought the biographical person before us. I am suggesting that texts make available to us that part of experience which manages to be subject to representation, to embodiment in writing—and that such embodiment does not give us historical persons but rather gives us what can be said of them. Not the self, but the self made manifest in writing.

Palmer's monuments are also "costly," and this is suggestive of several things. First, it suggests that writing is an enterprise to which expenses are tied—the expense of labor for one, and the expense of time for another. But "costly" also suggests that monuments exist "at the expense of" other things—at the expense, I would argue, of those features of the self and of experience that are not presentable, or that fail, for whatever reason, to gain representation. In this sense, a costly monument asks us to consider what it stands in the place of—what it makes invisible, what it keeps at bay, what it hides. And, finally, Palmer's monument is costly because it is "rich"—rich in texture, rich in density, richly embodied—and it is of course to this final meaning that I subscribe, because it speaks to the materiality of selves and texts with which, in the following pages, I shall be concerned.

part one

FICTIONS OF COHERENCE

chapter 1

"SO DID I WEAVE MY SELF INTO THE SENSE"

One of the first things I am doing when I begin to speak is insisting, in a new way, upon the fact that I am present. Even when my primary intention is to convey information or begin a conversation I can hardly do so without at the same time informing you that I am here or perhaps reminding you that I am still here. When I speak, then, I also make an implicit demand upon you—I demand that you attend to me. And so I make myself conspicuous when I talk—sometimes with your sanction and sometimes without it—and regardless of what else my words mean they almost always mean that.[1]

The beginnings of speech, in ordinary experience and in poems, illustrate the varying degrees of a speaker's interest in being counted present. Donne's secular speakers, for example, though celebrated for the drama of their opening words, are not always eager to appear. Pressed beyond endurance and impatient with their audience, they speak only long enough to silence those who would threaten their safety and privacy. "For Godsake hold your tongue, and let me love," cries the speaker of "The Canonization," and the speaker of "The

Sunne Rising" abuses that "Busie old foole" in hopes that it will depart and permit him to return to his lovemaking.[2] Speech in these poems interrupts the interrupter—and the speaker chooses silence again when outside interference has been neutralized or transformed.

Of course the fact is that Donne's lovers, for all their reluctance to appear, experience isolation as a special version of centrality: as long as they cannot see anyone else they can perpetuate the fiction that they are the only persons in the world. It is because interrupters threaten their convictions about centrality that speech becomes important—used in the service of persuasion, it transforms the threat of being crowded out into a guarantee of being singled out and saved. By the final lines of "The Sunne Rising" the speaker has stopped banishing and has begun inviting:

> Shine here to us, and thou art every where;
> This bed thy center is, these walls, thy spheare.

> (ll. 29–30)

And initially angry about interruption, the speaker of "The Canonization" is transformed at the end into someone who, instead of silencing the intrusive world, summons its collective voice. Of course the collective voice is scripted by the speaker, and its only concern is with the speaker and his lover: it invokes them, begs them, seeks to be like them (ll. 37–45). In the end, then, speech performs the same function as silence. It constitutes a world in which nobody else is present or in which nobody else counts. And so speech, even when it is a second-order experience, has saving powers nonetheless.

More frequently, speech in poems represents a positive *desire* to be conspicuous. The speakers in Donne's sacred lyrics, for example, find privacy both isolating and threatening, and here speech becomes a way of insisting upon one's presence in a world that seems far more hospitable to death and disappearance:

> I dare not move my dimme eyes any way,
> Despaire behind, and death before doth cast

Such terrour, and my febled flesh doth waste
By sinne in it, which it t'wards hell doth weigh.

("Holy Sonnet," ll. 5–8)

The world's monumental hostility is no secret in Donne, and speech serves as a temporary hedge against it. As long as the speaker of this sonnet can continue to speak he can "sustaine" himself another hour (l. 12)—or perhaps long enough to clarify the terms for escape from an annihilating present.

In Herbert's poems the speaker's situation is often less desperate than that of the speaker in Donne's *Holy Sonnets*, but speech does serve a similar function for both: it becomes a vehicle for self-manifestation in a world otherwise inhospitable to self-manifestation. It allows the speaker to provide for himself what Hannah Arendt has called, in another context, "the space of appearance"[3]: "With word and deed we insert ourselves into the human world, and this insertion is like a second birth, in which we confirm and take upon ourselves the naked fact of our original physical appearance . . . This beginning is not the same as the beginning of the world; it is not the beginning of something but of somebody, who is a beginner himself" (pp. 176–177). To speak is to *will* one's birth (to have a "second birth"), and to *consent* to the life of the body (to "take [it] upon ourselves"). Speech is an act of inauguration, and what it inaugurates is the self.[4]

But the speakers of Herbert's poems often make use of a language they also reject—so that the importance of speaking, and the difficulties associated with it, are analyzed and explored at once. In "Jordan (I)," for example, the speaker declares:

Shepherds are honest people; let them sing:
Riddle who list, for me, and pull for Prime:
I envie no mans nightingale or spring;
Nor let them punish me with losse of rime,
    Who plainly say, *My God, My King.*

(ll. 11–15)

And in "Jordan (II)":

> As flames do work and winde, when they ascend,
> So did I weave my self into the sense.
> But while I bustled, I might heare a friend
> Whisper, *How wide is all this long pretence!*
> *There is in love a sweetnesse readie penn'd:*
> *Copie out onely that, and save expense.*

(ll. 13–18)

These two poems have a common theme as well as a common form: they enlist the traditional language of secular literature only to dismiss it in the end—the first poem by returning to a simpler form of praise (the speaker takes his words from the Psalms), the second by permitting the speaker's voice to be usurped by a more reliable and a thriftier one, a voice that can dismiss the poem's first two stanzas as just so much "expense." Both poems, in addition, point to the dangers inherent in practicing the verbal arts: one risks getting lost in language, losing one's self or one's purpose or both. They suggest, in other words, that speech and writing are problematic activities and their conclusions emphasize the virtue of relinquishing the literary enterprise altogether.

But poems about not writing poetry, like speeches about not speaking anymore, rarely succeed in putting the effort entirely out of mind. The "Jordan" poems arrive at their conclusions at the end of some fifteen or more lines of exposition, and they seem more successful in raising and recording the ambivalent feelings of their author than they do in putting them to rest. The rhetorical questions of which "Jordan (I)" is composed—

> Who sayes that fictions onely and false hair
> Become a verse? Is there in truth no beautie?
> Is all good structure in a winding stair?

(ll. 1–3)

> Must all be vail'd while he that reades, divines,
> Catching the sense at two removes?

(ll. 9–10)

—readily answer themselves in the negative, encouraging us to dismiss both fictions and their needless complications. But while we condemn, along with the speaker, the winding stair and the sense caught at two removes, we necessarily participate in them as well—because the poem gives elaborate expression to the very tradition it would have us reject. It is a simple fact, in "Jordan (I)," that there *is no poem* if we attend only to the final words. And if we take to heart the instructions offered in "Jordan (II)" we will not read it again. And yet, of course, "Jordan (I)" and "Jordan (II)" remain: it seems we need to read them in order to know that we need not read them. So while the poems send us back to a reduced or minimal sort of speech ("plain" in one case and narrow—or at least not "wide"—in the other), their very presence stands as a contradiction of those instructions, suggesting that the representation of experience has virtues that cannot be ignored.[5]

One of those virtues is that representation brings before us not only the world but also the self—so that the competition in "Jordan (I)" between elaborate and simple language may also be seen as the competition between a fully articulated self and an extremely abbreviated, or underrepresented, one. But while "Jordan (I)" is merely suggestive of such ties between language and world and self, "Jordan (II)" makes their connection explicit.[6] In the poem's first two stanzas the speaker describes the process by which, in his effort to write of heavenly joys, he becomes more interested in the actual *business* of representation than in its object. And in the last stanza he identifies his enthusiasm for writing with an hitherto unacknowledged interest in the representation of the self.

To praise "heav'nly joyes" is, in stanza one, the speaker's stated intention, but his pleasure in this activity is quickly displaced by his pleasure in writing itself:

> When first my lines of heav'nly joyes made mention,
> Such was their lustre, they did so excell,
> That I sought out quaint words, and trim invention;
> My thoughts began to burnish, sprout, and swell,

> Curling with metaphors a plain intention,
> Decking the sense, as if it were to sell.
>
> (ll. 1–6)

The search for "quaint words" and "trim invention"—and for
the ingenuity and elegance they display—marks the shift from
an interest in language as service to an interest in language as
craft. But one of the curious things about "Jordan (II)" is that it
suggests a growing separation not only between the writer and
his object (his words no longer exist on heaven's behalf), but
also between the writer and his work:

> Thousands of notions in my brain did runne,
> Off'ring their service, if I were not sped:
> I often blotted what I had begunne;
> This was not quick enough, and that was dead.
> Nothing could seem too rich to clothe the sunne,
> Much lesse those joyes which trample on his head.
>
> (ll. 7–12)

The speaker's thoughts "burnish, sprout, and swell" in stanza
one, and in stanza two they develop faster than he does—so
that if he fails to manage well on his own (if he is not "sped")
his self-multiplying thoughts will be there to come to his aid.
Writing, as he portrays it, not only effaces its (divine) subject,
it also appears to outpace (and displace) its author, who gives
himself over to his craft.

Or so it seems until the poem's final stanza. For here the
speaker comments on his own description and calls the process he has just described a self-inventing, not a self-effacing,
one. To "work," "winde," and "deck" is necessarily to "weave
[one's]self" not out of but "into the sense" because the man
who works and winds mixes his labor with the world—in
order to make, in this case, a complex, rich, elegant, and inge-
nious object out of an otherwise "plain intention." Moreover
the speaker of "Jordan (II)" takes pride in the product of his
labor, in his capacity to produce lines which match in "lustre"

and "excel[lence]" their object, and he is therefore not only the maker of a thing but also its proud possessor. Whatever sense he may once have had that his work was independent of him, these lines assure us that, at least in this sense, it is not. He is, after all, both craftsman and owner, and as the craft elaborates itself it necessarily bears, and elaborates, his image. So does he weave himself into the sense.

When Christ interrupts in the final lines of the poem and reminds the speaker of his original purpose (praising heavenly joys), he also points to the fact that this purpose has been covered over by, and lost in, writing:

> But while I bustled I might heare a friend
> Whisper, *How wide is all this long pretence!*
> *There is in love a sweetnesse readie penn'd:*
> *Copie out onely that, and save expense.*
>
> (ll. 15–18)

But Christ really interrupts, substituting his words for the speaker's words and recommending that the speaker copy out a sweetness already written elsewhere, in order to suggest that the speaker weave himself back *out* of the sense. This un-weaving would be accomplished by the recognition that Christ's voice had priority over all personal voices and that one's proper work was not the original work of (conscious or unconscious) self-construction, but rather that secondary or derivative work of reproducing an already written text. "*Copie out onely that, and save expense,*" says the friend, knowing, of course, that saving expense is *necessarily* a way of weaving one-self out of the sense, since labor and expense are what weave the self into the sense—and into the world—to begin with.

Christ also recommends that the speaker give himself over to writing in a completely different way—as duplicator or scribe—and one might even say that this is what the speaker tries to do. He writes a past tense poem in which he reports for two stanzas a position with which he no longer identifies, and he records, as well, the usurpation of his writing by someone else's (Christ's) voice: in fact he quotes or copies that voice just as it recommends that he give up the labor of original writing and the elaboration of self which is its consequence. But the speaker does not, to begin with, *only* copy Christ's words. "Jordan (II)" is a retrospective poem, and the speaker who reports what Christ said also reports (and thereby conserves) what he himself thought and said as well. If he is a copier, he is not a copier of *"sweetnesse"* alone. Moreover the final lines suggest that the speaker should copy a sweetness *"readie penn'd,"* that he should copy, that is, from Scripture—though this solution is not one whose enactment we witness in the course of the poem itself. Indeed, "Jordan (II)" is more successful in recording a dilemma than in solving one, and it thus anticipates a practice characteristic of collapsing poems. For while it demonstrates just what it means (improperly) to weave oneself into and (properly) to weave oneself out of the sense, it offers no *demonstration* of what it would mean to copy out a *"sweetnesse readie penn'd."* The possibility of a new kind of writing is indicated in the final lines, but it has no representation in them.[7]

"Jordan (II)" presents us, then, not with the disappearance of the self, nor with its uncomplicated persistence, but rather with a central dialectic: first, it describes a method of composition (weaving oneself into the sense) in which self and text are identified with each other and appear, as it were, simultaneously; and then it describes a method of decomposition (weaving oneself out of the sense) in which the alliances of self and text are broken as the speaker is understood to have presented an experience with which he no longer identifies. Furthermore, the poem illustrates that process of displacement or evacuation in which the self acknowledges and gives way before the power and priority of another voice. And it points, significantly, to the *possibility* of a new kind of writing (duplication or copying) in which self would not be entangled in sense because the speaker who presented anything at all would offer not his own, but someone else's, work to begin with.[8]

In pointing to the dialectical nature of "Jordan (II)" I mean to emphasize something which should, in the course of the following chapters, become increasingly clear: self-representation is a vexed enterprise in Herbert's poems and we do the poems a disservice if we fail to acknowledge in them both the appearance of the self and the curtailment of the self's appearance, both the attachment of the self to language and the acknowledgement by the self that the domain of language is not always one over which he has full control. The displacement of the speaker's voice by Christ's voice is one sign of this, and the complex instructions offered by that voice are another.

A similar dialectic is also at work in "Frailtie," whose speaker, like the speaker of "Jordan (I)," begins with the knowledge that secular language is the language of deception:

> Lord, in my silence how do I despise
> What upon trust
> Is styled *honour, riches* or *fair eyes;*
> But is *fair dust!*
> I surname them *guilded clay,*
> *Deare earth, fine grasse* or *hay.*

(ll. 1–6)

But the speaker's efforts to rewrite (or "surname") the world prove themselves ineffective. When he looks about him in stanza two he still sees "both Regiments":

> The worlds, and thine:
> Thine clad with simplenesse, and sad events;
> The other fine,
> Full of glorie and gay weeds,
> Brave language, braver deeds.

(ll. 7–12)

Moreover the struggle between the two is no simple competition between noise (Babel as babble) and silence, between glory, gaiety, and brave language on the one hand, sad events and plain language on the other. For while this opposition is surely important in suggesting the speaker's wish to avoid the confounding of sense associated with Babel, the poem's last stanza suggests that the real problem in "Frailtie" is much like the one described in "Jordan (II)":

> O brook not this, lest if what even now
> My foot did tread,
> Affront those joyes, wherewith thou didst endow
> And long since wed
> My poore soul, ev'n sick of love:
> It may a Babel prove
> Commodious to conquer heav'n and thee
> Planted in me.

(ll. 17–24)

Those who build the Tower of Babel want to "make a name for themselves" and they build their tower in order to do precisely that: they fear the loss of identity that would come from being "scattered abroad upon the face of the whole earth" (Gen. 11:4), identified neither with each other, nor with a place, nor with a great deed. The building of the tower gathers them into one body and the tower identifies (makes a name for) them. In fact having a language, and being a people, are intimately tied to making one's name through one's deeds: "Behold," says God, "they are one people and they have all one language; and this is only the beginning of what they will do" (Gen. 11:6).

What the citizens of Shinar "do" is what Herbert would call weaving themselves into the sense. And when God comes down and confounds their language what he does is to weave them back out again: they do not understand each other; they can no longer build their city; and they are dispersed across the face of the earth. The speaker's fear that "brave language" and "braver deeds" "may a Babel prove" is first a fear that the desire to make something—to weave or write or build—is really a desire to make a name for oneself, to be inappropriately present in one's work, as the builders of Babel were. And it is then a fear that the punishment for this desire is the scattering and confusing of sense suffered by Babel's builders and, as I am here suggesting, by Herbert's speakers as well. Brave language is, in other words, a double-Babel, because it builds the self into the sense and then is subjected to that painful un-building—that multiplication and confusion of sense—which inevitably follows.[9]

If the ending of "Jordan (II)" suggests that the speaker who makes a name for himself must find a way of speaking (or writing) which points away from the self (copying Scripture is such a way), the ending of "Frailtie" suggests—as, I will argue, the ending of "The Collar" does—that the man who relies on language as a means of self-construction will find that language can be wrested from him and used against him—to multiply and complicate the sense until it no longer spells *his* name at all. The fear expressed in "Frailtie" is, in other words, a fear which might prevent or forestall the representation of self—though it is mostly a fear which speakers, here and else-where, both have, and hold at bay.

In "The Holdfast," for example, the speaker provides dra-matic evidence of his desire to gain access to sustained—and sustaining—speech, but the poem also illustrates that gaining such access is a difficult matter indeed. Though the speaker of "The Holdfast" is aggressive about self-assertion, he is blocked three times by an interlocutor who is clearly less in-terested in rejecting the speaker's admittedly flawed positions than in rejecting, and finally pre-empting, speech itself:

> I threatned to observe the strict decree
> Of my deare God with all my power & might.
> But I was told by one, it could not be;
> Yet I might trust in God to be my light.
> Then will I trust, said I, in him alone.
> Nay, ev'n to trust in him, was also his:
> We must confesse that nothing is our own.
> Then I confesse that he my succour is:
> But to have nought is ours, not to confesse
> That we have nought. I stood amaz'd at this,
> Much troubled, till I heard a friend expresse,

> That all things were more ours by being his.
> What Adam had, and forfeited for all,
> Christ keepeth now, who cannot fail or fall.

The boldness of the poem's opening assertion is its point. These lines are meant to be unassailable and the speaker therefore presents them as though his situation existed without alternative. He never questions the assumption that God's decree is a strict one, and he has, as a consequence, no real sense that an alternative response might be possible, no sense that it would be appropriate to bring to God's decree anything less than "all" his strength and determination. The speaker also presents himself as someone fully committed to the successful accomplishment of his plans: he neither thinks about observing nor promises to observe; instead, he boldly threatens.

The interlocutor, however, objects to the speaker's declaration and without offering any elucidation summarily dismisses his opening words and the world they confidently represent: "But I was told by one, it could not be" (l. 3). He does not point out that it was inappropriate for the speaker to threaten to observe, and he never explains that the speaker operated, at his peril, under the old rather than the new dispensation. But once the interlocutor speaks, the aggressive stance of the opening lines is radically compromised, its claims and threats are defused, and the idea that there is a relationship between the confidence with which statements are made and their capacity to sustain themselves quickly comes to an end.

Of course in one sense the dissolution of the speaker's position is both predictable and inevitable. Despite the fact that he proposed it with great authority his stance was surely a defective one: it is simply inappropriate to threaten God with obedience. But the problematic aspects of the speaker's second proposition are less easy to discern. When the interlocutor declares that, even if he can't threaten to observe, the speaker can still "trust in God to be [his] light," the speaker assumes that the interlocutor is offering him an alternative position, one he might adopt to take the place of the one he abandoned:

"Then will I trust," he replies, "in him alone." But the interlocutor declares this response as unacceptable as the first when he responds to the speaker this way:

> Nay, ev'n to trust in him, was also his:
> We must confesse that nothing is our own.
>
> (ll. 6–7)

Herbert's critics have often commented on the terrible unfairness of this exchange: the speaker accepts correction and adopts the terms of the interlocutor's counteroffer, but as soon as he does so the interlocutor declares those terms unavailable. But this speaker is not someone who accepts correction gracefully. Rather, he attempts to recover the territory he has lost by rewriting counteroffers in ways which suggest that he is not really adopting a corrective view at all but initiating a new and more acceptable one himself. Here he transforms an assurance that, in the absence of a position, comfort and aid will be forthcoming, into a suggestion that, deprived of one position, he is free to construct another: if he can't threaten, he may entrust. Furthermore, he rewrites the interlocutor's words and transforms them into first person speech—as though to suggest that he is not so much accepting correction as working at self-invention, not so much rewriting as writing anew. The insistence on speaking for himself, on saying it over again in the first person, is central, and it is also accompanied by the inclination to alter the statements he copies. At the end of line 5, when the speaker adds the phrase "in him alone," he denies, once again, his indebtedness to the interlocutor: the alteration dramatizes his desire both to originate statements and to exceed the boundaries and limits of the formulations given to him. He makes this statement his by making it idiosyncratic, he makes it his by making his choice conscious, and he makes it his by making his choice definitive.

But when the interlocutor declares that nothing, not even the ability to trust, is our own, the speaker understands that his second effort must also be relinquished. Acknowledging once again his failure to adopt an acceptable stance, he duplicates the interlocutor's language, transforms it into first person speech, alters it, and derives a new position from it—this one, perhaps, the most accommodating position of all. If nothing is my own, he declares, then I confess my reliance upon God, then "I confesse that he my succour is" (l. 8).

When the interlocutor objects,

> But to have nought is ours, not to confesse
> That we have nought

(ll. 9–10)

he seems to have trapped the speaker once again. But his counterclaim also points to the fact that the speaker's adaptability exists in the service of his own self-construction. He listens to the interlocutor's criticisms, but uses them only in order to create for himself positions for which he can still take responsibility and over which he can exert control. The interlocutor will not, however, permit him to appropriate language only to reorganize it and use it for his own purposes. When he declares that "to have nought is ours, not to confesse / That we have nought," he distinguishes between living with a state of affairs—having nothing—and making declarations about that state of affairs—confessing that we have nothing. His response insists, in other words, on the fact that the speaker's difficulties are not a function of the mistaken positions he holds but of the fact that, with every line, he asserts his independent agency as a speaker, the fact that, with word and deed, he inserts himself into the world.

Insofar as the appearance of the self is a function of the ability to present that self in language, "The Holdfast" is a record of the importance attached to, and the difficulty associated with, making a lasting appearance in the world: this speaker's words are presented with determination and rejected three times with equal force. By the end of the second stanza he has nothing left to say: he can only stand "amaz'd," "much troubled," incapable of further speech. In fact at this point speech is undertaken by someone else, a "friend," whose words the speaker now merely *reports:*

> ... I stood amaz'd at this,
> Much troubled, till I heard a friend expresse,
> That all things were more ours by being his.
> What Adam had, and forfeited for all,
> Christ keepeth now, who cannot fail or fall.

(ll. 10–14)

Here, as in the last stanza of "Jordan (II)," the speaker's voice is overtaken by, and given up to, the message Christ wishes to convey. And the poem becomes, also like "Jordan (II)," a lesson in the power and priority of Christ's voice.[10]

But it is not only a lesson in that. For the man who stops speaking on his own behalf and speaks, instead, on behalf of his "friend," does so in order to report that our losses (all things are not ours but his) become, through Christ, our gains (they are more ours by being his). If the poem provides an education in losing—losing positions, losing speeches, losing selves—it also provides a lesson in recovery. What we forfeit, the final lines declare, Christ keeps for us. And what he keeps for us we come to possess in a new way: we possess what we do *indirectly, by way of him.*[11]

Of course if Christ keeps what we lose in this poem, then what he keeps is our capacity to speak and to appear. He makes these available to us by speaking and standing for us, much as his words speak and stand for us in the last lines of the poem. And this exchange of direct for indirect representation is, in many ways, a good bargain, though it is also, as the speaker's struggle powerfully demonstrates, a difficult and costly one as well. For one gains the right to appear indirectly, in Christ's words and by way of him, at the expense of the (admittedly perilous) right to appear independently—in one's own words and by way of one's own exertions. The man who, with word and deed, inserts himself into the world, finds the world inhospitable to such insertions, finds them not only dangerous but, at least in the end, impossible.

Like its predecessors in this chapter "The Holdfast" has an ending that points away from the sort of representation gained through direct speech. Christ's capacity to act on our behalf is something that the speaker's friend "expresses"; but the speaker only reports—he does not appropriate—his friend's words. If "Jordan (II)" recommends copying another's words and "Frailtie" suggests that when we do not copy, our words are subject to multiplication and confusion, "The Holdfast" suggests that language becomes safe when it becomes indirect, and that representation becomes sure when it is turned over to another for safekeeping.

The competition between personal writing and divine appropriation is also Herbert's subject in two poems entitled "Good Friday." But the speaker of the first poem begins by *questioning* his ability to tell Christ's story: stanzas one through five make it clear that suffering is not subject to human measurement, and that, because it is not, Christ's story cannot adequately be told by the poem's human speaker. In the first stanza, for example, the speaker asks:

> How shall I measure out thy bloud?
> How shall I count what thee befell,
>   And each grief tell?

(ll. 2–4)

Measuring and counting—laying hold of, and gaining mastery over, Christ's suffering—would make telling possible, but in the absence of blood subject to measuring, and grief subject to counting, Christ's story, it seems, escapes the teller. In the remaining stanzas the speaker seeks analogies in his own world for Christ's incomparable grief—

> Shall I thy woes
> Number according to thy foes?
> Or, since one starre show'd thy first breath,
>   Shall all thy death?
>
> Or shall each leaf,
> Which falls in Autumne, score a grief?
> Or can not leaves, but fruit, be signe
>   Of the true vine?

(ll. 5–12)

—but as the grammar of the stanzas suggests, he rather imagines writing Christ's story than succeeds in writing it. How shall I? he asks in stanza one. Shall I number? he asks in two. Shall each leaf be the sign? he asks in three. By stanzas four and five the idea of writing Christ's story appears to have slipped into the background as the speaker imagines, instead, not writing Christ's story but rather internalizing it:

> Then let each houre
> Of my whole life one griefe devoure;
> That thy distresse through all may runne,
> And be my sunne.

(ll. 13–16)

Here the speaker's body becomes an arena in which Christ's story is enacted. Each grief occupies and thereby devours one hour of his day, and the passing of hours and days is marked not by the rising and setting of some external sun, but by the rising and setting of the internalized one.

This shift—from the idea that one might write Christ's story, to the idea that Christ's story is rather something one enacts in one's life—repeats itself, with alterations, in the following stanza, but here the speaker abandons the idea that he might write Christ's story himself, and *appeals to God to do the writing himself*. In the opening lines he offers his own blood as ink ("Since bloud is fittest, Lord, to write / Thy sorrows in" [ll. 21–22]), suggesting, still, that the story might be written the way stories usually are. By the stanza's last two lines, however, that notion has been turned around:

> Since bloud is fittest, Lord, to write
> Thy sorrows in, and bloudie fight;
> My heart hath store, write there, where in
> One box doth lie both ink and sinne.

(ll. 21–24)

Now the speaker offers not material for writing (blood for ink) but himself as the ground upon which writing proceeds (his heart as paper). Write with this, he says in lines 21–22. Write *on* this he says in lines 22–23.

The new story, written by God on the speaker's heart, would displace the sinful, personal story already lodged therein—and the speaker imagines, vividly, the conflict and competition between the two:

> That when sinne spies so many foes,
> Thy whips, thy nails, thy wounds, thy woes,
> All come to lodge there, sinne may say,
> *No room for me,* and flie away.

> Sinne being gone, oh fill the place,
> And keep possession with thy grace;
> Lest sinne take courage and return,
> And all the writings blot or burn.

(ll. 25–32)

The important point to be made about "Good Friday" is that it begins by asking the question "How shall *I* tell?" and ends, in its first half, by giving up the idea of telling altogether: instead of producing his own account of Christ's suffering the speaker gives his life over to a reenactment of it and he becomes, thereby, not the agent of Christ's story but rather its object. In the poem's second half his relinquishment of writing is made explicit, but—and this is the crucial point—rather than simply removing himself as agent and giving up writing altogether, he asks Christ to take on the task himself: he *invites* the rewriting imposed upon him in other poems.[12] But "Good Friday" makes explicit the implications of this rewriting: God's story would keep out alternative—here sinful—stories, though if the place were not "filled" sin might return and "blot or burn" God's account.

What the speaker describes is a competition between two kinds of writing: sinful—here identified with original—writing, and God's writing, which struggles to stay in place and prevent the disfiguring return of the personal. What would keep one safe from defective personal stories, "Good Friday" suggests, would be God's story, and what would keep one safe from the weaving of self into sense would be the transformation of self from agent to object of accounts.

In a sense, the solution wished for by the speaker of "Good Friday" is like the one imagined in "Jordan (II)"—God's writing, the speaker hopes, will occupy the space once reserved for stories by, or about, the self. But in "Jordan (II)" the displacing writing would be biblical writing copied by the speaker, and in "Good Friday" Christ's story would be inscribed *by him* on the speaker's heart. Of course neither poem shows us what such writing would look like, although both suggest that the alternative to personal writing is not *no writing* but rather *rewriting*, not silence but instead reinscription of a rather particular kind.

The conflict between self-representation and self-relinquishment, between personal and divine inscription, between the idea of the self as an agent of writing and a vision of him as writing's object, are central to collapsing poems—as they are to "The Reprisall," a poem which, though it begins with a sense of the exhaustion of possibilities, soon turns that exhaustion around. The speaker we meet in the opening lines has "consider'd it" and found that he can have nothing to do with, can take no action with regard to, can neither contend with, nor dispose of his obligations to, nor share in, Christ's passion. But while speech reflects the barren issue of contemplation—

> I have consider'd it, and finde
> There is no dealing with thy mighty passion
>
> (ll. 1–2)

—it also serves a contrary purpose. For speech *installs itself* in place of thought's barrenness, exchanging the exhaustion of possibilities for the generation of them. The possibilities here generated are those of narration itself, as it takes the vacant ground on which the speaker stands and turns it into discourse. The opening lines of the poem are not a sign of impotence at all; rather, they are an early sign of the speaker's pro-

ductivity: he reports a conclusion, which occasions a sequence
of explanations, complaints, and pleas.

> I have consider'd it, and finde
> There is no dealing with thy mighty passion:
> For though I die for thee, I am behinde;
>   My sinnes deserve the condemnation.
>
> O make me innocent, that I
> May give a disentangled state and free:
> And yet thy wounds still my attempts defie,
>   For by thy death I die for thee.

(ll. 1–8)

By the end of the first two stanzas the speaker's inability to
engage himself on the subject of the passion has evaporated in
face of his remarkable ability to manufacture articulations of
failure. His first explanation becomes, in the second stanza,
the occasion for a plea ("O make me innocent"), ends in the
discovery that his enterprise is hopeless ("And yet thy
wounds"), and leads him to reopen a dead issue (dead how
many times?) with this double complaint—

> Ah! was it not enough that thou
> By thy eternall glorie didst outgo me?
> Couldst thou not griefs sad conquests me allow,
>   But in all vict'ries overthrow me?

(ll. 9–12)

What all of this amounts to is engagement and activity on
every front. This is a speaker who, in the absence of means,
invents means: he transforms unproductive thought into argumentative speech, inactivity into sequence. The turn into discourse of which this poem gives evidence occurs at a moment
of great depletion, and masquerading as a complaint about the
absence of work it produces work of another kind—the work
of narration and, at the same time, the work of self-generation.

In the final stanza of "The Reprisall" we learn, however, that
this kind of work is an unacceptable form of activity:

> Yet by confession will I come
> Into thy conquest: though I can do nought
> Against thee, in thee I will overcome
> The man, who once against thee fought.
>
> (ll. 13–16)

Narration is identified here as the work, not of invention, but of opposition. For while the first three stanzas describe an effort to offer proper compensation for the Sacrifice, they turn the effort at recompense into an act of retaliation: what began as an interest in repaying an original and unprecedented gift ends in a statement about the impossibility of repaying an extremely burdensome debt: "Ah! was it not enough . . . ?" (l. 9). The discovery in the poem's last stanza is a discovery about the failure to be in control of intentions and suggests that the first three stanzas are essentially unconscious work, divorced from insight—not the work of generation, but the work of blind opposition. But narration is really the work of opposition because it constructs, in place of the speaker who has no work, a speaker whose work is warfare. It transforms a negotiating self into an opposing self, "The man, who once against thee fought."

Oddly enough, in the last stanza of the poem the speaker does find an authentic and acceptable labor, but it is not the labor of producing lyric discourse at all: rather, he takes on the task of overcoming the self who produces poems like this. Speaking of himself as another ("the man") is one way of indicating that he has already stopped identifying himself with the narrator of the first three stanzas, that he has divorced the text and, in a sense, abandoned authorship of it. He has not taken possession of his work and assumed the privileges of authorship but has disowned, and must dismantle, the dark work of narration:

> . . . in thee I will overcome
> The man, who once against thee fought.
>
> (ll. 15–16)

Moreover, he has turned from literary speech toward speech of another kind. "Confession," these lines suggest, will not complicate the ground but clear it, will not construct an opposing self but overcome one. The project the conclusion points to is the unmaking of narrator and narrative at once.

But the ending of "The Reprisall" also suggests that if narration takes the vacant ground and turns it into discourse, the new work of "confession" will revise discourse. In fact, the last stanza gestures toward a world in which the narrating speaker himself *becomes the ground* upon which revision proceeds. This new articulation, the poem implies, will be an enlightened one—it will take the old, false inscription (the blind work of stanzas 1–3) and, in effect, rewrite it. The man who once fought against God will be overcome, refashioned into His lover. Like the ending of the second "Good Friday" poem, this ending points to the rewriting of the history of the self *on the ground* of the old history—except the implication is that *re*-writing does not really occur as writing, but rather as unrecorded speech, confession. But in this sense "The Reprisall" is like many poems in *The Temple* whose endings reverse their own paths: in these poems the conclusion turns back upon the inscription, declares it deluded, and transforms it into an object of attention upon which a new reading must be inscribed. In "Jordan (II)" the speaker unhinges himself from a falsely embodying sense and the poem suggests that he copy, instead, a *"sweetnesse readie penn'd"*; in "Frailtie" the "brave" language of self-presentation will, the speaker fears, suffer a multiplication and confusion of sense if he does not keep his peace; in "Good Friday," the final stanza implies, personal stories may be rewritten as divine ones. But *re*-writing almost never takes place in the course of the poem itself: it is often promised, but it is rarely performed.[13] Instead, these poems suggest that the speaker who sings best is a speaker *without* a text, someone who has given up the fiction that he can generate appropriate discourse on his own. In a sequence of self-revising lines, the dedicatory poem to *The Temple* puts it this way:

> Lord, my first fruits present themselves to thee;
> Yet not mine neither: for from thee they came,

And must return. Accept of them and me,
And make us strive, who shall sing best thy name.

(ll. 1–4)

The speaker who sings best is clearly one who claims no ownership: he doesn't present his first fruits—they present themselves. He even errs when he calls them his: they are not his—
they come from God. In fact, they don't really present themselves at all—they return to their proper owner from whom, it
seems, they have shown a tendency to stray. And if the relationship of speaker to text is a contentious, indeed a rivalrous
one ("*Accept of them and me, / And make us strive*"), that is because the speaker sings best when he does not take himself as
the source of lyric or when he can relinquish an already-gen-
erated account; while texts sing best when they are thus released, freed from the tyranny of self-oriented meaning to
which narrators subject them.[14] Speakers and texts are often,
then, about the business of sundering themselves from each
other. Texts sing best without speakers, speakers without
texts.[15]

But if collapsing poems recommend in their final lines that
persons appear independently of texts or texts independently
of persons, they do not in fact *embody* the recommenda-
tion. Instead, these poems are, as I have tried to suggest in
this chapter, "resolutely dialectical":[16] the speaker of "The
Reprisall" sunders himself from the text in an act of self-
relinquishment, but he also binds himself to the text in an act
of self-generation. And while the poem suggests that the account before us is a defective one, it also suggests that an alternative account is possible—though because the alternative
remains to be spoken, there is in the poem no final *image* of the
regenerate man. In fact the presence of a *misconducted* story and
the absence of a *corrected counterstory* are, here and elsewhere,
the regular features of collapsing poems—which leave the
reader with the work of revising his own understanding and
leave the speaker with the work of dismantling and redesigning himself.[17]

chapter 2

COLLAPSING PERSONAL STORIES

One of the most interesting versions of the disturbed relation-ship between storyteller and story characteristic of collapsing poems occurs with the appearance of a poetic speaker who doubles back upon an already complete report. He offers a fully articulated, intact account of a significant set of events in his life, only to remind us that the account is retrospective and that there is a major discrepancy between his current feelings and those he has just described. He indicates that he has no faith in his account, that it no longer represents him, that he bears, in short, a different relationship to the story than we have assumed. His situation is different from that of the speaker who, like the speaker of "The Reprisall," discovers in the course of his story that everything he has said is inappro-priate or wrong. The narrating speaker discovers nothing in the course of the narrative. He knows what he knows *from* the start, even when he does not disclose what he knows *at* the start. Instead, he waits until the narrative's end to reveal a change that took place before the narrative began. This is the situation in two of Herbert's best-known poems, "Affliction (I)" and "The Collar."[1]

The suppression of information plays a crucial role in these poems, for one of the things the speaker suppresses is his awareness of the inappropriateness of the story he tells—so that the withholding of knowledge is precisely what permits him to tell the story. Of course the revelation of information plays an equally critical role, for it allows him to alter his relationship to the story—to disown it or reinterpret it after it has been told. In "The Collar," for example, an important part of the speaker's life is represented in a self-contained "interior story" complete with beginning, middle, and end (ll. 1–32), fenced off from the eroding influences of the narrative frame which surrounds it. The narrative frame, which appears at the beginning (l. 1) and reasserts itself in the poem's final lines (ll. 33–36), reminds us, as the end of "The Holdfast" does, of the inappropriateness of the story, the impossibility of adequately representing the self in language, and the obligation to relinquish personal stories altogether. But the frame's separation from the interior story ensures at least the partial safety of both. The narrative frame points to the defectiveness of the interior story and renders its usefulness suspect. But it also protects the story from extinction by keeping it manifest, in writing, before us:

> I struck the board, and cry'd, No more.
>   I will abroad.
>   What? shall I ever sigh and pine?
> My lines and life are free; free as the rode,
>   Loose as the winde, as large as store.
>   Shall I be still in suit?
>   Have I no harvest but a thorn
>   To let me bloud, and not restore
>   What I have lost with cordiall fruit?
>   Sure there was wine
> Before my sighs did drie it: there was corn
>   Before my tears did drown it.
>   Is the yeare onely lost to me?

Have I no bayes to crown it?
No flowers, no garlands gay? all blasted?
All wasted?
Not so, my heart: but there is fruit,
And thou hast hands.
Recover all thy sigh-blown age
On double pleasures: leave thy cold dispute
Of what is fit, and not. Forsake thy cage,
Thy rope of sands,
Which pettie thoughts have made, and made to thee
Good cable, to enforce and draw,
And by thy law,
While thou didst wink and wouldst not see.
Away; take heed:
I will abroad.
Call in thy deaths head there: tie up thy fears.
He that forbears
To suit and serve his need,
Deserves his load.
But as I rav'd and grew more fierce and wilde
At every word,
Me thoughts I heard one calling, *Child!*
And I reply'd, *My Lord.*

The beginning of "The Collar" observes scrupulously the boundary line between speechlessness and speech. The introduction to the interior story refers to the speaker's last non-verbal act (the striking of the board [l. 1]) and then reproduces, intact, the original speech of the man whose first words were "No more. / I will abroad" (ll. 1–2). Furthermore, because the opening lines of the interior story refer to an experience for which we have no context (they call an end to something we have not witnessed and therefore know nothing about), they suggest that the real event taking place before us has less to do with the meanings toward which the words eventually point than it has to do with the fact that suddenly there is speech where there was none before. The lack of context for the words permits them to serve more openly as signs, as indicators that something—untransformed, untranslated experience—has ended, and that something else—experience transformed into language—has begun. Of course, when the speaker's experience is transformed into language, what was once invisible becomes visible, what was undifferentiated gains differentiation, what was once impalpable achieves palpable form. The man who speaks has made a space for himself, and within that space he has made his appearance.

A speaker's emergence is a moment of great activity. It marks the coincidence of the desire to become manifest, the awareness that there is a subject of manifestation, and the consciousness that the subject is oneself. While in some ways this may seem an ordinary activity indeed—we do, after all, speak about ourselves all the time—it nonetheless represents a significant choice. The man who speaks reverses his status as an undifferentiated, unacknowledged member of a world that may never know of his presence if he makes no reference to it himself. The speaker who says "I" is self-reflexive: he indicates a desire not just to distinguish things but to distinguish *himself*. While later lines of "The Collar" make clear that, in the broadest sense, the poem's opening words mean something like "No more" relationship, or "No more" longing after it, the placement of these words at the beginning of the interior story also suggests a meaning something like this: no more speechlessness; no more invisibility; no more undifferentiated being.[2]

These statements indicate that self-manifestation is often achieved at the cost of continuity with the past: to speak is to stop being silent; to appear is to stop being invisible. And if this is true for human speakers in general, then it is emphatically true for the speaker of "The Collar," for the interior story does not just *begin* with its first line. It makes a point of declaring the discontinuity between present and past, of asserting its own newness, of announcing that what has happened before is ended and what is about to happen has never happened before: "No more. / I will abroad."

The declaration of discontinuity with which the poem begins develops in the following lines:

What? shall I ever sigh and pine?
My lines and life are free; free as the rode,
    Loose as the winde, as large as store.
        Shall I be still in suit?
    Have I no harvest but a thorn
    To let me bloud, and not restore
What I have lost with cordiall fruit?

(ll. 3–9)

In one sense, of course, these lines are an elaborate complaint by the speaker that he has not got what he has asked for. Neither sighing nor pining has produced a loving response from God, and even the speaker's harvest has produced only thorns. But the real problem here is that petitions that do not issue in a response must be either renewed or thrown over. This speaker has renewed them endlessly and has found himself in a situation in which it is impossible ever to begin anything new. His is a world in which the same gesture is repeated over and over again ("shall I ever sigh and pine?") and in which there is but one available posture—and that a posture held forever ("Shall I be still in suit?"). The lines also suggest, then, an alternative life, in no way bound to repetition or recurrence. "My lines and life are free," the speaker says; I need not repeat myself or remain in a world where each year the harvest will bring only thorns; there are endless, though as yet unimagined, possibilities for me if only I stop repeating the past and invent, instead, a new beginning. The world before him grows in size ("loose as the winde, as large as store") as it is contrasted with the narrow, repetitive world of the past he intends to leave behind.

The past to which "The Collar" refers, and from which it distinguishes itself, is inhabited by a (silent) self-duplicating person and is characterized both by the recurrence of a set repertoire of actions and by its restrictions upon new events. The obvious problem with this world is that it prevents the emergence of persons who, if they are to become known, must begin their own lives, chart their own paths. The world described in "The Collar" overdetermines the life of its speaker, prescribing in advance the course of events and effectively limiting the production in his life of original, or idiosyncratic, experience. It is against these limitations that the speaker of the poem rebels, and he rebels both by declaring his objections and by enacting them. The interior story enacts a dream of difference, originality, and novelty; it dreams what Edward Said has called, in another context, "the dream of privacy and freedom."[3] It does so by having the speaker end his silence, by inventing a communicable version of the self visible in these words, by declaring the intention to repeat already known actions no more, and by expressing opposition to life in a world that fails to acknowledge the speaker's presence ("Have I no bayes to crown it?" [l. 14]).

Furthermore, the interior story enacts its difference by disrupting the natural sequence of events and allowing the speaker to become the author of an entirely new sequence. The speaker becomes an intender; he has decided to stop being passive and to start taking active control of his life. The questioning man we meet in the opening lines has lived too long with the illusion that someone else will attend to his needs. When he begins to speak he does so because he has decided that his life is not fruitful and that he must intervene in order to change it and make it productive. In the first half of the interior story he asks whether he shall continue to be what he has, quite naturally, become, or whether he shall be something else entirely—something chosen, something invented. In the second half of the interior story the speaker answers the questions posed in the first half and begins to design a life for himself:

> No flowers, no garlands gay? all blasted?
>   All wasted?
> Not so, my heart: but there is fruit,
>   And thou hast hands.
> Recover all thy sigh-blown age
> On double pleasures.

>   (ll. 15–20)

The decision to take responsibility for his life—to speak, to become visible, to be new—also represents a demand upon the world: the once passive speaker now insists that the world make room for him, that it permit itself to be redesigned, that it subject itself to his mastery and bear his activity.

Of course the disruption of the natural sequence of events really begins the moment speech begins in "The Collar," for it is speech that interrupts the flow of life and halts the ongoing stream of experience. In a quite literal sense "No more" puts an end to the unfolding of events—not simply because the speaker substitutes an intended sequence of events for a natural one, but because he substitutes verbal for nonverbal experience, narration for participation. In fact, this speaker's safety inheres in his capacity for language, in his ability to bring to the surface and keep safe there what he cannot keep safe anywhere else—his own image. By virtue of his ability to generate an account of himself in language, he is able to withdraw from a set of experiences in which he is not safe, without at the same time vanishing from the world altogether. The account provides both visibility and security in a world whose wear and tear on the self are otherwise too great to sustain.

In the space of this safe withdrawal the dream of originality has its day. It is here that the speaker imagines himself at once distinguishable from the world and central to it, originator and inventor and manager of the unique story of his life:

> . . . Forsake thy cage,
> Thy rope of sands,
> Which pettie thoughts have made, and made to thee
> Good cable, to enforce and draw,
> And by thy law,
> While thou didst wink and wouldst not see.
> Away; take heed:
> I will abroad.
> Call in thy deaths head there: tie up thy fears.

(ll. 21–29)

It is also here that the events of life take on significance, at least in part because the space in which they occur is designated space and the time in which they occur is rescued (as opposed to ongoing) time. Frank Kermode raises the useful distinction between *chronos* and *kairos*, between "mere chronicity,"[4] or " 'passing time' " (p. 47), and "times which are concordant and full" (pp. 49–50). In Kermode's scheme the difference depends on the assignment of endings, since it is endings that organize time:

> The fact that we call the second of the two related sounds *tock* is evidence that we use fictions to enable the end to confer organization and form on the temporal structure. The interval between the two sounds, between *tick* and *tock*, is now charged with significant duration. The clock's *tick-tock* I take to be a model of what we call a plot, an organization that humanizes time by giving it form; and the interval between *tock* and *tick* represents purely successive, disorganized time of the sort that we need to humanize. (p. 45)

In the scheme I have been describing, the end of the interior story gives the story its intelligible shape and thereby completes its rescue from the disorder of experience. But I have also meant to stress, and I do so here again, the shaping force of the purposeful beginning—that beginning which intends the significant differences that follow from it, which imagines the shape of its own progress, and which must take upon itself the burdensome responsibility of having begun at all. Said describes the purposeful beginning this way[5]:

> This kind of beginning is suited for work, for polemic, for discovery. It . . . allows us to initiate, to direct, to measure time, to construct work, to discover, to produce knowledge . . . A beginning is a formal appetite imposing a severe discipline on the mind that wants to think every turn of its thoughts from the start. Thoughts then appear related to one another in a meaningful series of constantly experienced moments. (p. 76)

The interior story, when complete, is a fully articulated demand for livable, meaningful space, and it accomplishes its demand by intending *tock* from the moment it says *tick*, by humanizing time aggressively—from the start.

In other words, the transformation of *chronos* into *kairos* occurs from the beginning because the speaker imagines self-representation from the beginning, or is, at any rate, conscious of the difference between the past, in which he has no manifestation, and the present, in which he does. The concluding lines of the interior story serve to complete that intention and they do so in an extreme way, by closing the story epigrammatically: "He that forbears / To suit and serve his need, / Deserves his load" (ll. 30–32). It is the function of this statement to prevent the penetration of doubts, reservations, and fears, to seal the story against extraneous feeling by providing, in Barbara Herrnstein Smith's phrase, "maximal stability and finality": "To epigrammatize an experience is to strip it down, to cut away irrelevance, to eliminate local, specific, and descriptive detail, to reduce it to and fix it in its most permanent and stable aspect, to sew it up for eternity."[6] The conclusion that locks out alternatives is also designed to lock in, and protect, the person whose story is represented. For the conservation of the story is the means by which the speaker's image is preserved, the means by which he makes his presence known.[7]

But the reintroduction, at the thirty-third line, of the retrospective narrative voice reminds us of something we are, in this poem, rather inclined to forget. The interior story is not a present-tense account at all. It is the recapitulation of a present-tense account by a retrospective speaker who says, in the first line, "I struck the board and cry'd . . ." In the thirty-third line the speaker of "The Collar" resumes his own voice and, in so doing, at once makes clear that he has been speaking in a voice not his own and that he has finished speaking in that voice. The thirty-third line is, then, a critical boundary line, the line of multiple conversions: it marks the end of the speaker's ability to sustain the fiction that lines 1–32 are present-tense speech (the present-tense speaker never appears—it is his *image* that is preserved in these lines); it marks the re-discovery or re-cognition of the man who is a textmaker, who duplicates speech in order to conserve it (ll. 1–32); and it marks the appearance of the man who makes notes toward a secondary text by reading and interpreting the first (ll. 33–36).

Recognition that the speaker of lines 1–32 is not a present-tense speaker at all, that he is, in fact, a duplicator of present-tense speech, is critical. For while the words of the interior story have a way of insisting on their immediacy and spontaneity, line 33 (in which the retrospective speaker resumes his voice: "But as I rav'd") makes it clear that they are really the words of a man who has consented to the most extreme sort of constraint upon his freedom: he has relinquished the time and space of the present in order to take upon himself, intact, the life of an earlier version of himself. The narrator-as-duplicator relinquishes his voice to the voice of another, giving up whatever potential he has to tell a new story for the right to tell one that has all its features already determined. Insofar as men live by inventing their own careers moment to moment, the speaker who lends the space of his life to the duplication of an earlier career ceases to grow in the present and thereby ceases to have a career in it. The duplicator makes no real use of the present; he spends it reproducing the past.

This blotting-out of the self in the present is not, however, without its rewards. The narrator of "The Collar" acquires, for his pains, a designated space whose greatest defects are also its greatest virtues. The man whose present life is a quotation of his past life purchases a guarantee against surprise, change, instability, and vulnerability, for he purchases the sealed space of a journey already taken. For the duration of his account the constrained narrator is not subject either to the confusions or to the terrors of the present. He is already in possession of a finished story; he need not suffer the production, in pieces, of a new one. And while he has relinquished the capacity to have new experiences and invent new stories, he has won safety from that unwieldy, untraveled, potentially chaotic time in which we always live when we live in the present.

The reproducibility of a text has, then, far-reaching implications, and I should like to point here to one more. The ability to make something once again *assumes* the ability to make something once: reproduction attests, in other words, to the presence of an original, even when it does not insist upon it.

As J. Hillis Miller has suggested: "Even an exact repetition is never the same, if only because it is the second and not the first. The second constitutes the first, after the fact, as an origin, as a model or archetype. The second, the repetition, is the origin of the originality of the first."[8] Finally, then, duplication is the means by which the speaker is able to entertain the notion that he has got a text to begin with, that he has got something both stable and determinate, something that, because he can take it in hand and make it again, he knows he can take in hand.

But the speaker we meet in line 33 (now, as always, a retrospective speaker) no longer identifies himself with the man whose past he has reported. In fact, while duplication suggested an almost frightening degree of identification with the past (there was no apparent distinction between the first and the second sayings, though the implications of each were obviously different), the interpretation that begins at line 33—

> But as I rav'd and grew more fierce and wilde
> At every word

—suggests an almost frightening degree of *discontinuity* with the past. The speaker of that line does not simply stop identifying with the past, he stops being able to observe its integrity.

This is precisely what happens in Herbert's "Miserie" as well. The speaker presents himself, for seventy-seven of seventy-eight lines, as an authority on the activities of mankind, but his authority is both challenged and overturned by the poem's conclusion. In the first three stanzas the speaker portrays man's foolishness, folly, and sin, his excesses, pollutions, and blindnesses; in the fourth stanza he describes man as God's antagonist, a creature incapable of offering either proper service or proper praise. The poem is, in other words, a catalog of man's crimes, and chief among these are his refusal to acknowledge the inferiority of his vision ("No man shall beat into his head, / That thou within his curtains drawn canst see" [ll. 15–16]); his tendency toward self-inflicted blindness ("Oh foolish man! where are thine eyes? / How hast thou lost them in a croud of cares?" [ll. 49–50]); and, most particularly, his unwillingness to see that which is given to him to see ("But Man doth know / The spring, whence all things flow: / And yet, as though he knew it not, / His knowledge winks, and lets his humours reigne" [ll. 59–62]). But in the last stanza of the poem the speaker's own vision is precisely what is placed in question; for while he speaks as an outside authority on mankind's faults, someone whose superior knowledge exempts him from sins of blindness, the final line of the poem suggests that to imagine self-exemption is to exhibit the greatest blindness of all:

> But sinne hath fool'd him. Now he is
> A lump of flesh, without a foot or wing
>   To raise him to a glimpse of blisse:
> A sick toss'd vessel, dashing on each thing;
>   Nay, his own shelf:
>   My God, I mean my self.

(ll. 73–78)

"Miserie" is an account of the world outside of and separate from the self—until the final line, when it becomes clear that the self is not separate but implicated, not outside but inside. The speaker who says "my self" looks back upon a lengthy speech in which, he discovers, he makes no appearance at all; and suddenly he sees his speech not as an allied, but rather as an alien, text—not because he is not implicated in it, but because he is, and has not, until the end, been able to say so.

The speaker's discovery of his own complicity in those acts from which he has distanced himself represents, in one sense, a reversal of the discovery made in "The Collar." There, the speaker claims that he is present in his text only to discover, in the end, that he is absent from it; while in "Miserie" the speaker claims that he is absent from the story and discovers, instead, that he is (or ought to have been) present in it. But in both cases the speaker's relationship to his story is a relationship of *difference*. He fails to tell a story whose integrity he can affirm, fails to tell a story with which he is continuous, fails to tell a story which adequately represents him. In "The Collar" the duplicating speaker (the man who reproduces lines 1–32) is, by definition, scrupulous about the conservation of original intentions (quotation is a strategy designed to preserve the image of the justly rebellious speaker) and intent upon the notion that there is a central (reproducible) text of determinate meaning, the sign of whose determinacy *is* its reproducibility. But the interpreting speaker of the final lines of "The Collar" marks this notion a fiction. The speaker who stops quoting himself and begins to speak in the present provides instructions for the reinterpretation of his own text, knowing that the identification of self with sense is a fiction, and knowing that original intentions cannot be preserved.

The final lines of "The Collar" ask us to stop understanding the interior story as the account of a man who disengages himself from a repetitive past in order to engage in a productive future and to understand it instead as the story of a man who raves—a misguided man who grows wilder and wilder with every word he speaks. But what is significant here is not simply the way in which the lines alter the original story. What is significant is that the first reading has *no inherent stability*. The instruction to reread defeats whatever intentions this speaker has had to be either singular or determinate, marks an end to the duplicator's ability to preserve the fiction that the text has a fixed meaning, that it is a place in which the speaker is utterly manifest, in which meaning and being coincide. For the fact that there is a second reading marks the interior story a first reading—that is to say, marks it a "reading" rather than a determinate text. And insofar as it is only a "reading" it loses at once its claims to priority, stability, and centrality, and with them its claim to represent the speaker in ways either final or safe. The duplicating speaker, at great pains to preserve his story and thereby guarantee the representation of the person whose speech he reproduces, is superseded by an interpreting speaker, whose words puncture that sealed story and render it plural at a stroke.

When the interpreting speaker appears his words call for a revision of the notion that "No more" marks a radical departure, that what follows from it is either new or original or idiosyncratic. Instead, when the interpreting voice calls his early words "ravings" and thereby makes it clear that lines 1–32 tell the story of an unjust, misguided, rebellious man, he suggests that what he first conceived as a new beginning, charged with the importance and originality of all great departures, was in fact a rather conventional beginning, classically familiar to anyone schooled in the forms of rebellious behavior. Neither monumental nor radical, this beginning, seen retrospectively, is just another false start—the first step in a pattern of behavior as repetitious in its way as the one it meant to escape.

For the interior story is, after all, the story of a man who chafes against the obligations of the religious life, and while the speaker presents his plans for escape with great energy and seriousness, presents them as though he means them to stick, he gives them up as soon as he recognizes them for what they really are—one more set of complaints in a series of complaints, one more rebellion in a series of rebellions. The voice of the retrospective speaker is a knowing voice, and his knowledge floods the poem, suggesting that the idiosyncrasies of the interior story are almost wearying in their predictability, that the present is not really discontinuous with the past, that the boundary line between obscurity and visibility is often unclear, that the different is frequently rather ordinary and the strange sometimes painfully familiar.

The narrative frame further troubles the intelligibility of this text by providing a new end to a story whose end we thought we knew, suggesting, as the interpretive voice also suggests, that the text is no longer controlled by the intentions of the person who began it:

> But as I rav'd and grew more fierce and wilde
> At every word,
> Me thoughts I heard one calling, *Child!*
> And I reply'd, *My Lord.*

> (ll. 33–36)

The conclusion of "The Collar" (to which I shall shortly return) alters a once fixed story, opens a once closed account. If the interior story loses determinacy, if its beginning is, by line 33, deprived of the monumentality it seemed to have, its ending, as well, loses the sense of closure once attributed to it: it is no longer final in the way we expect endings to be final; it is, in fact, no longer the end. The extreme sense of closure with which the interior story concludes ("He that forbears / To suit and serve his need / Deserves his load") is pried open again by the story's true ending—ambiguous though that ending may be.

Furthermore, if the words of the interrupting speaker demand a reading of the interior story as the account of a man who moves further away from his heart's desire with every word he speaks, then the notion of intentional speech must itself be revised. The speaker of the interior story means his rightful liberation, but his words do not produce it. In fact, the interpreting speaker provides a framework in which it becomes possible to see the interior story as something the speaker never intended at all: the misreading of true relations, the misrepresentation of needs and solutions, the misuse of language. The speaker of "The Collar" and the speaker of "Miserie" both suffer from what Erving Goffman would call "errors in framing," and these involve them in

> systematically sustained, generative error, the breeding of wrongly oriented behavior. For if we can predict a fact by virtue of a framework within which it is formulated . . . then the misperception of a fact can involve the importation of a perspective that is itself radically inapplicable, which will itself establish a set, a whole grammar of expectations, that will not work. The actor will then find himself using not the wrong word but the wrong language.[9]

The speaker of "Miserie" uses the wrong language because he moves further away from his true subject with every word he speaks: the folly he describes really *means him* but he is unable to say so until the last line. Instead, he assigns to others everything that belongs to and characterizes the self, and he therefore ends with a text that cannot include him and therefore cannot represent him. In "The Collar" the speaker uses the wrong language—he "rav[es]"—because when he speaks in the interior story he *does not know what his words mean*. The intending speaker of lines 1–32 is, for example, never aware of the sacramental meanings of the words, meanings that the regenerate speaker surely knows. The regenerate speaker knows that the speaker who complains, in line 7, that he has "no harvest but a thorn" (the reward of his labor is not the cordial fruit that might restore and invigorate his heart but a thorn that pricks him and draws *more* blood) has, in fact, little to complain about. He understands that the thorn is a thorn of Christ's crown and that it is His blood that is the restorative "cordiall fruit." Jeffrey Hart, in "Herbert's *The Collar* Re-Read," provides a useful account:

> To Herbert's contemporaries the pun involved in "cordiall" would have been a routine matter: *cor, cordis*. "Cordiall" therefore refers to that which comes from the heart, or blood. But what is fruit? "Cordiall fruit," the restorative fruit for which the speaker longs, is thus "bloody fruit." . . . The Fall occurred when fruit was plucked from the forbidden tree. Because this theft introduced death into the world, the fruit Adam stole might plausibly be described as bloody. But Christ was the fruit which grew on a later tree . . . Christ's body and blood thus constitute one meaning of the bloody fruit, or "cordiall fruit," of the poem.[10]

Readers of "The Collar" have, of course, ventured alternative meanings for much of the interior story's language. The "board" of line 1 is the communion table (God's board), "free as the rode" suggests free as the Cross (rood), and the wine and corn of later lines clearly bear eucharistic meaning. To quote Hart again: "Wine and corn can represent natural food and drink, can represent the pleasures . . . he longs for, objects of desire comparable to fruit. But wine and corn (wheat) are also, of course, the elements of the Eucharist, wine and bread . . . To put it another way: [the speaker] *thinks* he desires natural pleasure, but the real object of his desire is supernatural, the cordial fruit of the Eucharist" (p. 252). Readers have also suggested alternative sources for the speaker's story in "the scriptural narratives of the Prodigal Son, the Resurrection appearance to Mary Magdalene, and Jesus' words on yokes and burdens." David Leigh claims that: "The three texts that . . . shed light on the poem are Matthew xi.29–30 ('My yoke is easy, and my burden is light'); Luke xv.13–21 ('And not many days after the younger son gathered all together, and took his journey into a far country, and there wasted his substance with riotous living'); and John xx.16 ('Jesus saith unto her, Mary. She turned herself, and saith unto him, Rabboni; which is to say, Master')."[11]

In one sense, then, the reinterpretation of the interior story points to the regenerative possibilities of the speaker's language: it provides the proper contexts for his story, assigns the correct meanings to what went before, establishes the proper relationship between the speaker's words and his God, fills language with meaning. But the interpretation is also—as it is in "Miserie"—an indication of crisis, for it points to the lack of precisely that congruence of intention and production, event and meaning, being and significance, which the interior story promised at the start. Meanings which *are* available to the speaker of "The Collar" 's narrative frame *are not* available to the "intending" speaker of the interior story. It may indeed be true that the speaker's new beginning is not, finally, new at all, that it is repeated in, and even modeled on, other stories. But the speaker who says "No more!" is not aware of that: he thinks he is starting a new life, not recapitulating an old one. The drama and the pathos of this poem are products of the discrepancy the speaker feels between his limited vision and that larger vision—sacramental and biblical—which finally surrounds and claims him. While the narrative frame is, then, corrective, it achieves its corrections at the expense of the suddenly obsolete notion that the interior story's speaker is in control of his own voice.

This lack of congruence between event and meaning is suffered by the speaker of Herbert's "Redemption" as well, and its significance there helps to illuminate the problem of reframing in "Miserie," "The Collar," and elsewhere. "Redemption" is the story of a man who does not thrive under an old lease and who goes in search of his landlord in order to arrange better terms. The poem is an allegory for the fundamental change occasioned by the Sacrifice—the change from an Old Covenant of laws and contracts to a New Covenant of grace—and in its concluding lines we witness the intersection of the two:

> Having been tenant long to a rich Lord,
>   Not thriving, I resolved to be bold,
>   And make a suit unto him, to afford
> A new small-rented lease, and cancell th' old.
> In heaven at his manour I him sought:
>   They told me there, that he was lately gone
>   About some land, which he had dearly bought
> Long since on earth, to take possession.
> I straight return'd, and knowing his great birth,
>   Sought him accordingly in great resorts;
>   In cities, theatres, gardens, parks, and courts:
> At length I heard a ragged noise and mirth
>   Of theeves and murderers: there I him espied,
>   Who straight, *Your suit is granted*, said, & died.

The intersection of two covenants (and the eventual domination of one) is also the point of intersection for two stories: the first story suggests a man who knows that something must be changed, but who is blocked from getting what he wants by a Lord who is unaware of his problem and who has better things to do with his time; the second suggests a man who wants something (though what he needs he does not truly know) and who is blocked from getting it by a Lord who takes better care of him than he ever imagined. In this second version the speaker who sets out to solve his own problem is already having his problem solved—in different terms—by a Lord who knows what he needs before he knows it himself.

Like "The Collar," "Redemption" is a retrospective poem: its speaker already lives under the New Covenant, but he produces, until the last lines, an account of himself under the Old—an account which is, therefore, not only obsolete but actually misleading. For it portrays the speaker as main actor in the particular drama before us, even though he knows, and finally permits us to know, that he is not the main actor and that the meaning of the story is not in his control. Christ's drama runs silently and invisibly behind the poem, coming to the foreground, and to center stage, only in the final lines. Virginia R. Mollenkott describes the situation this way: "The narrator is, strictly speaking, not the protagonist at all. He is simply the searcher; Christ is the protagonist, constantly acting in the background until finally He is picked up by the spotlight for the dazzling conclusion."[12] The narrator may not, strictly speaking, be the protagonist, but he *is* the main actor and main subject of the story for thirteen of the fourteen lines of the poem. While we say, then, that he is not the protagonist, we must not say that he never appears to be. For what is powerful about the ending of "Redemption" is precisely the fact that Christ's claim to the protagonist's role is a surprising one: to say otherwise is to minimize the force both of his claim and its costs, and therefore to reduce the impact of that potent drama which Mollenkott's words otherwise so powerfully evoke. When Christ's story—a collective story in whose meanings we are all implicated—overtakes the speaker's personal story, then foreground and background, the personal and the collective, exchange places.

"Redemption" is not, in other words, simply a poem about the change from Old Covenant to New, it is also a poem about the exchange of personal stories for background ones, and it demonstrates quite powerfully the way in which the collective stories and founding acts of one's belief are really foreground stories, and personal stories are really background ones. As the background story of "Redemption"—let us say its "frame story"—becomes, for a moment, manifest, *it* becomes the main story and as it does it dislodges and displaces the speaker's idiosyncratic account. While this solves his problem in the largest and most magnanimous of ways (his suit and all suits are granted), it also suggests that in the world of the New Covenant needs are met through just such a displacement of the personal by the collective solution, in just such an exchange of the idiosyncratic for the universal account, in just such a replacement of the manifest story by the one which has had, until the end, no manifestation. Like the speakers of "The Holdfast" and "The Collar," the speaker of "Redemption" loses control and gains salvation—loses his own story and gains another—all at the same time. He achieves what he does by disowning or disclaiming his own centrality to the poem's plot, and by returning to Christ the space of appearance to which he had mistakenly laid claim.[13]

The narrative frame that encases the interior story of "The Collar" functions in a similar way. It duplicates, and thereby preserves intact, the account that occupies the first thirty-two lines of the poem: the story of a man who reenters the world to begin the project of his own renewal, asserts his will in order to master the resources of his world, assumes his majority, and seals that activity in language—making it final, assuring its visibility, insisting upon its enduring value. But the interpreting speaker of the narrative frame also punctures the sealed text he has saved, eroding whatever belief in the story's coherence either speaker or reader may have entertained, and rendering the account vulnerable at every critical point: transforming its monumental beginning into a familiar, conventional "start"; opening its sealed conclusion (this poem dies twice) and providing it with a new, not to say ambiguous ending; rereading the story so that it becomes the account of a man who does not know either what he needs or what he means; and pointing to the possibility of a new interpretation which would come of reading the interior story in the contexts—both sacramental and biblical—to which it truly belongs.

The impulse toward self-representation, toward appearance in the world, is a crucial one, and it is this impulse that the speaker honors when he preserves the story of the first thirty-two lines of the poem. Ultimately, however, the idea that it is possible to represent the self in ways either coherent or safe is reduced to the status of a cherished fiction and is, at last, relinquished.[14] What replaces it is a vision of the world made vulnerable by interpretation, sensitive to the play of meaning, responsible to an alternative set of stories and, I would add, inhospitable to the representation of the individual self. In fact, the notion of a coherent, autonomous self is really in danger here. The plurality of readings available to insight points to the impossibility of settling on a univocal speaker. We can still read the interior story as a just rebellion if we are interested in recovering the intentions of the original speaker; we can read it as the speech of a madman completely out of touch with the richness of his own language; we ourselves can supply the sacramental meanings and biblical contexts the narrating speaker failed to supply; we can even, in places, read the account as though it were spoken by a man who *does* know what he means ("there *is* fruit and thou *hast* hands" [l. 12]).

Moreover, the poem's conclusion, powerful though it is in its ability to return to single things ("*Child!*" / "*My Lord*"), to reestablish the proper mode of address, and forcefully to restore the speaker to his God, illustrates at the same time the failure of the world to be simple, to provide anything so straightforward as sure intervention. I am not suggesting that there is doubt about whether the speaker returns to the fold; I am only suggesting that he does not do so out of a sense of certainty or out of a belief that the world will be easy for him. The ability to say "*My Lord*" and mean it, especially when it only *seems* God has said "*Child,*" is important precisely because it marks a willingness to persist, to speak, long after it is clear that speech provides no guarantees.

Of course it is just this sense of his (and the world's) vulnerability that encourages the speaker to preserve a story that is otherwise of no use to him at all (it is, after all, obsolete and embarrassing). The man whose speech is preserved in the interior story has a performance, has presence, has an image, while the man who knows enough to call his own words ravings never gets to display his knowledge at all. The clear-sighted speaker is shot through with the plurality of meanings, but he has no manifestation. Capable of pointing to the ways in which the speaker of lines 1–32 fails to know what he might have known, the retrospective speaker—like the speaker of "Miserie"—never makes manifest the ways in which he himself succeeds in knowing what he does know. The assignment of sacramental, eucharistic, and biblical meaning is an interpretive act *performed outside the narrative sequence of this poem:* it is sanctioned by the knowing voice of the narrator, but has no play in the temporal sequence at all. What we are left with, then, is an intending speaker who fails completely to understand the implications of his intentions and a clear-sighted speaker who displays his knowledge only when he says "*My Lord.*" These separations represent, finally, a surrender of the solace we often look for in lyric, the representation, all in one place, of something we have come to call meaningful life.

In pointing to the separation between the first telling of a story and the second, between the main plot and its background plot, between the beginning of a poem and its end, I do not mean to suggest either that the poem's writer, or that its reader, must be ignorant of the contexts about which the poem's speaker eventually learns. There is no question that some readers—whether they are seventeenth-century readers or learned contemporary ones—bring to their readings of these poems precisely the knowledge that is at stake in them. The reader of "Miserie," for example, may well understand that the speaker who exempts himself from his own presentation commits the sin of pride, and the reader of "Redemption" may be familiar with the way in which landlord/tenant metaphors convert themselves into purchase/sale metaphors and thereby provide analogies for the change from Old Covenant to New. But in both of these poems, and in this chapter's central example, "The Collar," it is important to observe that the knowledge to which speakers finally come is knowledge from which they are rigorously excluded as the poems proceed. These speakers are always in the position of persons who fail to have precisely the knowledge to which, in one form or another, readers and authors more easily lay claim.

The consequence of this, for the representation of experience, is a serious one. In the poems I have discussed in this chapter, as in collapsing poems generally, Christian truths are pressed outward—into the poem's end or into its frame—and this means that the speaker's portrayal of himself is necessarily a divided one: he presents us with a coherent self who has no access to Christian knowledge, and the knowledge he finally does acquire is knowledge that has no portrayal. In saying this I do not mean to suggest that Herbert could ever put his Christian knowledge away or that the meaning of a poem should be restricted to that consciously articulated by its speaker. But I do mean to point to the ways in which knowledge gains, and fails to gain, *representation* in these poems. In "Miserie," "Redemption," and "The Collar," Christian knowledge breaks in upon the speaker only as the poem ends, and because this is the case that knowledge, and the self who comes to bear it, have no real manifestation.

But insofar as fictions provide invulnerable texts and, with them, invulnerable presence, this poetry declares them both unavailable and unacceptable. The temporary separation of story from frame permits a story to be told in "The Collar" and permits a self to be represented, but the reappearance of the narrative voice at the story's end punctures the account, makes it porous, and threatens the notion that adequate self-representation ever really occurred. The self acquires (in ll. 1–32) a form for representation, but it does so only temporarily and at the expense of membership in a wider, a more open, present. Finding temporary safety in the closure that stories provide, the speaker also acknowledges his obligation to return to the present—always more unwieldy, more vulnerable, and less safe.

Herbert criticism would have it that "The Collar" describes the conflict between self-will and the will of God and that it provides, in one form or another, a lesson in submission and conformity. In an early analysis of the poem Joseph Summers wrote: "Until the final four lines, the poem dramatizes expertly and convincingly the revolt of the heart, and its imitation of colloquial speech almost convinces us of the justice of the cause. But the disorder of the poem provides a constant implicit criticism, and with the final lines we recognize that 'The Collar' is a narrative in the past tense: the message for the present concerns the necessity of order" (p. 92). In Summers' view self-will produces disorder, and the necessary return to order in the poem's final lines marks the submission of the speaker's will to God's. Louis L. Martz's view, though more consciously didactic, would prove essentially the same. Martz called the convincing revolt a "deliberate cultivation of blasphemous thoughts," an "outburst" that ends in a "whiplash of self-control and conformity with God's will."[15] Both views suggest a speaker who *returns* to the world he always belonged in, an ordered world in which outbursts are a deviation from the norm.

Arnold Stein, like Martz, has stressed the didactic features of "The Collar," but in Stein's view the speaker learns his lesson only because he is ready to do so. "God intervenes, having let His beloved child teach himself the steps and destination of his argument." When "the effort to escape love has demonstrated the logic of its own folly," then "the climax calls forth God's motion, which coincides with man's readiness, purged, to return to Him" (p. 124). Following in Stein's path, though offering amendments to it, Helen Vendler suggested that "we come to that submission with relief, because it means a return to Herbert's own nature, to which he has been so cruel in the course of the poem" (p. 135). The speaker, in Vendler's view, "works through his trouble until the resolution . . . shows the falsity of the problem proposed" (p. 136), shows that to give up is to return to a better, a more "natural," a truer self (p. 135).

While the positions outlined here offer different names for the problem—disorder or blasphemy, the effort to escape love or the effort to escape one's self—the solutions they propose are, in the end, virtually the same. When Summers posits a return to "order," Martz to "conformity," Stein to the "logic" of love, and Vendler to the "natural" self, each suggests that the conclusion of a collapsing poem places the speaker at rest on safe ground, having rescued him from the unsafe territory of the poem's opening lines. In fact, Vendler's position leads her to conclude that "nothing need be sacrificed for anything else. If it appears that one of these values must 'win' and the other must 'lose,' there is *a priori* something wrong with the way the problem is being seen or voiced" (p. 136). Here the notion of the safe return, pushed to its extreme, retroactively revises disruption until it is neutralized out of existence. The stability of the poem's solution has transforming powers and is a sign of the most thoroughgoing comfort and security— against the background of which rebellion is but a transitory fiction of difficulty.

The position I have been elaborating offers the opposite point of view, a view sympathetic in one important respect with the reading suggested by Stanley Fish.[16] Fish claims that poems like "The Collar" instruct both speaker and reader in the insufficiency of their perspective and the inappropriateness of their self-respect. The emphasis of his view is on the *devastation* of the poems' endings as they "render superfluous the mode of discourse and knowing of which [the poems] themselves are examples" (p. 158). This view occupies an interesting place in Herbert criticism because it refuses to be comforted by the reversals characteristic of the poet's conclusions. Instead, it locates in them the disruptive and eroding forces I have already described at some length.

If the general model suggests, then, that the interior story disrupts and disorders and that the poem's conclusion must establish order once again, the model I have just proposed suggests the contrary, namely, that the rebellious "interior story" offers the only fiction of coherence and stability available to the speaker of "The Collar," a fiction he constructs at first and deconstructs at the end. In other words, the conclusion of "The Collar" relinquishes—it does not purchase—the fiction of safe territory, and its real didacticism is a function of the way it instructs us in the costs of self-representation, asking both speaker and reader to exchange the desire to *witness* the representation of the self for the willingness to *conceive* a regenerate self, acknowledging all the while the enormous difficulty of doing so. Here, then, to return is to resume a retrospective voice sensitive to the failure of coherence, not to resume a voice skilled in the lessons of ease. And to return is to establish a relationship with God, not in a world where order is necessary, but in a vulnerable present where images cannot be secured.

chapter 3

AUTOBIOGRAPHY AND BEYOND

Like "The Collar," "Affliction (I)" gives testimony to the power and importance of telling stories about the self and to the power and importance of relinquishing them. The retrospective speaker recounts a tale—here, his autobiography—as though he were in possession both of his life and of its meanings, and yet he knows, as the speaker of "The Collar" does, that it makes no sense to tell stories, that their vision of life's workings is deluded. When, at the fifty-fifth line, he both completes and relinquishes his autobiography—and with it whatever safety closure has to offer—he finds himself in a world familiar to the speaker of "The Reprisall," a world neither bounded nor framed, a place in which conventional representation has become, in fact, impossible. But unlike the speaker of "The Collar," whose last words both reverse, and eclipse, speech, the speaker of "Affliction (I)" continues beyond the end, and the fact that he does, that he speaks even when speech provides no access to meaningful representation, is the great manifestation of devotion with which the poem concludes.

The first fifty-four lines of "Affliction (I)" recount the story of a man who, convinced that he lives in a world of possibilities, must learn that he lives in a world of none. But the speaker who tells the story is a man who already knows that he is utterly without means, and knowledge of his fate is present to him *at the beginning* of his retrospective account. So that while in one sense the story of this poem is a story of diminishment, in another sense there is no diminishment. The retrospective speaker knows that there *never were* either means or possibilities—only the illusion of them. The present in which he speaks bears down upon the past he describes, collapsing it into a mistake awaiting discovery.

But the man we meet in the opening lines of the poem describes the beginning, not the end, of a project. Like the speaker of "The Collar," whose first words separated the past from the present ("No more") and inaugurated something new ("I will abroad"), this man's thoughts are inaugural. We are told in the first two stanzas about the days in which the speaker "first" contemplated God's service:

> When first thou didst entice to thee my heart
>   I thought the service brave:
> So many joyes I writ down for my part,
>   Besides what I might have
> Out of my stock of naturall delights,
> Augmented with thy gracious benefits.
>
> I looked on thy furniture so fine,
>   And made it fine to me:
> Thy glorious houshold-stuffe did me entwine,
>   And 'tice me unto thee.
> Such starres I counted mine: both heav'n and earth
> Payd me my wages in a world of mirth.
>
>   (ll. 1–12)

And we are told, once he accepts the service, about its beginnings:

> At first thou gav'st me milk and sweetnesses;
>   I had my wish and way:
> My dayes were straw'd with flow'rs and happinesse;
>   There was no moneth but May.

(ll. 19–22)

This poem presents us, then, with a chronological sequence whose presence it promotes—and whose existence we credit—for fifty-four lines. But it also hints at, and finally emphasizes, its own despair about the viability of chronological life ("what thou wilt do with me / None of my books will show" [ll. 55–56]). When, for example, we read the opening line of the poem, "When first thou didst entice to thee my heart," we can read "entice" as "attract by offer of pleasure or advantage."[1] Read in this way there is nothing essentially duplicitous about the line, especially when we are told, in addition, that this early version of the self "thought the service brave" (l. 2). These lines describe a man with a genuine belief in self-direction, who lives in a world where "offers" are made and choice is possible. His words suggest that he could have the service or not have it, choose this position or some other. But we can also hear "entice" as spoken by a man who knows that God has designs upon the heart which the heart, in its innocence, does not see. This speaker also knows that the giving over of the heart is not, and never was, a matter of choice, that the service was neither brave nor not brave: it was simply inescapable.

And yet the world the speaker describes in the poem's early lines is a world invulnerable to change. The circumstances of the speaker's life seem unqualifiedly good and, by all accounts, the terms of his arrangement with God are excellent. This is a man with an ample "stock of naturall delights," whose riches would only be increased by the association he contemplates. The lines are an illustration of the speaker's confidence, not only in his own resources, but in his command of the world's. In the following lines, God's furniture becomes his furniture and even the stars are "counted mine." He writes down what he imagines his returns will be, he counts his share of the heavens, and well before the contract is sealed his wages are determined and are as good as paid. Even where conjecture takes the form of a question the question is rhetorical and sounds like a prediction. We can assume that to the query: "What pleasures could I want, whose King I served, / Where joyes my fellows were?" (ll. 13–14) the certain self would have answered, clearly, "None!" More to the point, of course, he sees no need to ask the question seriously, for he does not consider a world in which things fail to work out as he desires. The man who reaches, in one movement—

> Therefore my sudden soul caught at the place,
> And made her youth and fiercenesse seek thy face
>
> (ll. 17–18)

—both for his new position (his "place") and for the countenance of God (his "face"), does so with all the energy and rash confidence of a young man truly at the beginning of his life.

It is tempting to think that the speaker's eventual disillusionment is a product of his early overconfidence. But false confidence is subject to correction, and an unreliable man, appraised of the error of his way, may learn again to rely upon himself—in a world in which learning and reliability are possible. Stanzas 6–9, however, are a lesson in the futility of assuming such a world. When the speaker discovers, at the end of stanza 5, that he has failed to know what is going on before his eyes and that he has radically misread the terms of relationship with God, the error of the first four stanzas is, by and large, corrected:

> But with my yeares sorrow did twist and grow,
> And made a partie unawares for wo.
>
> My flesh began unto my soul in pain,
>   Sicknesses cleave my bones;
> Consuming agues dwell in ev'ry vein,
>   And tune my breath to grones.

Sorrow was all my soul; I scarce beleeved,
Till grief did tell me roundly, that I lived.

(ll. 23–30)

He knows that absence and loss are part of experience, that conjecture is subject to error, that he has failed to know himself well, and has little knowledge of the world. But stanzas 6–9 illustrate that the willingness to see clearly offers no guarantee that life will make sense, that it will be either better or more meaningful than it was before. The speaker's vision, though improved in the following lines, only renders more visible his vulnerable position and the radical unpredictability of his life.

When, in the fifth stanza, the speaker is consumed by sorrow and disease, he thinks his life lost—for he experiences the severity of his illness as the closest thing to death he has known. In the sixth stanza, however, he regains health—but again loses his "life / And more" (ll. 31–34). He has not, of course, grown ill again. Rather, the definition of life has undergone transformation: it no longer means "health," but the love and comfort of friends. The speaker gains life in stanza 6 only to lose it again on different terms in stanza 7. God's strategy in this stanza is also one of reduction:

When I got health, thou took'st away my life,
        And more; for my friends die:
My mirth and edge was lost; a blunted knife
        Was of more use then I.
Thus thinne and lean without a fence or friend,
I was blown through with ev'ry storm and winde.

(ll. 31–36)

The speaker experiences the loss of usefulness, the loss of joy in that which has no use, the loss of protection, comfort, and aid in the face of loss.

God's next strategy turns the self against its own instincts, so that what it knows is lost, and what it gets is somehow foreign:

Whereas my birth and spirit rather took
　　The way that takes the town;
Thou didst betray me to a lingring book,
　　And wrap me in a gown.

(ll. 37–40)

If it is difficult to keep pace with God in stanza 6—he is always capable of inflicting an injury greater than the one of which one last thought him capable—in this stanza man is also in arrears of himself, just coming to know one version when another is forced upon him.

In the eighth stanza the speaker witnesses God's ability to transform completely the very terms of existence. At first he thinks he has reached the end, thinks that paralysis is the final, static point:

Thou often didst with Academick praise
　　Melt and dissolve my rage.
I took thy sweetned pill, till I came where
I could not go away, nor persevere.

(ll. 45–48)

But he finds that even stasis can be turned around and redefined:

Yet lest perchance I should too happie be
　　In my unhappinesse,
Turning my purge to food, thou throwest me
　　Into more sicknesses.

(ll. 49–52)

In the final lines of stanza 9 we encounter the most sweeping statement about the nature of God's power with man:

Thus doth thy power crosse-bias me, not making
Thine own gift good, yet me from my wayes taking.

(ll. 53–54)

God is represented as he who cross-biases the self, but the way in which his "inclination runs athwart or counter to" the self is rather complicated.[2] The problem is not simply that God wants the speaker to be in a gown rather than in town, or that he wants him to be ill rather than well. In fact, even when the speaker resigns his own inclination (happiness, for example) and embraces instead that which he was once inclined to reject (unhappiness), the fact that he does accept becomes, itself, unacceptable. It is called being "too happie . . . In unhappinesse" (ll. 49–50). If God is he who cross-biases, it is not because he has specific plans which counter the plans one has for oneself. Rather, God cross-biases by countering every attempt by the self to have plans, to determine who he is, to define the terms of existence. If it is man's inclination to fix, and make peace with, experience, it is God's inclination that he shall not.

When, at the fifty-fifth line, we arrive at the conclusion of the retrospective account, what we gain, finally, is an accurate perspective, the rectification truth requires. The speaker who says,

> Now I am here, what thou wilt do with me
> None of my books will show,
>
> (ll. 55–56)

has not only been disabused of the notion that all choices are good choices, that the world is utterly hospitable, that his stock of delights is ample, God's riches an added abundance. He has been disabused of the very notion on which the entire beginning of the poem is based. By the fifty-fifth line it is clear not only that the terms of the contract were incorrectly figured, but that it makes no sense to figure the terms of a contract with God, and that conjecture has no bearing on reality. The speaker does not, in other words, simply know that he figured poorly, but knows, rather, that to figure at all is to act where there is no sanction to act, to participate in a decision where participation has already been pre-empted and is therefore illusory, to assume the reliability of judgment where reliability is not only unwarranted but in fact prohibited under any terms. He has learned, furthermore, that adequate self-knowledge is unavailable and reliability impossible; that he has the means neither to make sense of experience, nor to initiate it, nor to control it; that he is, and always has been, a man without means.[3]

While the fifty-fifth line provides us, then, with the rectification truth requires, it also exacts enormous costs in exchange. For when we gain the conclusion, what we are asked to relinquish is nothing less than the speaker's autobiography—which is, after all, the account of a man at the beginning of a project, in an indeterminate state of affairs, making choices, relying on his convictions, and adjusting to changing circumstances. Furthermore, if the implication of the account is that it is a story told by its narrator, the implication of the conclusion is that the speaker's story never really was his own. He is not its author because he was not running his life, and also because he did not know he was not running it. To acquire the end of the narrative account is, then, to stand corrected. But standing corrected means acknowledging the inadequacy both of one's former and of one's present life. The speaker we meet when the story of the past is done (and undone) is not a correct or even an adequate person. He is, at most, a corrected person who barely recognizes his own history and whose best news is that he has learned to say that he does not know what to do. The man who survives the end of this story does not speak in full knowledge—he speaks in full knowledge of his ignorance. And the man who arrives at the end of his autobiographical account does not arrive at the moment of life's greatest coherence, but at the moment of its most complete collapse.[4]

Of course we do have an *experience* of the speaker's past; in fact, most of our experience *is* of his past. Even if we are conscious, from the start, that the speaker is headed toward a "monumental dead end" (Stein, p. 124), we must also acknowledge his effort to prevent error from collapsing the past entirely. Retrospect represents in this poem an effort to sustain the past in order to substitute it for present life at a moment when the latter, if not threatened with extinction, is at least threatened with irrelevance. For past life, though erroneous and illusory, represents a more promising view of experience: the speaker believed he knew who he was, thought he was the agent of his own actions, had not yet witnessed the collapse of possibilities. And present life, though more fully conscious of itself, suffers great deprivation: there is no evidence that meaningful experience is any longer possible.

In fact, life proceeds in "Affliction (I)" as long as the speaker does not know that quest, growth, and freedom are illusions—or as long as the knowledge that they are illusions is postponed or suppressed. Of course, the living the speaker does is thereby rendered defective—not only because it depends on illusory terms, but because it fails to have adequate knowledge of itself. When, on the other hand, consciousness *is* achieved and the defect of life becomes clear, quest and growth become impossible. The poem suggests, in other words, the compatibility of life and impaired consciousness, and the essential incompatibility of life and full consciousness. For life flourishes as long as consciousness fails, and it comes to a dead end when consciousness is achieved: "What thou wilt do with me / None of my books will show."

The shifting emphasis of past and present suggests that the poem lives, and that we read it, on borrowed time: it supports the illusion of life as long as the end which collapses that illusion is suspended. In the broadest sense the illusion is that it makes sense to tell the story at all, and that the terms for life it illustrates have some validity. But, as Walter Benjamin suggests in another context, "It is a dry material on which the burning interest of the reader feeds."[5] For once the story's end is restored (and it always threatens to be restored), it renders visible what was true from the start—it makes no sense to tell the story, the terms for life it illustrates have no validity—and negates the illusion the poem's narrative exists in order to sustain. Benjamin continues:

"A man who dies at the age of thirty-five . . . is at every point of his life a man who dies at the age of thirty-five." Nothing is more dubious than this sentence—but for the sole reason that the tense is wrong. A man—so says the truth that was meant here—who died at the age of thirty-

five will appear to *remembrance* at every point in his life as
a man who dies at the age of thirty-five. In other words,
the statement that makes no sense for real life becomes
indisputable for remembered life.   (p. 100)

"Real life" in this poem is (or seems) possible only as long as
one of its poles is invisible. One gets the story's conclusion at
the expense of the story, or one gets the story at the expense of
its conclusion.

While in some sense, then, the conclusion of the retrospective account tempts us to think that the past has been rendered
"superfluous" (Fish, p. 158), to say so is to utter only half the
truth. The poem does tempt us in that direction: it offers a
rather long account of the personal past of its speaker only to
inform us, at the fifty-fifth line, that all of his experiences proceeded out of a basic misconception about the nature of relationship with God. But the dismantling and discarding of the
speaker's past is precisely what presents him with a problem.
The presence of an autobiographical account suggests a man
with an impulse toward having a history and representing it,
but that impulse is met by an equally powerful counter lesson
which teaches that these things are had only at the expense of
consciousness and veracity—and in the end those are expenses which render autobiography suspect. After all, what
value can be attached to an incomplete autobiography, a defective narrative account, a misrepresenting representation? At
the same time, the mere presence of autobiography—especially in its collapsing frame—points to the wish that representation were possible. In the face of God's lessons the
speaker really is at a loss, but knowledge is not immune to the
wish that things were otherwise, that life were possible, even
when God's lessons to the contrary are executed with the kind
of persistence and determination we witness here. The conflict
between these contradictory impulses—toward self-representation on the one hand and self-relinquishment on the other—
are the defining features of "Affliction (I)" until the fifty-fifth
line.[6]

I have treated line 55 as a point of significant demarcation because although the poem does not end here, the autobiographical account does, and the narrative bears characteristics which permit us to identify a complete "story." The fifty-fifth line is the point at which the speaker announces himself to be a storyteller: he is no longer a man to whom things happen, he is a man who distinguishes the present from the past and who identifies himself ("Now I am here") as the narrator of a story about his own life. As Hannah Arendt has said: "Action reveals itself fully only to the storyteller, that is, to the backward glance of the historian, who always knows better what it was all about than the participants . . . Even though stories are the inevitable results of action it is not the actor but the storyteller who perceives and 'makes' the story" (p. 193). Much as a storyteller, in Benjamin's words, "borrow[s] his authority from death," the man in this poem acquires authority from the extinction of his own possibilities. The fifty-fifth line is also the point at which the story is complete, its dimensions become clear, and it acquires "transmissable form"—even though its dimensions are problematic for the speaker, outlining as they do a defective past and pre-empted future.

The fiction is, then, that the story is over at the fifty-fifth line. But if it is true that "art 'represents' a self which is either insufficiently 'present' or feels itself as not 'presentable,' "[7] the speaker in this account faces a serious dilemma. For the story grants him temporary representation only to render him, at its conclusion, insufficiently present once again. But the speaker's undoing does not signal the end of his life; it only signals the end of coherence, the end of narrative, the end of *representational* life. Because the story does collapse when its coherent shape is achieved, it is true that life can no longer be "read" or "told." But life can still proceed—even when its procession lacks coherent form. Unlike the tragic situation in which life folds when its true dimensions are known, in which, for example, "Oedipus, killing his father and marrying his mother, simply elides individual identity and is allowed no being properly his own,"[8] the religious situation demands life's resurrection precisely at the moment when it is least obvious that a revival of any kind is possible or even desirable. The true difficulty this poem imposes, then, is *not* the humiliation of its conclusion but the obligation to revive itself, to continue *beyond* the humiliation of an end.

In lines 57–64 "Affliction (I)" relocates itself as the speaker entertains a series of alternatives all of which are attempts to imagine life in circumstances which fail to make clear that there *are* alternatives:

> I reade, and sigh, and wish I were a tree;
>   For sure then I should grow
> To fruit or shade: at least some bird would trust
> Her houshold to me, and I should be just.
>
> Yet though thou troublest me I must be meek;
>   In weaknesse must be stout.
>
> (ll. 57–62)

Neither withdrawal "into abstraction" (Vendler, p. 45) nor the commitment to resoluteness offers, however, a viable solution to the problem, and the lines which follow test a final, extreme alternative:

> Well, I will change the service, and go seek
>   Some other master out.
>
> (ll. 63–64)

The alternative tested here is, clearly, a blasphemous one, but not, I think, for the obvious reasons alone. Finding "some other" lord is a tempting solution precisely because it is a solution, because it suggests the possibility of obtaining a service whose terms are clear and subject, therefore, to mastery. It represents, in other words, an effort to make life coherent again, to provide it with meaningful closure, to withdraw from its devastating inconclusiveness into the safety of the knowable. For while it is true that the speaker of this poem resists conclusion for the first fifty-four lines, he does so in order to postpone his own demise: when the only coherent story is the story of one's undoing, endings seem unacceptable, conclusions humiliating. But the lesson imposed at the fifty-fifth line—and resisted until the final lines of the poem—is that one is required to live on the other side of coherence: beyond representation, beyond the devastation endings impose, beyond the safety closure provides. The speaker of this poem does not want to do that. He wants, as Stanley Cavell has suggested in another context, "to *do* something instead of stopping and seeing. So he goes on doing the very thing which needs making up for."[9] He goes on looking for solutions. Of course the solution he arrives at in the penultimate lines is simply unacceptable. It requires that the speaker live without his "deare God" (l. 65) and he discovers, as he says it, how enormous that loss would be.

The speaker's concern in the final lines of "Affliction (I)" is with the re-establishment of relationship with God, but the relationship is not—and cannot be—stated in positive terms (that is, Let me love you, for now I truly love you). Rather, the possibility of relationship is constituted through a complex negative injunction whose conditions are preventive and forestalling in character:

> Ah my deare God! though I am clean forgot,
> Let me not love thee, if I love thee not.

> (ll. 65–66)

The speaker declares: Let me not love you (think I love you, act as though I love you, love you partially), if I do not truly love you. And in the event that I only act as though I love you, let me be utterly forgotten, for I would rather be forgotten than be false with you.[10] The double negatives register, at last, the speaker's willingness to avoid generating the conclusion of an experience which is, in fact, not conclusive. They register a resistance to closure, to complete and coherent self-representation, to knowledgeable statement—at least insofar as speech can ever exist without insisting on its own presence, or endings can happen without drawing attention to their finality.[11]

In other words, the conclusion of "Affliction (I)" denies its speaker precisely that "substitution of representation for presence"[12] which literature traditionally makes available. While this fact is, in itself, difficult, it is especially difficult here because access to representation must be relinquished at the very moment when self-presence seems least secure. The speaker's willingness to accept a life which guarantees neither adequate presence nor adequate representation is the great manifestation of devotion with which the poem concludes.[13]

I have spoken at some length about the motive toward autobiography in "Affliction (I)," suggesting that the poem's speaker tells the story of the past because it is the only story he has and because it has the capacity to represent him. In a remarkable essay on the conditions and limits of autobiography Georges Gusdorf comments: "The man who goes to the trouble of telling his own story knows that the present differs from the past, and that it won't repeat itself in the future; he has become more sensitive to differences than to resemblances; in the midst of constant change, of the unsettled state of events and men, he thinks it is useful and valuable to fix his own image, thinking without this he might disappear like everything else in the world."[14] Gusdorf goes on to suggest that the man who tells the story of his own life thinks that story worthy of conservation: "he bears witness to himself; he calls upon others to bear witness to the irreplaceable features of his presence." The dual emphasis in Gusdorf's description—on the threatening features of existence (its capacity to erode individual identity or to see persons as replaceable) and the desire to recover and conserve the self ("to inscribe in nature the mark of [one's] presence" [p. 107])—is appropriate, also, to the situation of Herbert's speaker. The description becomes troubling, however, when we remember the specific nature of autobiographical account in Herbert. For while it is true that the speaker sustains the story of the past as a substitute for the deprivation of life in the present, he does so only temporarily: whatever beliefs we have gathered about the speaker's identity have, by the fifty-fifth line, been relinquished, undermining the notion that there *are* stable features of the self or that autobiography, if it has the ability to recover lost time, has the corresponding ability to "fix it forever" (p. 113). If, as Paul Delany suggests, seventeenth-century autobiographers "sought . . . to commemorate the particular destiny that chance or inclination had given them,"[15] the commemoration we witness here is short-lived and ends by giving testimony to the uncertain nature of the speaker's destiny.

Descriptions of autobiography consistently include the notion that it arranges life's experiences into a coherent shape, telling the story from the point of view of a man who, as Scholes and Kellogg point out, "comes to terms with himself, realizes his nature, assumes his vocation" (p. 215). Roy Pascal suggests that autobiography "imposes a pattern on a life, constructs out of it a coherent story. It establishes certain stages in an individual life, makes links between them, and defines, implicitly or explicitly, a certain consistency of relationship between the self and the outside world."[16] Gusdorf calls autobiography a total and "coherent expression of [a man's] entire destiny" and speaks of it as the reconstitution of his "unity" (p. 11). These descriptions hold true for "Affliction (I)" insofar as it offers a complete, chronological account of the significant, shaping events in the life of its speaker, told from the perspective of a man who "realizes his nature." But when the story's shape becomes clear and assumes its coherent form, the word "coherent" suddenly fails to describe the story accurately, becomes paradoxical and disturbing. For when the account comes to a close it simultaneously renders itself suspect: the speaker knows that "choices" once made were not really choices, decisions once contemplated had already been decided by another, understanding once assumed possible never was attainable. When the shaping moment is achieved in "Affliction (I)" it points to the collapse of a coherent view of the self, revealing a speaker estranged from his own history and even from his own account. The pattern of his life is hardly, in the end, a coherent one—unless we wish to say that coherence is the one thing he is *sure* he does not have.

One of the chief characteristics of autobiography is, as John N. Morris has said, its ordering of experience into a "shape that answers better than mere continuous sequence,"[17] its substitution, in Gusdorf's words, of the "completed fact" for the "fact-in-the-making" (p. 117). The narrator who takes himself as his own subject already knows the order and outcome of events and sees them from a perspective unavailable to the man who lived them. Open-ended actions become decisive ones, careless actions take on significance: "The illusion begins from the moment at which the account *gives meaning* to an event which, when it happened, might have had several meanings and probably had none" (p. 117). The problem presented to us when we look at "Affliction (I)" from this point of view is that meaning is not given until the conclusion of the account—not because its assignment might alter the sequence of events, but because it would annihilate sequence. Insofar as the meaning of this poem is a lesson in the radical inappropriateness of making meaning, the speaker who reveals his standpoint must acknowledge that all descriptions of experience—including this one—are unreliable, and that experience itself cannot be represented in traditional ways. To acknowledge this from the start is, of course, to *have* no account; to suppress its acknowledgment is to write a defective account; to reveal it in the end is to relinquish the "completed" account. In his role as autobiographer the speaker of "Affliction (I)" both sabotages—and serves—his own interests.

Analysts of the historical development of autobiography suggest that early accounts were encouraged by Christianity's imperatives: each man, responsible for the state of his soul, was obliged to examine carefully his personal life and conscience, and to confess his sins to the Creator. But the "theological mirror" of the Christian soul in the Middle Ages is, Gusdorf suggests, a "deforming mirror which exploits without kindness the least fault of the moral person. The most elementary law of humility obliges the faithful man to discover everywhere the traces of sin, to suspect, beneath the more or less flattering appearance of his person, the menacing corruption of the flesh." If the Reformation freed man to look in a mirror and see himself as he was, "without perversion and without flattery" (p. 110), it nevertheless did not bring with it that hospitality toward autobiography which characterizes the modern age. As Delany notes: "Fundamental to the autobiographical urge is a sense of one's importance as an individual; in the twentieth century this is usually taken for granted, but in the seventeenth it was neither taken for granted—except in so far as men claimed significance because they lived under God's providence—nor supported by a general theory of democratic individualism as it is today" (p. 108).

This brief sketch may suggest to us that the impulse toward self-representation—characteristic of all autobiography—does not necessarily achieve sanction when the distorting mirror has been removed. A man may look into a clear mirror and see himself as he is, without having attained the corollary freedom to secure what he sees, give it a shape, assign it a meaning, call an end to it, present it to the world. If the limitations imposed by medieval imperatives disintegrate in the Renaissance, they do not depart leaving an open field in their place. Herbert's poems have a reference outside of the self to which they owe whatever authority they have. When they temporarily suspend knowledge of their referential nature, autobiography— or lyric, or dream—grows up in the space that suspension provides. But their powers of self-representation are always, in the end, defined and limited by their relationship with the God to whom, ultimately, they are addressed, and to whom they always return. In the case of "Affliction (I)" God's restrictions complicate the shape of autobiographical account—not because they require the speaker to see himself as sinful, but because they threaten the permanence and coherence of the self and frustrate the making of meaning upon which autobiography depends. The autobiographical impulse—and its manifestation—are here; what is not present is the sanction for them.[18]

part two

CHRONICLES
OF DISSOLUTION

chapter 4

"NO CONTINUING CITTY"

The speaker of a collapsing poem uses language to generate experience, to build a world where none seems possible. If he begins in despair—"there is no dealing with thy mighty passion"—he soon leaves that despair behind, engaged by the dilemma his words have made palpable for him. He also uses language, or the extension of language into speech, as a means of declaring authorship and exercising control: he takes upon himself the role of a storyteller who makes judgments, establishes the sequence of events, commands his material, and delivers a coherent account of experience. And he uses language to differentiate himself from others, to engineer his emergence in the world as an articulate being capable of self-manifestation. Language provides him with the materials of self-construction and its use makes possible what, after Hannah Arendt, I have elsewhere called "the space of appearance."

The story a collapsing poem tells might be described, then, the way the speaker of "Jordan (II)" does it when he says, after two stanzas, "So did I weave my self into the sense." This notion—that self and sense are identified, that self is *embodied* in sense, and that it gets embodied as a function of the labor of writing, is what has interested me here, and it is central, as I have already suggested, to Herbert's "Affliction (I)" as well. There, the speaker presents for fifty-four lines an autobiographical account in which he demonstrates his impulse toward having a history and representing it, toward weaving himself into the sense—and this seems emphatically true, because the account produced is a retrospective one, so that self-representation is identified with the production, or rather the conscious *re*production, of a story. In "The Collar," speech is also a form of self-manifestation, but instead of autobiography, what we have is quotation—saved, or conserved, speech. In all of my examples speech and writing are methods of embodying the self, and in retrospective poems the act of preservation merely emphasizes this. Retrospective speakers are, by definition, text makers: they use the text as a way of holding onto the sense that selves and their stories have an intelligible shape, that it is possible to separate the self and its sense from the surrounding world, that psychic and textual coherence are possible. In fact in many cases conserved stories exist precisely in order to fend off the dissolution that surrounds them—to fend off the sense that life's events are recurrent and confusing and that in them the self appears undifferentiated or does not appear at all.

Of course the problem with collapsing poems is that the stories they tell endure only as long as their collapsing conclusions are suspended or postponed. For when the conclusion arrives, it turns back upon the story, declares it deluded, and transforms it into an object of attention upon which some new reading must be inscribed. The speaker of "The Collar" is not a man who solves his problems and takes care of his needs; he is, we learn, a raving man who grows wilder and wilder with every word he speaks. His story must be understood not to effect his proper separation from unproductive circumstances, but rather to effect his improper separation from God and from the sacramental and even biblical world to which he belongs.

But one of the things we discover when we discover this—

and here I speak of "Jordan (II)" as well as "The Collar"—is that by the end of the poem the self is *no longer embodied in the sense at all*. He is, rather, alienated from it, and this is especially problematic because the new contexts toward which the ends of collapsing poems point us do not *accomplish* the rewriting toward which they gesture. In fact this rewriting never takes place in the course of the poem itself: it is promised by it but not performed in it. What we have at the end is a complete but defective representation of the self, and instructions for displacing and reconceiving that self, but no new or corrected self to take the place of the old.

In other words, collapsing poems also dissolve, discredit, reinterpret, rearrange, and otherwise compromise the material existence of the speaker: they first create—and then contest—the space of appearance. These poems are hospitable to the presentation of the self, but they are also hostile to it, and their hostility is especially evident when the dissolution of one account does not occasion the construction of another designed to take its place. In the sacramental world to which the ends of Herbert's poems often return us—the world of Christ's presence in, and dominion over, all our acts—the self frequently has no manifestation at all.

The knowledge Herbert's speakers alternately reject and embrace is, then, not only sacramental knowledge, it is also knowledge about their own dissolution, knowledge about death. In "Affliction (I)" and "The Collar" speakers desire willfully to alter—or to ignore or to transform—that knowledge; they want a body that endures, that is coherent, meaningful, distinguishable from others, safe from change. In the absence of access to such a body the retrospective speaker even produces its illusion—a coherent account whose boundaries are fortified against dangerous knowledge, and within whose walls the self appears both to have substance and to be safe. The desire to conserve experience *as story* repeats, in other words, the desire to conserve the body, for both reflect the belief that having presence means being coherently manifest, means having material form—and in the poems we have explored so far that means making the self substantial and discrete, guaranteeing in some way its ongoing life, protecting it from dissolution, dispersion, mingling, swallowing, and "peremptory *nullification.*"[1]

But the problem with collapsing poems is that in them safe bodies (like safe stories) are really illusions. They are the illusions collapsing poems exist to *preserve*, but they are also illusions which do not survive the conclusions of the poems that generate them. In the following pages I hope to describe alternatives to the problematic solutions offered by collapsing poems and to consider possibilities hinted at, but not fully explored, in them—the idea, for example, that bodies, like stories and other forms of manifest life, offer the illusion of adequate representation while in fact blocking its possibility; and the corresponding idea that bodies, like stories, might be unnecessary obstructions. In fact in the poems I shall examine next, speakers do not first appear and then disappear, as they do in collapsing poems. Instead, they practice the lessons of dissolution *from the start*—learning them as the poems begin, absorbing and practicing them as the poems proceed. While it is true that fully elaborated, coherent appearances are never achieved in these poems, that is because they do not fend off the dissolution that surrounds them: they acknowledge it, make peace with it, sometimes, even, embrace it. When the speaker of "Church Monuments" sends his body to school he sends it there actively to learn the lessons resisted so vigorously elsewhere. He sends it to embrace the inevitable fact of bodily corruption and to see in it opportunities for an alternative vision of what it might mean to be present both to oneself and to God.

"Church Monuments" begins this way:

> While that my soul repairs to her devotion,
> Here I intombe my flesh, that it betimes
> May take acquaintance of this heap of dust.

> (ll. 1–3)

The speaker's first act is to call attention to the body's individuality by separating body from soul: while the soul repairs to

her devotion, the flesh is sent to school below. This initial separation is crucial because it discriminates not only between
body and soul but between two kinds of discourse as well: the
soul's discourse with God, to which we are not party, and the
body's discourse upon matters of the flesh, to which we are.
But while in one sense the poem marks off for our attention,
and makes available to us, the body and its concerns, it does
so only to explore more fully the *problematics* of bodily existence.[2] The knowledge whose acquaintance the body is encouraged to make is not friendly knowledge at all—it is
knowledge about the *vulnerability* of manifest life. The
speaker's body is accessible to us throughout "Church Monuments" (it is in fact displayed), but its continuity is often impossible to grasp.

Nevertheless, the poem begins with a phrase—"Here I intombe my flesh"—which inaugurates the discourse of the
body in several ways. It identifies the body with the text before us (the body is "here" in the poem) and it calls attention
at the same time to the body's position (it is "here" in the
tomb), to its density (it is made of flesh), and to its coherence
(it can be owned, it can be placed, and it can also be enclosed).
Moreover, in taking acquaintance of the things before him, the
speaker suggests that the objects of his attention are palpable
too—as palpable as he. He will make friends with, and gain
knowledge of, something concrete, something outside the self:
this monument will learn about other monuments, this body
about other bodies. But if the opening lines stress both the
body's density and its concrete relation to other things, they
also suggest, paradoxically, that the real business of the body
is to abandon the concerns of the present and to learn not
about present things but about future ends:

> Here I intombe my flesh, that it betimes
> May take acquaintance of this heap of dust;
> To which the blast of deaths incessant motion,
> Fed with the exhalation of our crimes,
> Drives all at last.

> (ll. 2–6)

The dust to which these bodies are driven is the dust to which all bodies are driven, so that to study the ends of others is to study one's own ends as well. When the body "intombe[s]" itself it is a palpable body, a body with coherent form. But its project pitches it toward knowledge about, and even identity with, the disintegrated bodies which are here its object of concern.

Of course the opening lines have already complicated in other ways the very question of an "object" of concern. The speaker of "Church Monuments" puts his body into a tomb in order to learn what's in that tomb, in order to learn about human ends. But in so doing he also commits his body to the grave in what can only be described as an act of *self*-burial. And so he takes acquaintance of that heap of dust which is not only others but also the self. The double nature of the referent in "this heap of dust" suggests that the speaker learns about the ends which are outside of him (about the bodies that monuments mark), but also that he learns lessons in which he is deeply implicated himself. Stanley Fish has described the situation this way: "As the poem opens, 'intombe my flesh' seems merely a fancifully witty way of referring to the speaker's immobility while at prayer. Now we see that the witticism is a tautology: his flesh *is* its own tombe, one more heap of dust, exactly like those that are the objects of its contemplation. To take acquaintance of *this* heap of dust is to follow (with a vengeance) the Socratean injunction, 'know thy self' " (p. 166).

This early confusion about the object of contemplation—do I study others or do I study myself?—points to a difficulty which is really the poem's theme: the difficulty of maintaining the body's integrity in face of the tendency of one body to merge with another, of dust to merge with dust. When present bodies study future ends they press themselves, dangerously, toward those ends. But "Church Monuments" even suggests that ends have already been (in the true sense of the word) "incorporated," that *this* body is already perceived as identical with *that* heap of dust.

The school to which the speaker sends his body is, then, not a school in which some alien set of lessons will be administered. It is rather a school in which one elaborates upon the lessons one has already learned—uncovering, exploring, and representing them in surprising ways. In fact as stanza two makes clear, the body goes to school not only, as we had thought, to learn about distant ends, but to learn about, and to explore, origins:

> . . .Therefore I gladly trust
>
> My bodie to this school, that it may learn
> To spell his elements, and finde his birth
> Written in dustie heraldrie and lines.
>
> (ll. 6–9)

Of course the exploration of origins does not help the speaker to compose (that is, to arrange and to construct) himself, nor, by bringing his birth to consciousness, does it help him to rediscover and rebuild. Spelling one's elements might mean naming, and thereby reconstituting, the parts of the whole; but it can also mean decomposing those parts, distinguishing them from each other, separating and dispersing them. And finding one's birth "written in dustie heraldrie and lines" might mean tracing one's ancestry and locating the relationship of one's own life to the lives and histories of others (a reassuring activity). But it can also mean understanding one's beginning as something founded not in the lives, but in the deaths, of others. Here, one finds one's origins in the virtually unreadable chronicles of the dead, and this suggests that lives have their foundations not in other bodies but in other graves, in the remnants, or rather the dissolving accounts of the remnants, of others. The speaker explores and elaborates his knowledge—he goes to school, he learns, he spells, he finds his origins—but exploration and elaboration are not, here, acts of composition; they are acts of decomposition. The beginnings about which the body learns are the same as the ends to which death "drives all at last," so that while bodies appear to hold origins and ends asunder, they do so only to illustrate their ultimate identity.

Tombstone inscriptions also conserve, however imperfectly,

the appearance of a difference between origins and ends. Inscriptions are accounts of the lives of persons—they conserve human names and note the duration of human lives—and their dissolution, when it comes, is therefore significant. Of course in one sense it means little—only that the *record* of a separation between origins and ends will be obliterated, for the relationship itself, already a relationship of identity, will then only be confirmed. But the disintegration of histories is nevertheless crucial because it marks that moment—in what will soon be understood as a sequence of moments—when yet another illusion ends: first bodies have no body, and then accounts are of no account.

Herbert points to a direct relationship between the dissolution of bodies and inscriptions when he remarks in line 10 that "dissolution sure doth best discern" dissolution. The body, he declares, is the best reader of disintegrating inscriptions because it is in a state of disintegration itself. Made of dust, he adds, the body can read dust; made of earth it can read earth. Bodies and stories are also here resolved into common matter, and this means that neither is able to distinguish itself from, and thereby to point to or represent, the other. In fact at this point in "Church Monuments" it is also impossible to distinguish between the school to which the speaker entrusts his body and that body itself, for all comparisons turn out to be comparisons not between different but between identical things: *"Comparing,"* Fish suggests, "becomes an exercise in tautology," as dust is compared with dust, earth with earth (p. 167). This merely demonstrates, however, that the lessons have been properly learned: here, to learn one's lessons is to *be* indistinguishable both from the text and the teacher. In other words the successful student brings his body to school, but he doesn't take it home with him again. He understands his lessons (or demonstrates that he understands them) when he knows that his body isn't really his own.

But one of the most interesting things about "Church Monuments" is its determination not only to dissolve the distinction between beginnings and ends, between bodies and accounts of bodies, between students and schools, but even to dissolve the distinction between the signs that mark out the areas once occupied by bodies and the areas themselves. As the histories recorded on tombstones disintegrate, the lines

> . . . laugh at Jeat and Marble put for signes,
>
> To sever the good fellowship of dust,
> And spoil the meeting. What shall point out them,
> When they shall bow, and kneel, and fall down flat
> To kisse those heaps, which now they have in trust?
>
> (ll. 12–16)

They laugh, in other words, at the pretense involved in the gravestones' effort to conserve the body each has "in trust" and thereby to facilitate the memory others have of the individuality of the persons whose graves are marked. The separation of one person's dust from another's is a way of marking the autonomy of persons and remembering it. But here it is not only the case that one's body is dust, and that the story of one's body is dust, but also that neither the body's integrity, nor the representation of its integrity, can be conserved.[3] This poem demonstrates that the body is but a temporary (and finally inadequate) way of holding origins and ends asunder, and also that the body has integrity neither as a physical fact nor as a fact of *memory*. What disintegrates in "Church Monuments" is not just bodies but the systems of record that note whatever worldly presence, whatever definition, bodies had, and the systems of conservation by which, when records are gone, the brute fact of a body's prior individuality is marked. The mocking question, "What shall point out them?," itself suggests a time when all systems of recollection will disappear. The fact is that while tombstones represent absent persons, nothing represents tombstones, nothing points them out. As Joseph Summers has suggested, the monuments "are an ironic commentary on mortality; their states and messages mock at their composition of 'Jeat and Marble'—too obviously fleshly attempts to deny the dissolution of the bodies which they contain. Can there be monuments to monuments? Can monuments hope for a memorial . . . ?" (p. 131).[4] The answer, of course, is that they cannot: they are the last markers in the system, and when they are gone, nothing is subject to recall. When they "bow, and kneel, and fall down flat / To kisse those heaps, which now they have in trust," there will be no way of distinguishing the conserver from the conserved, and the poem's reversal of hierarchical relationships is a sign of this: proud guardians become supplicants (they bow and kneel) to those over whom they once watched. Sir Thomas Browne would later make the same point in *Urne-Burial:*

> Our Fathers finde their graves in our short memories, and sadly tell us how we may be buried in our Survivors. Grave-stones tell truth scarce fourty years: Generations passe while some trees stand, and old Families last not three Oaks. To be read by bare Inscriptions . . . to hope for Eternity by Enigmaticall Epithetes, or first letters of our names, to be studied by Antiquaries, who we were, and have new Names given us like many of the Mummies, are cold consolations unto the Students of perpetuity . . . Time hath spared the Epitaph of *Adrians* horse, confounded that of himself.[5]

In Browne, as in Herbert, the illegibility of inscriptions (they are "bare" and "enigmaticall" and they scarce "tell truth" for forty years) is tied to the confusion of relationships and roles: fathers are buried in the memories of their children; human families are measured in tree-lives; agents (antiquaries) become the objects of study (antiques); and the epitaph of the horse, but not of the rider, endures.

In the last lines of "Church Monuments" Herbert again makes clear the point with which he began:[6]

> Deare flesh, while I do pray, learn here thy stemme
> And true descent; that when thou shalt grow fat,
>
> And wanton in thy cravings, thou mayst know,
> That flesh is but the glasse, which holds the dust

That measures all our time; which also shall
Be crumbled into dust. Mark here below
How tame these ashes are, how free from lust,
That thou mayst fit thy self against thy fall.

(ll. 17–24)

Learning one's origins, one's "stemme and true descent," is the same as learning one's end. Origins do not clarify the originary terms of some personal project, some individual adventure. They do not *inaugurate* experience. Instead, they point to the fact that inaugurations are illusions because beginnings and ends are identical, and that middles, like bodies, are illusions as well. To learn one's origins is the *same* as to fit oneself against one's fall: origins and ends are dust, and the systems of presentation, conservation, and recollection are illusions as well. In this poem there is no means of conserving either persons, or their histories, or the memory of them.

"Church Monuments" chronicles the process of dissolution to which the ends of collapsing poems only point, but while representations of the integrity of the body are, in Herbert's poems, subject to collapse, representations of the body's vulnerability apparently need not be. There is, it seems, no sanction at all against representing the body's failure to acquire self-definition, its failure to be, or to remain, whole. In fact "Church Monuments" really suggests that certain forms of manifest life may well be a *barrier* to communication with God: after all, the speaker who prays leaves his body behind and his colloquy with God is, at least here, not only bodiless but wordless. If the self becomes present to God by leaving material life—and coherent representation—temporarily behind, then the process by which it learns to do that, or, perhaps, a chronicle of that process, may be just the sort of representation to which one should aspire.

Of course there is no getting around the fact that the representation of self in "Church Monuments" is the representation of a self in the process of losing its identity, the representation of a body in the process of relinquishing its boundaries:

> . . . flesh is but the glasse, which holds the dust
> That measures all our time; which also shall
> Be crumbled into dust.
>
> (ll. 20–22)

But the knowledge to which the body comes is knowledge to which it comes intentionally: the speaker puts himself to the task of knowing, becoming conscious of, and *elaborating upon,* precisely those things from which he protects himself in "Affliction (I)" and "The Collar"—as though to embrace this knowledge, to bring it to the surface and *represent* it, were to accept, and at least in one sense to offset, the full force of that knowledge. Instead of keeping dissolution at bay, poems like "Church Monuments" and, as I shall later suggest, "Mortification," *perform* the dissolution of the body in public—as an act of acknowledgment. And they suggest, thereby, that one alternative to a collapsing representation of the self is a dissolving representation of the self. It is precisely because, in this poem about the body, the body is always being effaced, and precisely because, in this unfolding lesson in physical dissolution, the poem unbends its readers' very ability to keep the objects of attention distinct—precisely because, in other words, the poem resists representing the self as an orderly, coherent, and bounded self, that it is able to avert that alienation of self from sense characteristic of collapsing poems.

In order to explain more fully the implications of what I mean I shall turn in the next pages to a discussion of Donne's famous meditation on the dissolution of the body, *Deaths Duell:* first, because it stands behind both "Church Monuments" and "Mortification," and second, because it explores in great detail the issues that are of concern to us here. Donne's sermon is a meditation on Psalm 68, verse 20, "And unto God the Lord belong the issues of Death," and this is the way it begins: "Buildings stand by the benefit of their *foundations* that susteine and *support* them, and of their *butteresses* that comprehend and *embrace* them, and of their *contignations* that knit and *unite* them: The *foundations* suffer them not to *sinke,* the *butteresses* suffer them not to *swerve,* and the *contignation* and knitting suffers them not to *cleave*" (p. 374). One of the interesting things about this statement is that its opening assertion—buildings stand—is precisely the statement the rest of the sermon exists to undermine. But the phrase "buildings stand" places buildings before us in all their materiality and strength. These buildings already exist; their parts have been put together and fashioned into a shape; they have been reared. In fact the entire passage supports the understanding that buildings which stand at all stand firmly and have a kind of permanence about them. Because their buttresses "comprehend and *embrace* them," their identity and coherence as objects seem assured: they can be embraced because they have a determinate shape, a shape that buttresses reaffirm in comprehending. And because their contignations "knit and *unite* them," the parts of the building are bound together—not as disparate parts are bound but as related ones are organized into a harmonious whole.

In the second sentence of this introductory statement, having explained the function of foundations, buttresses, and contignations, Donne also points to the ways in which these ward off dangers—as though in elaborating on possible dangers only to insist they will not be suffered, he demonstrates that he is not unaware of the problems to which buildings are heir: buildings can sink and swerve and cleave—but these buildings cannot. Their firmness, straightness, and integrity are reaffirmed.

But what is the source of strength for this building of ours? Of what are our buttresses, foundations, and contignations made? "The body of our building," Donne continues, "is in the former part of this verse" (p. 374). This statement means that the body (foundations, buttresses, and contignations) of our building (our body, our physical life) is in the verse from Scripture upon which his sermon comments: "And unto God the Lord belong the issues of death." Of course in many ways this statement is an odd one: it sends the reader back to the beginning of the sermon in search of the verse that is to serve as foundation for the building whose construction he has so patiently followed. And it takes the listener out of the world in which physical buildings are constructed, and places him in a world in which buildings have, for foundations and buttresses, lines of text. Moreover at this point we are merely referred to the text—our support "is in the former part of this verse"—and the fact that Donne refers to his line rather than quoting it only emphasizes something that is about to become startlingly clear. The building he has so carefully constructed for us and whose palpability, integrity, unity, and permanence have been so painstakingly described, is held together by its utter reliance on the belief that "our *issue in death* shall be an *entrance into everlasting life*," or, as Donne suggests in a restatement of this idea, "our deliverance . . . *from death, in death*, and *by death*, will abundantly doe all the offices of the *foundations*, of the *butteresses*, of the *contignation* of this our *building*" (p. 376). But what is the nature of a building whose foundation and support is its belief not in the permanence of buildings but in their impermanence?

The building we are building is—in the ordinary sense of the term—no building at all, and though we have not yet arrived at the point of giving up this sense of ourselves as structures on firm foundations, it is nonetheless the case that we are encouraged to entertain, simultaneously, several increasingly incompatible ideas: that we are buildings; that we are buildings whose support and foundation is a belief; and that we are buildings whose support and foundation is a belief in the insubstantiality and insupportability of buildings. If the opening lines ask me to understand that the building being described is my body, the fact remains that the body I have, once I have acknowledged as source the statement "unto God the Lord belong the issues of Death," is a dying body, a body supported, comprehended, embraced, and united, by a belief in its own terrible mortality. In other words, the image of the body created in the first lines of the sermon is radically revised by the rest, as we discover at each point—at each corner and wall, at each limb and joint—that the body is held together by and is suffused with, knowledge of its own dissolution.

In fact the image of the body as a positive building never returns again. Quite the contrary: what Donne develops with a vengeance is the idea that the body is a body of corruption—as he complains with the apostle Paul, "Wretched man that he

is, who shall deliver him from this body of death?" The building he describes, in other words, comes to stand for the body
built for unbuilding, the body constructed on the premise that
all bodies are prisons—all wombs are tombs—from which we
pray for deliverance, the body built from, joined by, founded
in, held together with, a faith in its own corruption. The language of support and stability is, finally, a language that can
only refer to the *thoroughness* with which this faith informs
us—a thoroughness that at once binds and unbinds, strengthens and dissolves. The image of the body in the opening lines
turns out to be an Herbertian illusion (now you see it, now
you don't), a vision of the body's composition which becomes
a vision of its decomposition in a stroke.[7]

First, man's body is a body of death because its beginning
and its end are the same and because, as a consequence, man
cannot plot for himself a middle ground in which freedom of
action, or freedom of development, is possible. He has no
body, no middle, no world which, having begun, unfolds, develops, grows, endures. The fact is that in this world all exits
are entrances, all entrances exits, all "periods" are really
"transitions": "But then this *exitus a morte* is but *introitus in
mortem*, this *issue*, this deliverance from that *death*, the death of
the *wombe*, is an *entrance*, a delivering over to *another death*, the
manifold deathes of this *world*" (p. 377). The passage begins by
suggesting that deliverance from the death of the womb (it is
a death because in it we do not know we live, do not have
consciousness of life) is not only a deliverance *from*, but also a
deliverance *over to*, death, so that what appears to be a
"period"—life in the womb—marked on one end by imprisonment and on the other by liberation, is really no period at all
but rather a transition or passage. It is a passage because the
liberating end provides no closure, and also because the
deathliness of the womb is identical with that death *into* which
we are delivered. There are two important points to be made
here. Periods become passages when they have no closure,
when their terminal points become points of entry; and periods become passages when they have no identity and therefore cannot be differentiated from one another. In this double
transformation of periods into passages what we have

are not corridors that lead us into rooms, but corridors that lead us into other corridors. And what drops out of sight is the coherent, identifiable middle, the middle understood as something which keeps origins and ends apart, the middle as a world that *continues*. In the universe Donne describes there is no middle and it is, in fact, impossible to travel anywhere at all: "Wee have a winding sheete in our Mothers wombe, which growes with us from our conception, and wee come into the world, wound up in that *winding sheet*, for wee come to *seeke a grave* . . . We celebrate our owne funeralls with cryes, even at birth; as though our *three-score and ten years of life* were spent in our mothers labour, and our circle made up in the first point thereof" (pp. 377–378). Beginnings and ends fold in upon each other and make progress impossible, as though "our circle [were] made up in the first point thereof." The implications of this passage, as of the next one to which I shall turn, are precisely that our circle is made up in the first point, that birth cries and death cries are the same, and that growth, development, and change are illusions. The passage also makes clear, as does the language of periods and transitions, that narrative life, like daily and worldly life, is impossible: lives that make no progress are not subject to representation in ordinary narrative accounts, for the latter depend upon the very notion of sequence so completely annihilated here.

The body is a body of death because its periods are transitions, and its transitions are indistinguishable from one another. And the body is a body of death because it translates progress into inertia, into the absence of movement and growth. Donne reiterates and expands upon these two points when he adds that God has given men *"earth* for their *materialls* to bee made of earth, and he hath given them *earth* for their *grave* and sepulture, to *returne* and resolve to *earth*, but not for their *possession"* (p. 378). Man is given materials with which to constitute his body when he begins, and a material resting place into which he can deposit his body when he dies, but his material life and material end (grave and sepulchre mark doubly the empty space once occupied by the human person) fail to provide him with a means of self-definition. Made of earth and returned to earth he is indistinguishable from the materials of which he is formed. These materials are, as Donne says later in the same line, "not for [his] *possession*," which is to say, he cannot either hold them or hold onto them, cannot keep them from resolving into earth. Neither the materials that make up the body, nor the materials of which the body's grave is made, can resist resolution into the common matter from which both have been constructed—so that to be made of materials at all ceases to be a mark of distinction. When Donne adds that *"here wee have no continuing citty*, nay no *cottage* that continues, nay no persons, no bodies that continue" (p. 378), he therefore probably means something like, "for here we have no cities that last, no cottages, persons, or bodies that last." But his statement also suggests that bodies in time are so completely vulnerable that their lives from moment to moment hardly seem continuous at all. The passage also makes clear that persons and bodies are subject to exactly the same dissolution and resolution into earth as cities and cottages are. This failure to "continue" means that persons, like bodies, have no safe temporal life, or that the life they do have is a life threatened with dissolution at every moment. The body is a body of death because it cannot resist its own resolution into earth, because it cannot "continue," because it cannot maintain its own integrity in time.

The dissolution of the body is also, at least in part, a function of the multiple attacks the body suffers "from the manifold deaths of this world, the *omni die* and the *tota die*, the *every dayes death* and *every houres death*" that precede what Donne calls "the *final dissolution* of body and soule, the end of all" (pp. 379-380). But even this, the dissolution we think of as final, is not final: "But then is that the end of all? Is that dissolution of body and soule the last death that the body shall suffer? . . . It is not. Though this be *exitus a morte*, it is *introitus in mortem:* though it bee an *issue from* the manifold *deaths* of this *world*, yet it is an *entrance* into the *death of corruption* and *putrefaction* and *vermiculation* and *incineration*, and dispersion in and from the *grave*, in which every dead man dyes over again" (p. 380). Once again, exit equals entrance and the process of dissolution which seemed at once so thorough and so final actually begins again as our bodies are dispersed both "in" the grave and "from" the grave, and our death to this world is repeated by the physical dissolution we suffer in the grave and beyond. Donne is vivid in his description of this *"posthume* death" and his language stresses the way in which the destructiveness of death in this world is repeated in, and doubled by, the death of our bodies in the next: "we must al passe this *posthume* death, this *death* after *death,* nay this death after buriall, this *dissolution* after *dissolution,* this death of *corruption* and *putrefaction,* of *vermiculation* and *incineration,* of *dissolution* and *dispersion* in and *from* the grave" (p. 382). Like Herbert's description of the hierarchical reversals which occur when monuments "kisse those heaps, which now they have in trust," Donne's description of the dissolution of the body is characterized by the violence it does to orders, hierarchies, and rules of governance, to social and familial relations and taboos: "Miserable *incest,* when I must bee *maried* to my *mother* and my *sister,* and bee both *father* and *mother* to my *owne mother* and *sister, beget,* and *beare* that *worme* which is all that *miserable penury;* when my *mouth* shall be *filled* with *dust,* and the *worme* shall *feed,* and *feed sweetly* upon me" (p. 382). The body in dissolution observes no boundaries—not the boundaries between self and other, not the boundaries between other and other, and not, therefore, the boundaries between mother, father, sister, and self. Later in the same passage, Donne declares, "This is the most inglorious and contemptible *vilification,* the most deadly and peremptory *nullification* of man, that wee can consider," and this is especially true because in this *"death* after *death"* man is so completely dispersed ("mingled . . . with the dust of every high way, and of every dunghill, and swallowed in every puddle and pond") that his image can no longer be picked out— that is, neither his image, nor the record of his image, nor the memory of that record endures. This is the same difficulty described by Herbert's speaker in "Church Monuments"—not only the failure of bodies to continue, but the failure of their materials to remind us that they ever lived. As Donne points out, when God asked Ezekiel, *"can these bones live?"* there were, at least, *"bones* to bee *seene,* something visible, of which it might be sayd, can this thing live? But in this death of *incineration,* and dispersion of dust, wee see *nothing* that we can call *that mans"*

(p. 383). The absence of "something visible" that we can call man's, the utter absence of distinguishing shape and of image, and, in Herbert's terms, of the record and memory of images, threatens at their core the notions both of having and of representing the self.[8]

But I want to return for a moment to an earlier passage in the sermon, a passage which suggests, I think, the necessity of understanding the ways in which this body is a body of death, and of comprehending as well the importance of relinquishing the vision of the body first created, and then dispelled as illusion, in the first sentences of the sermon. The passage to which I refer begins, again, this way: "hee hath *given* them *earth* for their *materialls* to bee made of *earth*, and he hath given them *earth* for their *grave* and sepulture, to *returne* and resolve to *earth*, but not for their *possession: Here wee have no continuing citty*, nay no *cottage* that continues, nay no persons, no bodies that continue." And it goes on:

> Whatsoever moved Saint *Jerome* to call the journies of the *Israelites*, in the wildernes, Mansions, the *word* . . . signifies but a *journey*, but a peregrination. Even the *Israel of God* hath no mansions; but journies, pilgrimages in this life . . . And though the *Apostle* would not say *morimur*, that, whilest *wee are in the body* wee *are dead*, yet hee sayes, *Peregrinamur*, whilest wee are *in the body*, wee are but in *a pilgrimage*, and we are *absent from the Lord*; hee might have sayd *dead*, for this whole *world* is but an *universall churchyard*, but our *common grave*; and the life and motion that the greatest persons have in it, is but as the shaking of buried bodies in their graves.   (p. 378)

Let me clarify the sequence of transformations upon which this passage turns. Man is made of materials; he does not hold onto these materials forever (that is, does not "possess" them); nothing else holds onto its materials either—neither cities nor cottages nor persons nor bodies "continue." In fact, because the material world does not "continue," it can hardly be said to be made up of things—of cottages and mansions—at all. Rather the world is constituted of (passing) activities—of wan-

dering, for example, and journeying. But since, when we journey, our destination (like that of the Israelites) is not present to
us, and since God is always our destination, we are, when we
journey in this world, *"absent from the Lord."* To be absent from
the Lord is to be dead, and therefore all "life and motion" is
but a "shaking" in the grave. The lines move, in other words,
from a description of man's material constitution, to the assertion that nothing material lasts, to the suggestion that material
life, when it does not last, cannot be said precisely to be material at all. It can only be said to be in transit—to be passing or
wandering or journeying—like the Israelites, who were not
mansion-builders but pilgrims. Of course when you are a pilgrim you are not so much a person as a person-in-transit, a
wanderer pitched toward, but absent from, your destination;
so that it is probably more accurate to say, even though a pilgrim lives in his body in the world, that insofar as he is in his
body he is not so much present as absent, for he is absent from
the destination that counts, absent from the Lord.

The conclusion of the argument points, then, to a fact at
once comforting and frightening. To be in the body is not to
be manifest and therefore present to God, it is to fail to "continue," to be in transit (on a pilgrimage), and really to be absent from God. The thought is frightening, I would contend,
because as collapsing poems suggest and as this sermon con-
firms, it is not easy for speakers to accept the idea that embodiment is both an obstruction and an illusion: in "Jordan (II)"
the embodiment of self-in-sense *alienates* the speaker, however
unintentionally, from God. And in "The Collar," though embodiment is a strategy designed to *produce* for the rebellious
speaker the separation from God which he desires, the discovery of what it really means to be absent from the Lord occasions a return to him, and that occasions, at the poem's end,
the speaker's *dis*embodiment. To be present to the Lord is to
die, however reluctantly, to one's story and to one's body and
to one's self. Of course the power, and the pressure, of
Donne's sermon are themselves designed to overcome the te-
naciousness with which men hold onto the idea that being in
the body means being present.[9] But here, though the sermon is

morbid and terrifying, it also offers unusual comfort. For if being in the body means being not present to God but separated from him and *absent from him*, then giving up the body or, more particularly, acknowledging its dissolution, permits one to accept—rather than to resist or to oppose—the facts of bodily life, and even to embrace dissolution, to learn its procedures, to practice them in public as conscious acts. And it permits one to be, as a consequence, less *in*accessible to the Lord, and therefore as present to him as one can be to him in this life. "Hast thou gone about to *redeeme thy sinne*," Donne asks, "by *fasting*, by *Almes*, by *disciplines* and *mortifications*, in way of *satisfaction* to the *Justice* of *God?*" (p. 391). He might also have asked, Hast thou gone about practicing—as I have done here—the dissolution of this body already in dissolution? Hast thou gone about practicing death—as I have done here—in way of satisfaction to the justice of God?

The forcefulness with which Donne's sermon presses its point is, I want to suggest, an indication that it means to practice, to rehearse, to teach death, and thereby to acknowledge the dissolution which, though we resist knowledge of it, nonetheless characterizes our "life and motion" in this world.[10] Herbert's "Church Monuments" is also, clearly, a means of teaching its speaker to absorb and practice the lessons that monuments teach: he sends his body to school; he instructs it to "learn" (l. 17) and to "mark" (l. 22) that it might "fit [it]self against [its] fall" (l. 24). Like Donne's sermon, Herbert's poem teaches its lessons with remarkable and often terrifying rigor, but its intentions are not narrowly grim ones. Poems about the dissolution of the body are, in Herbert, designed to teach us the lesson Donne's sermon makes abundantly clear: that being present to the Lord has nothing at all to do with being present to oneself in any of the ways practiced by the speakers of collapsing poems. Rather it is a function of one's willingness to give up the body's obstructive and illusory access to presence in favor of the unobstructive access that comes of relinquishing the body, of learning, practicing, and chronicling its dissolution.[11]

Herbert's "Mortification" is just such an effort to chronicle the dissolution of the body, and when the speaker exclaims, in the first line of the poem, "How soon doth man decay!" he brings to the very beginning of his account of man's life knowledge about its end. But if the opening line narrows the distance between the first moment and the last ("How soon . . . !"), the remaining lines collapse that distance altogether:

> When clothes are taken from a chest of sweets
>   To swaddle infants, whose young breath
>   Scarce knows the way;
>   Those clouts are little winding sheets,
> Which do consigne and send them unto death.

(ll. 2–6)

The "chest of sweets" from which swaddling clothes are taken suggests that parents prepare for a child's arrival and compensate for his lack of worldly knowledge by bringing to bear upon his life protective designs of their own. But the stanza's final lines point both to the futility and to the violation of beginning intentions. The child who "scarce knows [his] way" simply has no way (lack of knowledge is not his problem) and those who would protect him only send him to his grave. As in "Church Monuments" and *Deaths Duell* the end flattens itself into the beginning so that there is no space at all between the two: swaddling clothes *are* winding sheets; there is no middle; there is no developing plot; there is no life.

This transformation of beginnings into ends, of entrances into exits, is a familiar subject to the reader of Donne's sermon, and its point in "Mortification" is essentially the same: where we intend growth or progress or development we find only that the materials out of which we mean to shape them are the materials out of which ends are made. Herbert presents us, in the first lines of his stanzas, with beginnings which are *prior* to decay—but our experience in this poem is the repeated experience of their violation, of their difficult transformation into, and rewriting as, ends. The regularity with which these transformations are wrought teaches us to see the ways in which ends are built into beginnings, teaches us to learn what Donne asserts all along: that the "circle [is] made up in the first point thereof."[12]

In stanza two, for example, infants are boys and they step into "voluntarie graves" under their own power:

> When boyes go first to bed,
> They step into their voluntarie graves,
>   Sleep bindes them fast; onely their breath
>   Makes them not dead:
>   Successive nights, like rolling waves,
> Convey them quickly, who are bound for death.

> (ll. 7–12)

Of course what these lines really mean is that boys who step into *bed* voluntarily step, *without knowing it*, into graves. But when Herbert calls their beds "voluntarie graves" he eliminates the interval between their intentions (they want to sleep) and the results of those intentions (sleep binds them faster than they know; they go to a final, not a temporary, rest). And so intentions are not simply violated, they are revised, because the end so overpowers the beginning that original motives are, quite literally, rewritten by their outcomes. These boys appear to embrace death, to move toward it with open arms.

In the remaining stanzas the process of violation and revision repeats itself three times:

> When youth is frank and free,
> And calls for musick, while his veins do swell,
>   All day exchanging mirth and breath
>   In companie;
>   That musick summons to the knell,
> Which shall befriend him at the houre of death.

> When man grows staid and wise,
> Getting a house and home, where he may move

Within the circle of his breath,
　　Schooling his eyes;
That dumbe inclosure maketh love
Unto the coffin, that attends his death.

　　When age grows low and weak,
Marking his grave, and thawing ev'ry yeare,
　　Till all do melt, and drown his breath
　　　When he would speak;
A chair or litter shows the biere,
Which shall convey him to the house of death.

(ll. 13–30)

Whether youth is "frank and free" and life appears to have scope, or man is "staid and wise" and life is lived within modest limits, the result is always the same. For the materials out of which life is fashioned are identical to those out of which death is made: the music that fills one's veins also summons mourners to the funeral; the house one builds "within the circle of his breath" proves but an imitation coffin. The world described in these stanzas is parsimonious in the extreme, and because that is true, because the materials of the end are always available in the beginning (breath and death are interchangeable), action is of necessity suicidal.[13] The building of a home is not followed by, nor does it even postpone, the building of the tomb; it *is* the building of the tomb. Actions do not generate alternatives and add to the repertoire of events. They only repeat past events (or repeat the same event) and close the repertoire down.

In fact though the stages in "Mortification" resemble, in certain obvious ways, those stages which together compose a life, the real business of this poem is not composition but decomposition, the dissolution both of life and of the narrative line that represents it. Unlike the speakers of collapsing poems, who labor at continuity and coherence by practicing the most complete sort of denial, the speaker of "Mortification" brings to the center of his discourse that knowledge which exists only at the periphery of collapsing poems— knowledge of our vulnerability as human persons, knowledge that our bodies are bodies of death—and chronicles the dissolution of continuity and coherence which such knowledge makes inevitable. The consequences for an understanding of what it means to have a life and what it means to tell a story are manifold. Stanley Fish and Joseph Summers have both suggested that in "Church Monuments" the effects of dissolution can be traced in the structure of Herbert's sentences: references are multiple or unclear; the subject of one phrase becomes the object of another; the boundaries between sentences (there are more semicolons than periods) and between stanzas (they often begin in midsentence) have a tendency to disappear.[14] In "Mortification" the effects of dissolution—or rather its implications—can be traced both in the structure of the speaker's story and in the shape of the poem's plot.

When beginnings and ends do not organize into some shape the materials of each stage of our life, and when, instead, ends dominate all our beginnings, then they do so at the expense of each stage's development. In "Mortification" the infants of stanza one have not grown toward boyhood when the stanza ends, nor have boys grown into youths at the end of stanza two. Instead, infant beginnings are immediately rewritten as infant ends (birth equals burial), so that infancy is over as soon as it has begun. This means that no stage of life has any real extension and that no episode of the story either develops or endures. But this means, in turn, that the relationship between stages will be a peculiar one. After all, when each episode's primary relationship is to its own end—when the relation of infants to boys and boys to youths is broken by the more powerful relation each bears to his own death—then the linking of episodes or stages to each other, and the consequent production either of a life or of a plot, becomes virtually impossible. Instead, this poem disjoins elements and produces not sequences but fragments, not plots but pieces. By the end of stanza two, boys are bound for death, and in stanza three, youths have no boyish origins: death intervenes at boyhood's end and makes those origins inaccessible. The same is true for the men of stanza three and the old men of four: theirs is a history whose episodes never knit themselves together to produce a plot because each episode has its own conclusion and each new episode must therefore begin as though it were the first.

But it is not enough to say that death transforms all beginnings into ends and all sequences into mere stages. One must say, as well, that it transforms all stages *into the same stage.* For no stage has a content which distinguishes it—for long—from another. Instead, dominated by death, infants do what boys and youths do: they prepare for their own funerals. The point I want to make is one on which Donne's sermon is absolutely clear: death resolves all matter into common matter. Episodes, stages, the sequences they compose—all are dominated by death, all speak of death, all mean death. When chronological stages fail to develop and differentiate themselves, when sequences fail to develop and leave us instead with episodes, when episodes are all composed of common matter, then death has returned to dust not only cities, cottages, persons, and bodies, but also poems.

Of course neither Donne's sermon nor Herbert's death poems accomplishes death and finishes with the body. In fact much of the power of *Deaths Duell* derives from the experience that in it the body is under *unremitting* siege: each time one thinks the final death has come, there is, it seems, another death to suffer, another transformation of exit into entrance to undergo, a new *"vermiculation* and *incineration"* to endure. In many respects the same thing is true of "Church Monuments": the speaker sends his body to school to learn the lessons of dissolution, but those lessons are taught with greater rigor than one might wish. To fit oneself against one's fall is to learn and to relearn the dissolving lessons whose acquaintance we have only just begun to make, so that the end of the poem suggests not that the task has been accomplished, but rather that it is a task one must take to heart and practice—over and over again.

I have already suggested that when we practice dissolution we practice our deliverance from this body of death, from the body conceived as obstacle and barrier to God. But it is also the case that when one practices dissolution one practices a mode of being in the world in which one rests neither in one's being nor in one's body nor in one's self. In fact one practices a mode of being in which there is no rest at all: the self is transitory, in pilgrimage, subject to virtually ceaseless transformation. To practice one's disembodiment is not to accomplish it and then to rest in the accomplishment; it is, rather, to find in the activity of disembodiment a mode of being which is the very expression of the self's vulnerability and instability in this world. When Herbert says, at the end of "Mortification," "Yet Lord, instruct us so to die, / That all these dyings may be life in death" (ll. 35–36), we must understand him to mean at least two things: "All these dyings" are "life in death" not only because they bring yet another transformation—life *after* death for the faithful—but also because life is made up of, *is constituted by*, acts of relinquishment, acts of disembodiment.[15]

Now in some respects collapsing poems practice dissolution too: they first hold the body in place, and then point to its disintegration, so that in them the self is alternately embodied and disembodied. But collapsing poems demonstrate the *incompatibility* of representation and dissolution: one lives, resolutely, in the body, but only as long as knowledge of death is suspended or delayed. When that knowledge arrives—as inevitably it does—it renders both bodies and stories unfit for habitation, and thereby brings with it an end to representation. Dissolving poems, on the other hand, suggest that to *chronicle* one's own dissolution is not to lose but to *gain access* to representation, albeit to a new kind of representation. When Summers suggests that "Church Monuments" is a hieroglyph which "image[s its] subject" (p. 135) I am inclined to agree because I am interested in the way the poem *represents* dissolution. But Summers does not mean to suggest, as I do, that "Church Monuments" images the poem's speaker. For there is, in Summers' view, a "sharp distinction between [Herbert's] poems and himself which still warns the reader." The speaker may use "himself" in order to produce "the objective creations which [are] his poems" (p. 85), but he does not use his *poems* in order to produce *himself*. The materiality of "Church Monuments" is not, as Summers understands it, a sign of the speaker's capacity to appear before us. It is, rather, a sign of his capacity to produce orderly objects and to contribute them to the world. Indeed, one of the odd facts about Summers' reading is that it offers, at once, a powerful description of the dissolution to which proud flesh is driven, and suggests, at the same time, that the poem's materiality is a way of *ordering* the disorder it describes. Because the poem is a *"memento mori"* (p. 133), "construct[ed] so that its form image[s] the subject" and becomes "an integral part of the meaning" (p. 135), the dissolution Herbert describes is neither—as Fish would say—a sign of personal and textual dissolution nor, as I am suggesting, a sign that personal dissolution has a textual representation. Rather, divorced from the self that produces it, the text's "formal organization" domesticates and harmonizes the dissolution it exists to portray.

Fish's reading follows, and elaborates upon, Summers' reading; but Fish suggests that poems like "Church Monuments" "become true (accurate) hieroglyphs only when their pretensions are exposed" (p. 168). In Fish's view the poem's efforts at specification are *always* being undermined—and he takes this to mean that specification has become "impossible" (p. 169). Indeed Fish argues that "Church Monuments" is "a *profoundly* unsatisfactory poem, for there is no position one can assume in relation to it without compounding and extending the error it exposes" (p. 179) and he thus argues that the poem both describes and enacts its own dissolution and disappearance: "Summers tells us that the hieroglyphic form of 'Church Monuments' serves to 'reinforce the message,' but that message itself crumbles just as we are about to carry it away" (p. 169). I want to assert, however, that Herbert's poems do not—in the ordinary sense of the word—vanish before our eyes. Rather, "Church Monuments" and "Mortification" *embody disembodiment:* they represent the self in the very process of losing its access to conventional representation. Indeed, when the self does its dying work properly, it gives expression to that restless mode of being in the world with respect to which no *additional* relinquishment of self is required.[16]

The dissolution of self and story is not, moreover, a feature unique to death poems. In fact I would like to suggest that dissolution is often Herbert's theme, that its lessons are taught, learned, and practiced with great frequency in *The*

Temple. In some poems, however, dissolution is simultaneous with what one of Herbert's readers has called "reinvention,"[17] so that the violation and disintegration of self so prominent in "Church Monuments" becomes, in "Artillerie" and "The Flower," the variability, indeed the *multiplicity,* of story and self. In any case, what all of these poems have in common is their understanding that death is not outside of us—either as a danger to be postponed or as an end to be at once feared and desired because of its finality—but rather that it is inside of us (the body is a body of death) and that all periods are therefore transitions, all transitions passageways. The speaker of Herbert's "The Pilgrimage" sets out on a journey whose end, he hopes, will bring spiritual, physical, and narrative completion. But the boundaries of his journey are, from the start, problematic in the extreme. The poem opens "in the middle of things," so that origins have a curious status in it; and death intervenes (also, as it were, in the middle of things) before any of the speaker's ends have been acquired. Death's intervention makes the acquisition of wholeness an impossible project, but that is exactly the point: the boundaries of the speaker's journey—and of his body and of his story—are precisely what the poem exists to undermine. "The Pilgrimage" provides an allegory of the relationship between events and ends—of the relationship between self-representation and death—upon which all chronicles of dissolution are founded. And because it does I shall turn, in the following pages, to an analysis of it, and then to a discussion of its consequences for poems which are *not* meditations upon death, but which nonetheless chronicle the instability of self and story about which death poems teach us.

chapter 5

THE DISSOLUTION OF BODIES AND STORIES

Because "The Pilgrimage" opens "in the middle of things"—
its speaker merely says "I travell'd on"—it gestures toward a
history whose features are unrecoverable; it hints at a beginning utterly absent from view. And so the opening of "The
Pilgrimage" both indicates and empties the past, which appears as a category whose content has been erased. What appears, however, in place of a beginning capable of specifying
the speaker's generative circumstances is the constitutive end
capable of specifying his goal. The story of "The Pilgrimage"
comes into view just as the hill toward which the speaker
moves becomes visible, so that against the failure to provide
an adequate account of origins, the poem immediately sets a
defining end, the accomplishment of which is the speaker's set
purpose:

> I travell'd on, seeing the hill, where lay
> My expectation.

(ll. 1–2)

In fact the poem suggests that, especially in the absence of beginnings, access to ends is a *condition of representation:* the sighting of the hill is simultaneous with the appearance of the speaker and with the initiation of his story. It locates him; it makes his journey available as an object of consciousness; and it establishes the arena in which travel and quest and narrative will occur. If the absence of a beginning prevents us from fully imagining the organizing shape of events, the presence of a visible, and in fact dominating, end performs that function instead: it provides an anchoring goal to take the place of an anchoring origin. So that while we do not know when the speaker set out on his journey, how he lost what he lost, or why he decided to find it, we do come to know that he has a purpose in mind, that his desire to achieve it is the motivating force behind his actions, that it is the accomplishment in whose light all other accomplishments will be read.

Of course the fact remains that while the hill marks out the dimensions of the journey and establishes a critical relationship between ends and events, it is unclear in the first three stanzas just what the journey is actually a journey toward. We know that the speaker moves toward a specific destination and that its achievement motivates his activities, but why the hill is valued is not entirely clear. In fact, the poem asks us to read toward a second term about whose content we really know nothing at all: what lies on the hill is what the speaker expects to find there, but the substance of his "expectation" remains a mystery. The poem sets the speaker's destination before us at the outset, but as soon as it is established as a reality it is, simultaneously, masked and postponed—access to it and to its contents deferred.[1]

Nevertheless, it is in relation to this (masked) ending that the poem's events are actually construed—or in relation to which its meanings are not so much decided as deferred. The speaker's desire to get "unto the gladsome hill" makes him yield all interest in present events, all questions about their meaning. He is interested, almost exclusively, in the way present events signify a future one—the way they signal progress, mark speed, and predict arrival. He is not interested in, and the poem does not make available to us, the sort of experience one might have living in a present *not* dominated by ends, a present in which events are seen as meaningful trials to the spirit, reflections of struggle, and occasions for understanding and growth.

In the early phases of the journey, for example, the traditional dangers of the swing between Despair and Pride are allegorized in the form of a gloomy cave and a rock, set opposite each other on the traveler's path. The antithesis represents a familiar Christian problem, the danger born of the conviction that the speaker will never get what he wants, and the danger born of the certainty that he will—both sins of confidence.[2] But the poem mentions these trials only to point out that they have already been overcome:

> The gloomy cave of Desperation
> I left on th' one, and on the other side
>   The rock of Pride.

                                (ll. 4–6)

The speaker's lack of surprise, both at finding them and at surviving their dangers, suggests that if he understands anything at all it is the importance of putting both trials behind. What we do not know is whether he understands fully their function in a Christian pilgrimage, whether he feels tested by their presence, or justified by his ability to pass through. Like markers along a route, the cave and rock refer us to a set of familiar but unexplored trials whose most salient feature is their failure to pose any serious threat to the forward progress of the poem.

To cave and rock we soon add meadow and copse, and with them a second set of antitheses:

> And so I came to Fancies medow strow'd
>   With many a flower:
> Fain would I here have made abode,
> But I was quicken'd by my houre.

                                (ll. 7–10)

Fancy's meadow is a place whose joys are hallucinatory, whose flowers, for example, are images formed by the imagination to entice the pilgrim and prevent him from proceeding. Care's copse is a place of sorrow and trouble, but it presents a similar danger: if fancy's meadow encourages the speaker to forget his goals and obligations in favor of the pleasures of the present, Care's copse threatens to make him forget his destination by absorbing him in difficulties. But while both traps are laid to retard a pilgrim's progress, this pilgrim hurries through barely conscious of their design upon him. He simply doesn't seem to know that his desire to stay in fancy's meadow is not an accidental response to an otherwise pleasant place, but is a function of the place's intention to keep him from continuing on his way. In the same fashion, he speaks of the difficulties of getting through Care's copse as though they represented unfortunate annoyances. The lines show little recognition that having a hard time is precisely what being in Care's copse *means.* Again, the meadow and the copse both represent successful crossings, but their interest as trials is bypassed. The speaker tells us nothing about how he managed his survival; he only tells us that he did so "With much ado" (l. 22). And so we attend to his success in passing through difficulties, in overcoming all efforts to retard his movement, even when he does not seem to understand that overcoming trials is part of what a pilgrimage is about.

The next stage of the journey incorporates the antitheses of two stages into one stage and one place:

> That led me to the wilde of Passion, which
>   Some call the wold;
>   A wasted place, but sometimes rich.
>   Here I was robb'd of all my gold,
> Save one good Angell, which a friend had ti'd
>   Close to my side.
>
>   (ll. 13–18)

This stanza does not tell of a pair of dangerous sins or dangerous delays, but rather that set of difficulties one encounters in an uneven and dangerous world. The landscape of the stanza is frightening precisely because the antitheses are not separated either in space or in time, but come together in chaotic, arbitrary, and agentless combination: the world is described as both wasted and rich; the speaker says he is robbed here but does not say how or by whom; he says he is left with "one good Angell" but does not say whether that affords him significant protection or not.[3]

Meaning is, in other words, regularly suspended on this journey, though the end of the pilgrimage promises to settle meaning and close suspension down. The sighting of the hill made the speaker's journey visible at the start and provided it with an organizing shape; and now arrival at the hill promises to explain the journey, to conclude our suspense with respect to its meaning, and to make the story, and as it turns out the speaker, whole. But the pilgrim who arrives at his "gladsome hill" finds neither meanings, nor solutions, nor wholeness:

> At length I got unto the gladsome hill,
>> Where lay my hope,
>> Where lay my heart; and climbing still,
>> When I had gain'd the brow and top,
> A lake of brackish waters on the ground
>> Was all I found.

> (ll. 19–24)

It is true that suspense about the content of the speaker's desire is settled here, but it gets settled (his *heart* is on this hill) only a moment before we discover that his heart is *not* on this hill. And so the solution to the mystery does not provide an end to the poem's suspense. Quite the contrary: it reconstitutes it. We find out, at last, what the destination was supposed to hold, but we also find out that the destination is empty.

If the appearance of the hill at the opening of the poem provided the journey with a purpose, that purpose has now been discredited. And if the promise of future wholeness made the speaker delay the making of meaning, future wholeness—and meaning itself—have now been deferred once again. The transforming connections imagined at the start simply do not materialize, and so the segments of the journey lose their ana-gogic promise and retain, only, the diminished episodic value to which they were reduced by their reliance on the transfig-uring end. The brackish water the speaker finds on the hill is evidence of the ending's failure to produce the transforming connections it promised. Brackish waters are salty, like tears, and this means that "both the way and end" *are the same:*

> With that abash'd and struck with many a sting
> > Of swarming fears,
> > I fell, and cry'd, Alas my King!
> Can both the way and end be tears?

(ll. 25–28)

This end has no transforming power because it cannot differ-entiate itself from the middle. It is indistinguishable as an epi-sode from the episodes it is supposed to transform.

But the failure of the conclusion to be a conclusion is espe-cially troublesome in "The Pilgrimage" because the idea of the end provided the only sense of closure available anywhere at all. The "beginning" provided no foundation or limiting ori-gin; the deferral of meaning along the journey postponed our understanding of the middle until the end; and now the open-ended end provides no access to closure. Like the boundaries in "Church Monuments" that separate tombstones from other tombstones and bodies from other bodies, the boundaries that traditionally organize and control experience have also been defeated here.

Moreover the journey's end does not simply fail to provide a clearly defined narrative space and a coherent narrative ac-count. It also fails to provide a coherent shape for its speaker. The journey was undertaken by an incomplete person and its successful termination meant, we now know, gaining union with what would make the self whole. The vision of harmony, whose projected shape was that of the completed journey, was also, in other words, a vision of *corporeal* unity—though this

vision is a failure at the end of stanza five. The speaker pro-
jects its fulfillment from the beginning of the poem and moves
toward it in stanzas one through four, but on the verge of its
achievement it is unexpectedly postponed, so that the self
whose completion was sought remains uncomposed.

As soon as the full impact of the empty conclusion begins to
make itself felt, however, the possibility of finding a proper
ending is, once again, revived:

> I was deceived:

> My hill was further.

> (ll. 30–31)

These lines suggest that empty endings are sometimes only
false endings, and that a proper destination is still within
reach. And so once again we entertain the possibility that
there is access to the content of one's desire; that openness is
in fact subject to closure; that there is a transforming end with
the capacity to make pieces of a story parts of a narrative
whole, and pieces of a self parts of a personal one.

In one sense it might even be said that the disappointment
about, revival of, and simultaneous deferral of the end promotes the representation of experience because it prevents the
story from meeting its own demise. But *this* particular reloca-
tion causes no simple delay: it does not promise concord at the
end of a subsequent episode. For the hill toward which the
speaker is pitched is, in fact, no longer available inside the
limits mapped by the narrator at the start:

> My hill was further: so I flung away,
>   Yet heard a crie
> Just as I went, *None goes that way*
> *And lives:* If that be all, said I,
> After so foul a journey death is fair,
>   And but a chair.

> (ll. 31–36)

Now the hill is on the other side of experience, available across a divide, and access to it becomes a complex matter indeed. By removing the speaker's destination from the arena in which narrative is at work, the poem proposes entirely new possibilities for the relationship between ends and events.

The representation of experience has been identified in this poem with having (but not having arrived at) a purpose, aiming at (but not having acquired) wholeness, solving (but not having yet solved) a mystery. Access to ends has been described throughout as a condition of representation, though it has also been noted that narratives thrive on the absence of the very ends they propose. Indeed, this is precisely the dialectic on which representation often hinges: in exchange for that access to closure which is the constitutive condition of narration, one relinquishes, in the end, the right to wander, the right to explore and persist. One also gains, of course, in exchange for an end to narrative-in-the-making, the satisfactions of a completed account.

But the final lines of "The Pilgrimage" suggest that meaning, closure, and psychic coherence are unavailable in this life. They are available in the next life at the expense of this (*"None goes that way / And lives"*), but they are not conferred either on this journey or in this world. Hannah Arendt has described a related—but, finally, radically different—exchange this way:

> Only a man who does not survive his one supreme act remains the indisputable master of his identity and possible greatness, because he withdraws into death from the possible consequences and continuation of what he began. What gives the story of Achilles its paradigmatic significance is that it shows in a nutshell that *eudamonia* can be bought only at the price of life and that one can make sure of it only by foregoing the continuity of living in which we disclose ourselves piecemeal, by summing up all of one's life in a single deed, so that the story of the act comes to its end together with life itself. (pp. 193–194)

In Arendt's analysis of the Achilles story the hero stops disclosing himself "piecemeal" and becomes, when he dies, the "master of his identity" because his "last great deed" occurs at the same time as, and is therefore sealed by, his death. The bargain he strikes is a costly one—he completes his story and pays for its completion with his life—but the life he exchanges for representation, and the representation itself, are both, in their own ways, complete. He "sum[s] up" his life in his last deed, and death has the double power both to end, and to confer meaning upon, his existence.

"The Pilgrimage" too proposes the notion that the self completes itself only at the paradoxical price of physical annihilation—the speaker's heart is on the hill and if he is to complete the journey, finish the story, and acquire wholeness, he will do so "at the price of life." But unlike Achilles, this speaker does not *first* acquire wholeness and then seal the acquisition with his death. Quite the contrary: death intervenes *before* the speaker can take possession of his heart. Reintegration is something to which he can look forward *after death*, but death has nothing at all to do either with completing him in this world or representing his completion to it. When representation happens in a world in which access to closure is annihilating (we pay for our hearts with our lives), then we must gain our ends at the price of our lives—or representation must function without access to authoritative ends. In either case (and it is impossible to tell, in the ambiguous final lines of "The Pilgrimage," just what the speaker actually chooses to do), the vision of representation thus conceived is profoundly different from the one imagined in collapsing poems and in Arendt's example of the Achilles story—both instances in which death (real or imagined) provides lives and stories with significant closure. For if, in "The Pilgrimage," we cross the divide and surrender our lives, we do so without either fulfilling or conferring meaning upon them in this world. And if, on the other hand, we defer death, then journeys and stories continue to function in relation to worldly and contingent ends, but not, as we had thought, in relation to final and authoritative ones. These views—they are, essentially, the same view, since both point to the inaccessibility of closure and to the consequent impossibility of coherent self-representation—are the ones upon which "Church Monuments" and "Mortification" also rely. For as I suggested in my discussion of these poems, death's presence to us in the world—its intervention in our lives—does not provide us with knowledge about boundaries or with access to closure. It provides us with knowledge about the *violation* of boundaries and *denies* us access to meaningful closure. The body is a body of death precisely because its limits, like the limits of this journey, *take in* rather than *exclude* death, because its "periods" are therefore "transitions," its transitions passageways. To meditate upon death is not, in "Church Monuments," to imagine and actually to confront some final and meaningful end; it is, rather, to surrender such imaginings—as Donne's sermon does when it resubmits the body to "this *death* after *death*, nay this death after buriall, this *dissolution* after *dissolution*" (p. 382) when "every dead man dyes over againe" (p. 380). Poems about death are not, paradoxically, poems about final ends. Rather, they *forestall* such ends by preempting all *premature* closure. These works point to the dissolution of self which occurs when boundaries—bodily boundaries, narrative boundaries—are extended to *include* death and when death provides, at the same time, no real sense of completion.[4]

This is not to say that fulfillment is available nowhere or that representation is impossible. It is rather to suggest, as Donne does in *Deaths Duell*, that coherent images are reconstituted not in this world but in the next, not at the end of the worldly journey but, rather, at Judgment Day, when *"wee shall all be changed. In an instant we shall have a dissolution, and in the same instant a redintegration, a recompacting of body and soule, and that shall be truely a death and truely a resurrection"* (p. 382). This is precisely the point Herbert makes about Death in his poem of the same name. Death is "uncouth" and "hideous" (l. 1) when we look "on this side of [it], shooting short" (l. 9). But there is an image available on the other side, a doomsday image in which

> . . . souls shall wear their new array,
> And all [death's] bones with beautie shall be clad.

> (ll. 19–20)

In this world, however, no such images of wholeness are available—so that to be on a quest is not, as the speaker of "The Pilgrimage" had hoped, to be on a journey whose end will make foul journeying fair.[5] It is, instead, to be "uncouth" (unknowing) and "hideous," to be in transit, incomplete and dispersed—as the speaker of "The Pilgrimage" is in the indeterminate grammar of the poem's final lines.[6] There is no declaration about the journey's meaning, no transformation of its fragmentary events, no self made significant or whole. If the speaker does cross the boundary and acquire his heart, he does not do so in the course of the poem itself. Fulfillment is available across that divide, but it is not available, and it has no representation, here.[7]

If the representation of experience in "The Pilgrimage" is barred from access both to original and to final limits, and barred, therefore, from "recomposing" the self, it must nevertheless be said that the poem establishes and violates *erroneous* limits repeatedly. In the absence of originating circumstances, for example, the beginning *in medias res* provides us with an opening occasion—whose appearance is contingent on the sighting of an end—which is really not an end at all. And the speaker we meet in the opening stanza first sees his destination ("travell[s] on, seeing the hill"), then finds it empty ("a lake of brackish waters"), then discovers he has only misplaced it ("my hill was further"), and finally finds that authoritative ends are not accessible in this world (*"None goes that way / And lives"*). The absence or disappearance of one limiting circumstance always occasions the production of another, so that the narrative proceeds by defining a territory whose (threatened) borders are reconstituted only to be threatened again. In the end, of course, one loses the sense that the territory is, or ever was, a firmly established one. Instead it becomes clear that beginnings and ends have neither originating nor concluding force, that they have no power to limit experience and close it down, and that their authority with respect to the events they organize is questionable in the extreme. And yet the fact remains that experience has been represented in this poem. The discovery that the hill is a disposable boundary rather than a place of completion and exchange does not alter the fact that events, under its auspices, have appeared. What it does alter is our sense of the status of those events and our vision of the self they represent. When all ends are provisional ones, narrative ceases to be a discourse whose form makes determinate meaning available, and whose events have been chosen for their *enduring* importance and value. Instead, as constitutive borders are erected and dismantled, the stories they make possible, and the selves those stories represent, change their shapes as well. Where access to ends is a condition of representation and the *available* ends have no authority, then representation is a contingent activity at best.

Herbert even invents a fable to explain this uneasy state of affairs when he declares, in "The Pulley," that "when God at first made man," he planned to "let the worlds riches, which dispersed lie, / Contract into a span" (l. 1; ll. 4–5). But at the last moment, "when almost all was out" (l. 8), God held back, leaving the creature unfinished. The blessing he withheld was "rest"—the one whose absence made all the others uneasy and inadequate possessions:

> Yet let him keep the rest,
> But keep them with repining restlesnesse:
> Let him be rich and wearie, that at least,
> If goodnesse leade him not, yet wearinesse
>   May tosse him to my breast.
>
> (ll. 16–20)

Repining restlessness is the design of life both in "The Pulley" and in "The Pilgrimage" because in both poems the values and characteristics associated with structured selves and structured scenes—the preservation of boundaries, the projection and fulfillment of desire, the development of character, the interest in psychic coherence and in the relation of part to whole—have necessarily been abandoned. The speaker of "The Pilgrimage" experiences the absence of such traditional limits (and his own resulting discontinuity) as a form of compelled liberation—imposed by a God who reserves fulfillment for another world and who, in this world, disorders, segments, violates, and opens both narrative speakers and their accounts. The openness of selves and texts is a function of the fact that all access to closure, and to the narrative and psychic stability closure brings, has been abandoned or relinquished, overturned or overcome.[8]

Barbara Lewalski has suggested that one of the "most pervasive of the metaphors for the Christian life is that of pilgrimage," and she offers, as an example of this, a passage from a funeral sermon by Thomas Taylor which "describes very vividly the pilgrim's path as interior landscape" (p. 93):

> In this way be content if sometimes thou art weary, as one that goeth up a steepe hill, if sometimes thou sighest and pantest in thy painfull travell, through a foule way, and stormie weather; Let the tediousnesse of the way make thee desire the wayes end, and to covet to be at home with Christ . . . But be sure in thy wearinesse thou sit not downe . . . but *presse hard forward to the marke* [Phil. 3:13], as one resolved to goe through and persevere to the end; considering that after an hill commeth a valley; after foule way commeth fayre; and after a storme a faire shine and gleame againe; *heavinesse may endure for a night, but joy returneth in the morning.*[9]

Taylor's description of the pilgrim's journey resembles Herbert's in many of its details, but it is especially striking for its suggestion that the pilgrim *"presse hard forward to the marke . . . considering that . . . after foule way commeth fayre."* In Taylor's description the foulness and "tediousnesse" of the way are a function of the fact that ways *are ways* and *not ends*, that the joy of the morning, the joy of being "at home with Christ," is a joy that can only be acquired after death. In other words, the absence of ends *makes journeying foul*, but Taylor also encourages his pilgrim to be "content" in his weariness, to accept both journeying and its consequences. If "The Pilgrimage," "Church Monuments," and "Mortification" are not only grim but also oddly promising poems, their promise lies in the knowledge that, while journeys are difficult, they are also both necessary activities, and activities subject to (noncollapsing) representation.

The mixture of weariness and contentment with which pilgrimages are associated is also central to a group of Herbert's poems in which the grounding or rooting of self in some fixed conception is an enterprise speakers learn to abandon. The insight to which the speaker of "The Pilgrimage" necessarily comes—that the ways of the world are without worldly ends, and that stories and selves are therefore extremely vulnerable—is the insight upon which the poems to which I refer are founded. Their pervasive metaphors are not those of journeying and dying, but the lessons about which death poems teach us, and the understanding that informs pilgrimage accounts, are nonetheless embodied in them. In "The Temper," "Artillerie," and "The Flower" speakers learn to accept, to explore, and to elaborate upon the instability of stories and selves, and as they do their understanding of what it means to be a self and to have a story undergoes transformation as well.[10]

In "The Temper," for example, the speaker begins by complaining that he cannot praise God because his feelings about him are unstable. Representation, as he understands it, is an expression of the unvarying relationship between persons and feelings and it is, moreover, a sort of permanent inscription— what the speaker calls, in the first stanza, "engrav[ing] in steel":

> How should I praise thee, Lord! how should my rymes
>   Gladly engrave thy love in steel,
>   If what my soul doth feel sometimes,
>   My soul might ever feel!
>
> (ll. 1–4)

This poem is not, however, the stable poem of praise the speaker would like it to be. It is a description of the transformations about which the speaker complains, and a plea for the steadiness that would make praise possible.

In stanzas two through four instability of feeling is identi-

fied first with bodily instability, and then with that disorganization and dispersal of the body which is the result of physical
torture:

> Although there were some fourtie heav'ns, or more,
> > Sometimes I peere above them all;
> Sometimes I hardly reach a score,
> > Sometimes to hell I fall.
>
> O rack me not to such a vast extent;
> > Those distances belong to thee:
> The world's too little for thy tent,
> > A grave too big for me.
>
> Wilt thou meet arms with man, that thou dost stretch
> > A crumme of dust from heav'n to hell?
> Will great God measure with a wretch?
> > Shall he thy stature spell?

(ll. 5–16)

The speaker's complaint about the variability of his feelings
becomes, in stanza two, a complaint about the way in which
God's actions prevent him from being one individual and
make him feel, instead, like a plurality of persons: the one
who "lives above them all," the one who "hardly reach[es] a
score," and the one who "to hell . . . fall[s]." Geographically
distinct from each other and identified by wholly disparate
sets of feelings, these selves (each of whom is assigned a gram-
matically independent line) barely recognize one another, so
different are they in content and in location.

But the self as a plurality of selves, driven to multiplication
by God's punishing changefulness (he has forty heavens "or
more" and he makes sure we visit them all), becomes, in
stanzas three and four, the self stretched beyond its breaking
point—not so much multiplied as divided by God's insistence
that man meet arms with him. God's body is here an instrument of torture (a rack) upon which the speaker's body is
stretched, "a crumme of dust" dispersed across that "vast"
distance between heaven and hell. When God meets arms

with man he becomes an instrument not of organization—
where taking one's measure would mean coming to know
one's size and shape—but of disorganization and dispersal—
because measuring oneself against God means measuring oneself against the infinite, an impossible and finally body-
endangering task. In stanza five, therefore, the speaker retreats
from the difficulties he faces:

> O let me, when thy roof my soul hath hid,
>   O let me roost and nestle there:
> Then of a sinner thou art rid,
>   And I of hope and fear.
>
> (ll. 17–20)

The desire to hide, to "roost and nestle," is really a desire to
live within safe limits, protected from the dangerous forms of
relationship described above. But even this desire is quickly
revised: the speaker of "The Temper" complains in stanza
three, argues in four, and begs in five, but in stanza six he relinquishes his argument altogether: "Yet take thy way, for sure
thy way is best." As he abandons his argument, and with it his
complaint, the language in which he speaks also marks a complete transformation of the problem at hand:

> Yet take thy way; for sure thy way is best:
>   Stretch or contract me, thy poore debter:
> This is but tuning of my breast,
>   To make the musick better.
>
> (ll. 21–24)

The tuning metaphor, as Vendler, for one, has noted (p. 40),
transforms God from torturer to temperer, but it also transforms the hope that the speaker might avoid being an unstable
self (stanza one), or a set of discrete selves (stanza two), or a
fragmented self (stanza three), or a hidden self (stanza four),
into a notion that these are all versions of the self—however
discontinuous the self might therefore be. This solution recov-
ers the idea that there is a self—one version recognizes an-

other; they are versions of each other; a single breast is tuned—but it sacrifices the hope expressed in the first stanza, that the self might be stable, that the experience of being many might be reduced to the experience of being one. In fact that hope is not only relinquished (in stanza six), but is reversed (in stanza seven) as the speaker actually gives thanks for being many instead of being one:

> Whether I flie with angels, fall with dust,
>   Thy hands made both, and I am there:
> Thy power and love, my love and trust
>   Make one place ev'ry where.

(ll. 25–28)

These lines reverse the poem's initial plea for reduction—make all places one place, make all feelings one feeling—and give thanks for the multiplication of one into many—make one place all places, make one place everywhere. This means that all states of the self become recognizable as self (a unifying experience), but it also means that the concept of self as centered, stable, permanent, and coherent has been completely transformed. The explosion of one place into many is acceptable as an idea because all places share now a common ground ("thy hands made both, and I am there"), but it is nonetheless a dizzying notion. The speaker's acceptance of his plural location represents a major concession: on the strength of his faith he relinquishes entirely the dream of being all together in one place at one time (stanza one) and with it the dream of producing an enduring representation of his experience. The self exists only in versions, exists exploded, remains vulnerable to change. And because it does, the idea that the self ought to produce a monument to the stability of feeling is also relinquished. Engraving in steel is seen, at last, as an inappropriate mode for the self-in-versions, whose proper mode is, rather, the variable tune.

Like "The Pilgrimage" "The Temper" offers us a restless vision both of the self and of the self as representer. But in "The Temper" the disorganization and dispersal of the body (however difficult to manage) are *affirmed*. The distance across which the speaker's body is stretched expands the body, much as its plural location disperses it. So that while the desire for and absence of closure in "The Pilgrimage" unsettle and empty the speaker, in "The Temper" they unsettle the speaker and multiply him. The disintegration of self in "The Temper" is, simultaneously, a celebration of its *plurality* and *openness*.

The idea of the poem as a variable tune is precisely what stands behind Herbert's "Artillerie" as well. And though this poem does not speak the language of bodily dissolution, it shares with "The Temper" and also, as I shall later suggest, with "The Flower," that shifting vision of both self and text whose ground is the belief that we live in the world without access to closure, that periods are really transitions, transitions passageways. There are in this poem no holding actions, no efforts to produce a stable account, to reconcile opposing positions, or fashion a coherent tale. On the contrary, the plot of "Artillerie" takes at least a dozen unexpected turns, and each time it swerves it renders obsolete an earlier position and puts a new one in its place. But the capacity to sink and swerve— rather than rigidly to stipulate—is precisely what the poem means to cultivate. The speaker of "Artillerie" demonstrates exactly that mobility of self and sense sought, and practiced, both in "Church Monuments" and in "The Temper."

"Artillerie" begins much as a conventional tale might: it establishes the time and place. On a perfectly ordinary evening, and possessed of no special expectations, the speaker of the tale "sat before [his] cell" (l. 1). And if the second line alerts us to the possibility that this will be no ordinary evening—a star shoots into the speaker's lap—that possibility is quickly dismissed by the cautious speaker who responds without either excitement or curiosity and merely rises to shake out his clothes, "knowing well, / That from small fires comes oft no small mishap" (ll. 3–4). If the calm of the evening is disturbed in line two, the disturbance it causes is, in other words, quickly managed: the speaker knows, and knows well, that events like this one are potentially dangerous, but his knowledge permits him to act quickly and surely and thereby to domesticate whatever danger was potential in the situation. But an outside voice "suddenly" speaks in the second half of the stanza:

> *Do as thou usest, disobey,*
> *Expell good motions from thy breast,*
> *Which have the face of fire, but end in rest.*

(ll. 6–8)

Our vision of the speaker as someone who "knows well" and handles difficult situations with style and dispatch is here seriously challenged. For this speaker is accused of disobedience, and his disobedience is a function of precisely that inclination to *"do as* [he] *usest,"* a function of his uncritical self-reliance. Instead of seeing the speaker as a man confident in a crisis, someone who prevents small troubles from becoming large ones, the interrupting voice portrays the speaker as a man who *"expell*[s] *good motions from* [his] *breast,"* motions which merely have the *"face"* of fire. It accuses him, in other words, of taking things at face value, of reading both too quickly and too finally, and therefore of *misreading.* To reject trouble, this voice suggests, is really to *"expell good motions,"* which, while they upset the equilibrium of the present, do so to good purpose and bring, in the end, a different and better kind of rest.

This reversal of the speaker's initial view of things, and of our vision of the speaker himself, is rather stunning in its completeness. But the speaker we encounter at the beginning of the second stanza seems neither to appreciate the thoroughness with which he has been countered, nor to know the identity of the counterer. When he speaks in lines 9–10 he speaks with the same confident, self-possessed mastery which characterized him at the start:

> I, who had heard of musick in the spheres,
> But not of speech in starres, began to muse.

(ll. 9–10)

These lines suggest that the speaker is surprised and somewhat mystified by what he has heard: he is a man of both knowledge and experience (he has, after all, heard of music in the spheres) and yet he has neither knowledge, nor experience, of speech in stars—a fact which causes him to muse. But just as this comfortable, self-confident man seems to dismiss the suspect outside voice and to return to the peacefulness of the evening, it suddenly becomes clear that he does indeed know whose voice this is and, furthermore, that he understands fully what that voice is trying to say:

> But turning to my God, whose ministers
> The starres and all things are; If I refuse,
>   Dread Lord, said I, so oft my good;
>   Then I refuse not ev'n with bloud
>   To wash away my stubborn thought:
> For I will do or suffer what I ought.

(ll. 11–16)

The self-sufficient, independent man of the first stanza gives way to the self-critical man who has taken his own measure not only this time but many times before, a man who acknowledges his own prior excesses of confidence, and who is quite straightforward about his willingness to reform. In fact one of the interesting things about this stanza is that it suggests a man who has many times gone through just such a process of self-revision—a man who has come to rest comfortably in himself only to discover that, from God's point of view, he rests altogether too comfortably and must be stirred to change. As he says in line 13, he often refuses his good; but as he also claims in line 15, he never refuses to "wash away [a] stubborn thought" once he has seen he is guilty of one.

In the third stanza, however, the speaker suggests that it isn't really he who puts up resistance. Despite the disclaimers of earlier lines he declares that he understands perfectly well the language of stars and that he uses it day and night in vain efforts to win God's love:

> But I have also starres and shooters too,
> Born where thy servants both artilleries use.

My tears and prayers night and day do wooe,
And work up to thee; yet thou dost refuse.
   Not but I am (I must say still)
   Much more oblig'd to do thy will,
   Then thou to grant mine: but because
Thy promise now hath ev'n set thee thy laws.

(ll. 17–24)

The third stanza reverses, in other words, the revision effected in the second (the transformation of a comfortable and self-sufficient man into a self-critical and repentant one) and presents the speaker as the one who woos and God as the one who refuses.

But even this view has a short life. In the fourth stanza the speaker understands that he and God are "shooters both" and that they enter combat with each other. This view makes sense of the poem's prior events, for it permits the speaker to see them as episodes in an extended contest. It also encourages him to request an alteration in the terms of his relationship with God—as though understanding it as a kind of combat makes available as well the idea that a peace treaty might be effected and the conflict brought to an end:

Then we are shooters both, and thou dost deigne
To enter combate with us, and contest
With thine own clay. But I would parley fain:
Shunne not my arrows, and behold my breast.

(ll. 25–28)

But what the speaker really seems to want here is not so much a peace treaty or armistice (as the word "parley" suggests) but a set of rules for engagement and for mutual beholding. He does not want a suspension of the conflict; he wants God to agree to take in his arrows (to shun them not) and he offers in turn to make himself vulnerable to God's (to make his own breast subject to beholding). In many ways this is a good compromise position: neither one party nor the other will do all the work (both are shooters) and the relationship will be a cooperative venture. But this view of things is, it seems, as vulnerable as all the others, and in the last lines of the poem, lines reminiscent of those at the end of "The Temper" ("Yet take thy way . . ."), it too is relinquished:

> Yet if thou shunnest, I am thine:
> I must be so, if I am mine.
> There is no articling with thee:
> I am but finite, yet thine infinitely.

(ll. 29–32)

The hope that he might insure, by way of provisions or articles, the shape of his relationship with God, is here abandoned—not because the desire to have a relationship is seen as improper, but only because the relationship *cannot be articled*. It is impossible to arrange, by treaty or stipulation, its shape, and in the absence of access to stipulation, the relationship one gets resists fixity, becomes mobile, remains vulnerable to change. Furthermore, while it may be the case that, independently of God, one perceives oneself as "finite," in the context of a relationship with him the experience of one's finitude is dramatically altered. To be "thine infinitely" is to be God's in all the ways in which the absence of stipulation in my relationship to him makes me his. Whether I see myself as confident or critical, argumentative or passive, beheld or shunned, I am his.

One of the interesting features of "Artillerie" is that it is itself a demonstration of the truths arrived at in the poem's conclusion: this speaker, it seems, can stipulate to nothing—or rather, and this is the critical point, he can *stipulate multiply:* he speaks and lets go of speech, imagines a self and lets go of a self, conceives one relationship with God and then alters his conception, shifts his point of view and tone of voice almost as often as sentences begin and end. And while this may seem worrisome behavior—has this speaker no integrity?—it is, in fact, the reverse. Absence of integrity is a virtue here, a sign that the speaker is able to accept the sort of fluid identity which makes him properly vulnerable to God, which shows him "infinitely" his.

When Stanley Fish suggests that the speaker's dilemma, "both as would-be praiser and God-seeking man, exists only in his formulation of it," and that "its solution is effected when that formulation is abandoned or let go" (p. 160), he means to demonstrate the way in which dissolution ends in the self's disappearance into God.[11] Letting go of the formulation means letting go of the view that the world is divided, and it means passing, instead, to a "*uni*verse" (p. 161). What I am suggesting, however, is that "Artillerie" and "The Temper" are less poems in which distinctions are dissolved (so that all places become one place) than they are poems in which distinctions are mutiplied. When "one place" becomes "everywhere" and the "finite" self becomes God's "infinitely" then what we have is not the end of specification but the persistence of partial— and multiple—specifications.

In this sense Vendler's term seems the right one, for it stresses what is "provisional" (p. 25) in Herbert's poems. Unlike collapsing poems, in which the need for revision is indicated once, at the end, in a final and radical way, "reinvented" poems are provisional from start to finish and they show their revisions to us as they do them, quite literally, "in public" (p. 27). The visible nature of revision is, in fact, precisely what is interesting both about these poems and about Vendler's description of them. They externalize and make available those corrections toward which collapsing poems point but about which they tell us so little.

And yet in Vendler's view reinvention is not a sign of instability. The emphasis in her view is, she asserts, an emphasis on "coherence, order and resolution" (p. 5). Reinvented poems are characterized by their "constant reinvention of [their] way" (p. 27) and yet this produces not instability but refinement—as the poem "unfolds toward its final form" (p. 30). Vendler and Fish take, in one sense, opposing views of these poems—Fish stresses the disintegration of distinctions, Vendler their proliferation—but both end by pressing the poems toward some principle of unification. In Fish that single principle is God ("all others . . . are but by a distinction"),[12] and in Vendler it is aesthetic form (poems can end when they have refined themselves toward originality). What I would like to suggest is that the dissolution of a coherent view of self and sense is indeed Herbert's subject in these poems. In fact, it is *persistently* his subject: neither the self's disappearance into God's word, nor his acquisition of an aesthetic victory, brings the tentative and restless making of distinctions to an end. In "Artillerie" and "The Temper" dissolution and reinvention go hand in hand—and they do so from start to finish. The speakers of these poems are not mansion builders; they are pilgrims. And while the dissolution of the ground upon which they stand makes their journeys seem, in one sense, perilous, perilousness must be understood as a fact rather than a fault of their situations. In the introductory poem to "The Church" Herbert says as much when he declares:

> Avoid, Profaneness; come not here:
> Nothing but holy, pure, and cleare,
> Or that which groneth to be so,
> May at his perill further go.

The opening line addresses Profaneness and asks it to steer clear of the Church, and the second line suggests that, instead of profane persons, "holy, pure, and cleare" ones will be welcomed. But the third line qualifies that statement and thereby makes possible the entry of precisely those persons excluded in the first place—as long as the profane persons who come are also persons who groan not to be. Nevertheless, the fourth line suggests that, whether "holy, pure, and cleare," or only desirous of being so, all those who enter the church do so at their own risk. There simply is no safe journey here—even the man who stands corrected proceeds at his peril. What makes the journey difficult is the fact that in its course one is subject to the same revision and self-correction to which one is subject upon entering. The openness to self-correction is a prerequisite to journeying, but it is also what journeying *means*.

This vision of the self as both provisional and open to revision is central to all chronicles of dissolution and it provides, as I have already suggested, a striking contrast to the poem whose central account—like the interior story of "The Collar"—preserves boundaries, develops the speaker's character, and offers an image of psychic and narrative coherence. In the opening lines of "The Flower," for example, the speaker welcomes God much as one greets with pleasure someone who has been, unavoidably, away.[13] In words that indicate newness, purity, and freedom from taint, he expresses his unqualified pleasure in God's returns. But what appears to be a complete comparison at the end of the second line—

> How fresh, O Lord, how sweet and clean
> Are thy returns! ev'n as the flowers in spring
>
> (ll. 1–2)

—is unexpectedly extended in lines 3–4[14] as we encounter the first hint that God's returns are, perhaps, more complicated:

> To which, besides their own demean,
> The late-past frosts tributes of pleasure bring.
>
> (ll. 3–4)

These lines suggest that God's returns, though sweet in themselves, are sweeter still because they bring an end to his absence and to the coldness absence necessarily means. From the point of view of lines 3–4 the unalloyed pleasure of the poem's beginning now seems a pleasure complicated by prior grief— and the stanza's last lines confirm this:

> Grief melts away
> Like snow in May,
> As if there were no such cold thing.
>
> (ll. 5–8)

The purity and sweetness of God's returns is not a function of the fact that his absences are easy to bear. Rather, his returns are described as "sweet and clean" because pleasure in them makes past grief virtually unrecognizable: the present, in other words, effaces and rewrites the past—makes it vanish, almost as though there had been "no such cold thing."

But the repetition of this process—in which one present displaces and makes alien another—has profound consequences: for in rendering the past vulnerable it suggests that the present is subject to displacement as well.[15] In the second stanza of "The Flower" the "grief" of stanza one is recalled with some intensity, but its very recollection makes present pleasure seem incomprehensible—and this causes the speaker to rewrite past history from the perspective of the present with which he wishes to identify himself:

> Who would have thought my shrivel'd heart
> Could have recover'd greennesse? It was gone
>   Quite under ground; as flowers depart
> To see their mother-root, when they have blown;
>   Where they together
>   All the hard weather,
> Dead to the world, keep house unknown.
>
> (ll. 8–14)

In these lines the speaker suggests that his life is like the cyclical life of a flower—whose times of blossoming, resting, and revival are predictable. But this notion is dramatically at odds with the belief expressed everywhere else in this poem: that God's actions are unpredictable, that he kills and quickens in an hour, that, as Herbert says elsewhere, we "cannot skill of [his] wayes" ("Justice [I]"). Stanza two rewrites the inexplicable grief of stanza one in order to make sense of the happy present with which this grief is incompatible. The seasonal and natural language of the poem belies the speaker's experience of God's unpredictable agency, portraying it as regular and intelligible, even when experience tells him that it is not. The alienation and virtual disappearance of the past in stanza one is replaced in stanza two by a rewriting of the past which secures the speaker's view of the world in which he now lives—bringing the past into line with the present instead of permitting it to remain incomprehensibly alien.

In the third stanza, however, the speaker's perspective on his difficulties changes once again:

These are thy wonders, Lord of power,
Killing and quickning, bringing down to hell
    And up to heaven in an houre;
Making a chiming of a passing-bell.
        We say amisse,
        This or that is:
Thy word is all, if we could spell.

(ll. 15–21)

He understands in these lines that God kills and quickens with a sense of purpose, that he is, by nature, a God of transformations, who makes bells of celebration out of death knells. The effort here is to see God's actions as deliberate actions rather than arbitrary ones, and to see both the difficult past and the happy present as pieces of a single design. The perspective this demands is not, however, easy to come by, for it means that the speaker must see his own experiences from a distance—he must not experience God's absence as simple abandonment, and he must not see his presence as a guarantee of grace, for God's power is the double power both to throw down and to raise. In some respects, stanza three means to rewrite one and two because it means to see God's actions from the outside in a total, rather than in a narrowly personal, way. But stanza three also suggests that all of our perspectives are limited—even those which seem most nearly in sympathy with God's totalizing vision. When the speaker declares, at the end of stanza three:

        We say amisse,
        This or that is:
Thy word is all, if we could spell

(ll. 19–21)

he means that all our ways of designating reality are partial and "amisse." "This" and "that" are names for the incomplete realities in which, mistaking them for complete ones, we necessarily live. When we say "this" or "that" we say something amiss because we have no access to God's word, to that collection of statements whose totality is itself a complete language. But these lines also suggest that we live in a world in which all that is available *is* saying amiss, for we live first in this, and then in that, world.

Nonetheless, in the next two stanzas of "The Flower" the speaker wishes that it were possible to escape the world of this and that, to escape the world of partial views and limited perspectives, and to live in a world "past changing":

> O that I once past changing were,
> Fast in thy Paradise, where no flower can wither!
> Many a spring I shoot up fair,
> Offring at heav'n, growing and groning thither:
>   Nor doth my flower
>   Want a spring-showre,
> My sinnes and I joining together.
>
> But while I grow in a straight line,
> Still upwards bent, as if heav'n were mine own,
> Thy anger comes, and I decline:
> What frost to that? what poll is not the zone,
>   Where all things burn,
>   When thou dost turn,
> And the least frown of thine is shown?
>
> (ll. 22–35)

One of the interesting things about this section is that its content resembles that of the interior story in "The Collar," since in both the poem's speaker imagines himself the agent of his own experience, capable of making meaning in the world, capable of growth toward an end. But here present tense speech is not really quotation. It is speech about a recurrent event or recurrent dream, and there is no effort at all to fence it off from the larger sense that such dreams of accomplishment and coherent growth—"grow[th] in a straight line"—are necessarily illusions. If these two stanzas do make up an interior story, then the frame, rather than the enclosed dream, predominates. Like the conviction that one's heart has been permanently destroyed ("shrivel'd"), or the conviction that God's returns are "clean," this dream is another one of the ways in which the speaker says amiss—lives fully an experience which he soon comes to see as a partial rather than a complete one.

In fact when the sixth stanza begins, this dream (like the dreams of the stanzas before it) has already been shed, and the "death" (or "decline") it represents is added to the growing tally of deaths the poem continues to record. The loss of this particular dream of coherence, so powerfully felt in "Affliction (I)" and "The Collar," is here felt rather differently—as one loss in a sequence of losses, one change in an endless sequence of changes—for change itself has become the norm.

This does not, I think, make change easy to bear, though surely it seems, in "Artillerie" and "The Flower," far less annihilating than it does in collapsing poems. The speaker who suffers one defective world after another to die away and be replaced before it dies away again comes, as the speakers of "Church Monuments" and "Mortification" do, to understand his losses in a new way. They do not signify, as in "The Collar" they seemed to do, the final loss of access to meaning in the world. Rather, they reconstitute the very idea of being in the world until it no longer means having a *continuous* presence in it at all. The loss of one's vision, or one's view of the world, or one's view of the self, is a death—a relinquishing or letting go—not different in kind from the deaths suffered by the speakers of collapsing poems, but different in consequence. For here, death comes, finally, to be incorporated into life, to be understood as one of its characterizing features, so that one sees oneself not as someone who grows, or fails to grow, "in a straight line," but rather as someone who dies many deaths and experiences many renewals. If death is incorporated into life, then the threat of death in collapsing poems—a threat at once generative and destructive—undergoes a dramatic alteration. The speaker who "dies" at the end of "The Collar," or at the fifty-fourth line of "Affliction (I)," fears that his story is, though defective, the only story he has, the only story subject to narration. But the speaker of "The Flower" has both no stories and many: his first story is an incomplete representation of the world, displacing as it does some earlier story of a (now hidden) grief; his second representation is revisionary, a way of acknowledging the power of grief while at the same time masking it; his third story frames the smaller perspectives of stanzas one and two in a larger view in which grief and joy form an alliance; his fourth story denies the possibility of such framing, and represents, instead, a dream of growth, continuity, and accomplishment—before giving them all up; and the fifth, to which we now come, sees death and revival as perpetual, extraordinary, and inevitable, and then, once more, declares them utterly incomprehensible:

> And now in age I bud again,
> After so many deaths I live and write;
>   I once more smell the dew and rain,
> And relish versing: O my onely light,
>   It cannot be
>   That I am he
> On whom thy tempests fell all night.

> (ll. 36–42)

The speaker's pleasure in being alive—in budding, growing, and working—is precisely a function of his acknowledgment that such births follow deaths, that they are the other side of dying, that dissolution and rebirth are companions. In this stanza—at least in its opening lines—the speaker is a survivor, someone who carries with him the memory of his own death, and a sense, therefore, of the miracle of his life. He enjoys "the dew and rain" because he had missed them; he relishes writing because he had lost it. In the next lines, however, he makes a comment worthy of the poem's last stanza—"It cannot be / That I am he / On whom thy tempests fell all night"— suggesting that pleasure and grief, held together momentarily in stanza three, once again separate: the past seems alien, the pleasure of the present total and without alternative, the current self utterly new.[16]

Nevertheless, the repetition of this process—or rather these processes—ends in a perspective which openly asserts the position finally taken by all chronicles of dissolution:

These are thy wonders, Lord of love,
To make us see we are but flowers that glide:
Which when we once can finde and prove,
Thou hast a garden for us, where to bide.
    Who would be more,
    Swelling through store,
Forfeit their Paradise by their pride.

(ll. 43–49)

The critical notion here is that God teaches us, "make[s] us see," that "we are but flowers that glide." Flowers that glide are not natural flowers at all, and this is extremely important because it reminds us that we must not take the natural as a sign that life, though changeful, is predictable in cyclical ways. The flower of this poem is a shifter from the start: it is at once an annual and a perennial flower (shrivelled beyond hope of recovering greenness; a ground bulb waiting some known revival); it is killed and quickened not yearly but hourly; it does what flowers naturally do (it grows "upwards bent") and yet is cruelly rebuffed. In stanza seven, then, God tells us something we ought, already, to know: that we are not natural flowers whose growth and death are predictable, but that we are, rather, flowers without roots, flowers that pass from one place to another, flowers that "glide." To wish, furthermore, to be anything else, is to wish to be past changing, and such wishes are identified here with wishing to be in Paradise before one's time.

This insistence that our lives are shifting and restless ones, lived by creatures among other creatures, actually legitimates a form of *misreading* regarded, in collapsing poems, as short-sighted and extremely dangerous. In the final lines of collapsing poems speakers alienate themselves from their own defective words. But in "The Flower" experience is always in the process of changing, and descriptions of it are always in the process of becoming obsolete. This speaker is a misreader *by necessity*—someone who can only say amiss because, as a creature, he has no access to that total and unchanging vision represented by God's word in stanza three and by Paradise in stanza seven. In "The Flower" creatures are *in the business* of being and saying amiss, and the recognition of that fact makes saying amiss the only real way of saying aright.[17] Or, to put it another way, saying amiss is saying aright when the speaker acknowledges the *impossibility* of any full saying, when he acknowledges that our sentences, like our bodies and like our stories, are provisional. The valorization of saying amiss is like the valorization, in death poems, of practicing the body's dissolution, for both acknowledge and struggle against the forbidden desire to have a coherent body, to have true sayings, to be represented in orderly and structured ways. In collapsing poems this desire presses all opposing knowledge to the side and asserts body and story with great energy—until it no longer can. But dissolving poems acknowledge the inevitable—that neither bodies nor stories are safe from dissolution, that neither bodies nor stories are past changing. As I have, however, tried to suggest, the dissolution of the continuous story, like the dissolution of the continuous body, does not leave the speaker featureless: instead, it shows him *multiply and discontinuously featured.*[18] If dying and saying amiss exist on the other side of the desire to live completely, to speak truly, and to have a coherent body, then they do so because, in transforming these desires, they make life, and representation, available to us in radically different ways.

CONCLUSION:
THE BIBLE AS COUNTERTEXT

In *The Arte of English Poesie* George Puttenham describes the rhetorical figure he calls *metanoia* or *correctio*, the figure of "making straight" or "setting right":

> Otherwhiles we speake and be sorry for it, as if we had not wel spoken, so that we seeme to call in our word againe, and to put in another fitter for the purpose: for which respects the Greekes called this manner of speech the figure of repentance: then for that vpon repentance commonly followes amendment, the Latins called it the figure of correction, in that the speaker seemeth to re-forme that which was said amisse. I following the Greeke originall, choose to call him the penitent, or re-pentant.[1]

Puttenham's definition provides an apt description of the poems I have described in Part One: their speakers often say amiss, reform what they have said, and then say it over once again. This is certainly true of the speaker of "Artillerie," for example, whose errors are acknowledged and corrected many times in the course of the poem. And it is equally true for the speaker of "The Flower," whose corrections are literally performed, as Helen Vendler has suggested, "in public" (p. 27). But Puttenham's description is oddly *in*accurate for the poems it seems in one sense most accurately to describe. The speaker of a collapsing poem is precisely a man who "call[s] in [his] word againe," but, as I have often remarked, it is precisely in the nature of collapsing poems that they do not "put in another [word] fitter for the purpose." Puttenham calls *correctio* the figure of the "penitent" (after the "Greeke originall") and his description is, again, an apt one for the speakers of Herbert's collapsing poems. But it is nevertheless the case that while these speakers do reform *themselves*, they do not, as it turns out, "reforme that which was said amisse." As I commented in chapter two and remarked throughout my discussions of the poems in Part One, the *suggestion* of a proper counterstory is only a suggestion. It is the absence of such stories, the absence of rewriting, that characterizes collapsing poems—which leave both speaker and reader with the problematic task of dismantling and redesigning themselves.[2]

In the following pages I hope to describe those true examples of *metanoia* or *correctio* with which Herbert's poems provide us. These are, I shall argue, typological poems, and they are significant, in my view, because their speakers begin by telling idiosyncratic, independent stories, but end by rewriting them as biblical accounts. They "call in [their] word again," but they also "reforme that which was said amisse." The erosion of the personal account is, in these poems, compensated by its rewriting as a biblical account, so that the self who corrects himself actually *has a story*. The alignment of personal with biblical stories offers, in other words, a solution to the problem of self-representation with which we have been concerned—though it does not do so without, of course, importing problems of its own.

In Herbert's "The Bunch of Grapes," for example, the speaker begins by referring to a past in which, as he here recalls, he gained possession of joy and took it out of the public domain. He enclosed it, secured it, made it safe:

> Joy, I did lock thee up: but some bad man
> Hath let thee out again.

(ll. 1–2)

Of course his memory is a double-edged one, for the lines really gain force from the speaker's sense both that once he accomplished something difficult and that now the accomplishment is a feat of the past (some "bad" man has undone *his* "good" work). Here, as elsewhere in Herbert, speech about the past grows out of a desire to preserve it—to rescue the image of the act (and the image of oneself in the act) when the act itself is lost. And so the opening line reflects a double conservation: the speaker's initial success in locking joy up, and his secondary participation in that success whose form is its preservation as memory and account.

I go to the trouble of stressing the speaker's memorializing work because the use of narration in the service of conservation is associated here, as it often is in Herbert, with the desire to enclose, isolate, seal, and keep separate, an independent world once the speaker's exclusive possession. That world locks up both Joy and Joy's keeper in a seven-year imprisonment whose image is conserved in the opening line—resurrected as narration by a man who does not refrain from representing it.

Of course the speaker's desire to lock Joy up is, at least in part, a response to his sense that the terms of existence are those of imprisonment, struggle, and release. Here, success is wrested from others (to lock something up is not simply to make it safe, but to prevent others from gaining access to it) and maintained only as long as others are kept at bay. The anonymity of the person who releases Joy ("some bad man") underlines the importance of maintaining separation from the world—a world conceived as indifferent or distracting at best, hostile at worst. When Joy is "let out," released into the world, the speaker loses his sense of control over destiny, a control only available to him when he lives in a world set apart.

But the desire to lock Joy up is *not* a desire for protection against growth. On the contrary, the speaker's purpose is at once protection and *advancement*. He identifies the acquisition of Joy, and his separation from the world-at-large, with his own capacity to proceed toward the promised land:

> Joy, I did lock thee up: but some bad man
> > Hath let thee out again:
> And now, me thinks, I am where I began
> > Sev'n yeares ago: one vogue and vein,
> > One aire of thoughts usurps my brain.
> I did towards Canaan draw; but now I am
> Brought back to the Red sea, the sea of shame.

(ll. 1–7)

The opening lines identify advancement with isolation because they understand progress as something only a man himself can generate. The speaker who would protect his forward movement must know his project, overcome resistance to it, press his own case in the world. The stanza suggests, in fact, that the loss of control (some bad man has taken charge) is the cause of the speaker's trouble. When he had joy "lock[ed] . . . up" he proceeded toward Canaan, but now that it is "out again" he is back "where [he] began."

Of course claiming responsibility for his own salvation does not make salvation happen, nor, by making it seem possible, does it offer a consoling fiction. Instead, the speaker's progress is reversed in this poem *precisely because* he attempts to be its agent. His failure is not the outcome of his inability to maintain the control he once so successfully exerted. It is, rather, the *consequence* of whatever success he has had. The punishment for wresting one's world from the world at large, for constructing an alternative world and alternative self, is the reversal of world and self alike: the script is run backward, narrative progress—like time—is reversed, and the speaker whose intention was the generation of experience finds himself back at the beginning. Unlike the journey composed of distinct experiences, this speaker's journey has neither variety nor particularity: his "brain" has been usurped and his mind is occupied by a single set of obsessional thoughts ("one vogue and vein") over which he has no control.

The explanation for this difficult state of affairs can be found, I think, in the biblical and typological insistence that historical life is the realm of encounter with God—so that to exempt oneself from it is to separate oneself from the only world in which it makes any sense to live at all: the world of God's "unrepetitive, unprecedented, and demanding" activity.[3] And to exempt oneself from it in an effort to alter, divert, or control history is tantamount to a rejection of the realm of encounter, a rejection which, as Alan Charity has suggested, causes one to experience history "in reverse" (p. 41). The key passage here is Deut. 28: 67–68, in which God promises that the failure to meet the terms of his covenant will bring ruin upon the people. And reversal is the shape ruin takes: "In the morning you shall say, 'Would it were evening!' and at evening you shall say, 'Would it were morning!' because of the dread which your heart shall fear, and the sights which your eyes shall see. And the Lord will bring you back in ships to Egypt, a journey which I promised that you should never make again." To ignore the lessons of history is, in this description, to be utterly undone—cursed with reversal, doomed to the repetition of beginnings. Nor is God's punishment at all arbitrary: he who would live apart, saying "I shall be safe, though I walk in the stubbornness of my heart" (Deut. 29:19), will never be safe at all. He who would escape and conduct *his own journey* will be brought back to Egypt in a ship.

The punishing character of reversal is significant here because it makes nostalgia for the past, and for the independent life associated with it, extremely difficult to maintain. Unlike "The Collar"—whose only manifest story is the completely articulated one available in the poem's interior, a story which, despite its defects, is valued for its capacity to bear the speaker's image—"The Bunch of Grapes" constructs a story associated only momentarily with the capacity to represent the self. For here storymaking has become suicidal: the exemption of the self from the world of men and the corresponding construction of an independent account produce, as I have already suggested, a narrative reversal that eliminates the story and returns the exempt self to its own origins in history—to its beginnings at the Red Sea. The speaker who is "brought back" has no story, and his desire to have one has been the *cause* of his having none.

Of course in many respects this puts him in a position identical to the one occupied by the speakers of collapsing poems: the speaker of "The Reprisall" who declares that his real task is the overcoming of persons who produce contentious texts like the one he has just made ("I will overcome / The man, who once against thee fought" [ll. 15–16]); the speaker of "Affliction (I)," who announces that he no longer identifies with the autobiographical account he has just produced ("Now I am here, what thou wilt do with me, / None of my books will show" [ll. 55–56]); or the speaker of "The Collar," whose alienation from his own words (finally called "rav[ings]" [l. 33]) leaves him, too, without a text he can comfortably call his own. The common difficulty in these poems is that their conclusions point to the defective character of the once-valued poetic account without offering any alternative to it: the conclusion of "The Reprisall" suggests that the story must be unwritten; the last lines of "Affliction (I)" resist using language to re-establish the self on firm ground; and the conclusion of "The Collar" leaves us with a self whose only fully articulated performance has lost its stability altogether. At the end of the first stanza of "The Bunch of Grapes" the speaker's life (his seven-year journey to Canaan) has been reversed, and like the speakers of collapsing poems he has been deprived of his independent experience: he stands at the Red Sea with no story properly his own.

But the reversal of the speaker's story occurs at the end of the first, not the end of the last, stanza and the terms in which it is cast suggest that, while deprived of one account, the speaker is already participant in another. For what reversal does is to uncover, beneath the text it strips away, another story already in place. Behind the fiction of an independent journey, locked up and exempt from time, lies the biblical story of the Exodus whose account, the speaker acknowledges fully in the second stanza, is the true account of his life:

> For as the Jews of old by Gods command
>   Travell'd, and saw no town;
> So now each Christian hath his journeys spann'd:
>   Their storie pennes and sets us down.
>   A single deed is small renown.
> Gods works are wide, and let in future times;
> His ancient justice overflows our crimes.
>
>   (ll. 8–14)

This acknowledgment is difficult, not only because it involves accepting the fact that his own story has been rewritten (he once drew toward Canaan, but now, it seems, Canaan was never within view; like the Jews who traveled and saw no town, he too has wandered in a wilderness and seen nothing), but also because the story that takes the place of his own was *never* his own and was *always* there. The futility of self-invention is highlighted by this discovery: the speaker's error in the first stanza is not just a function of the fact that he misread the journey; it is a function of the fact that he thought the journey was a private one and thought he could conduct it himself. Stanza two suggests, on the contrary, that behind the evasion that personal stories represent lies a prior account, already written and in place, an account toward which one might turn if one were not occupied with inventing alternatives. And that account, we would find, not only precedes us but also anticipates our actions. Whether we know it or not (and our own stories merely prevent us from knowing it), we are on a journey whose shape has already been determined: their story not only "pennes" us, it "sets us down." In two lines of a poem entitled "Faith" the discovery made in the first two stanzas of "The Bunch of Grapes" finds succinct expression. "Faith makes me any thing, or all," the speaker declares—and then he concludes his sentence this way:

> Faith makes me any thing, or all
> That I beleeve is in the sacred storie.
>
>   (ll. 17–18)

And in a poem called "Judgment" the speaker even suggests that when God asks him for his own "peculiar book" (l. 5), he will not comply with the request:

> But I resolve, when thou shalt call for mine,
> That to decline,
> And thrust a Testament into thy hand:
> Let that be scann'd.
> There thou shalt finde my faults are thine.

(ll. 11–15)

In both poems the speaker declares that personal and sacred stories are identical, but in "The Bunch of Grapes" this discovery is a difficult one precisely because it alters so radically the idea of composition imagined at the start. The speaker who thinks he writes his own account finds his account is written; the man who thinks himself an original finds he has ancestors; the person who believes he plots his own story finds the plot has been designed by another with him in mind. I am not suggesting that the speaker first discovers his Old Testament origins in stanza two. The language of stanza one is, after all, Old Testament language itself. But the speaker of stanza one uses that language without realizing in any way the collective nature of his involvement in sacramental history. It is the very notion that one might have an independent or isolated account that is so drastically altered in stanza two—when the speaker discovers, as he says in line 12, that "a single deed is small renown." The speaker's *participation* in the Exodus story is the crucial matter: he does not begin something for the first time; he participates in a story that is already under way. And as the language of the lines suggests, the story is a collective one: the biblical account does not lie beneath his life alone; it lies beneath the lives of all Christians who wander in search of Canaan. Their story pens and sets all of us down.

The uncovering of the biblical story, and the speaker's discovery that he is a participant in it, appear as parallel accounts in stanza two: for as the Jews of old traveled . . . so now we travel. But the discovery of affiliation in stanza two leads, in stanza three, not to the retelling of the biblical Exodus, but to the translation of the speaker's life into Exodus language:

> Then have we too our guardian fires and clouds;
>   Our Scripture-dew drops fast:
> We have our sands and serpents, tents and shrowds;
>   Alas! our murmurings come not last.

(ll. 15–18)

The speaker whose experience was reversed in stanza one uncovers the biblical text as pre-text in stanza two—but in stanza three he *rewrites his own history* (now a collective history) in the terms of the story to which he belongs. The catalog of Exodus incidents and events—the guardian cloud in which the host of Egypt was separated from the host of Israel, the dew that became manna for the wilderness travelers, the murmurings of the Israelites who complained at the Red Sea that "it would have been better for [them] to serve the Egyptians than to die in the Wilderness" (Exod. 14:12)—is here employed as a way of describing the author's temporal experience. We see his life *as* an exodus story, not as an idiosyncratic account whose terms are independently conceived. This open rewriting of the history of the self points to the way in which the alignment of personal with biblical stories makes representation possible: the speaker's life becomes manifest because the way in which it enacts the biblical exodus comes into focus and can be elaborated on. The unraveling of the personal story in stanza one clears the way for its reconstitution as a biblical story in stanza three.

This rewriting depends, however, on the fitness of the biblical story as a description of the personal one. And in the last lines of stanza three that fitness is challenged:

> But where's the cluster? Where's the taste
> Of mine inheritance? Lord, if I must borrow,
> Let me as well take up their joy, as sorrow.

(ll. 19–21)

The speaker does not deviate from the language of his borrowed account, but he does suggest that there is one sense in
which the story outstrips him: he finds nothing in his life that
is comparable to the cluster of grapes carried on a pole from
the valley of Eshcol as a sign of the bounty of Canaan. Moreover it is just when the personal and the biblical story fail to
match up, to cohere, that the self makes its appearance: the
collective language of stanza two ("Then have we too") becomes the personal and self-presenting language of stanza
three ("Lord, if *I* must borrow").

What is significant about the poem's last stanza, then, is that
the speaker does locate something in his life capable of being
rewritten as "cluster"—"But can he want the grape, who hath
the wine?"—and yet the effect of this is not to establish the fit
between his individual life and the Old Testament account,
nor to complete, thereby, the rewriting of the former into the
latter. Rather, the fit between them is established:

> I have their fruit . . .

only to be surpassed and extended:

> I have their fruit and more.
>
> (l. 23)

These lines do suggest that the speaker who asked, in line 20,
where the cluster was, had in fact failed to perceive that his life
already contained it (he had Christ, the fruit of the vine) and in
that sense they point out that the Old Testament account does
not exceed (and thereby fail to represent) the speaker's experience. But the lines do suggest another problem: the Old Testament story, because it is really a segment of a larger story,
cannot, in fact, contain—it cannot limit or hold—the speaker's
experience:

> But can he want the grape, who hath the wine?
> I have their fruit and more.

Blessed be God, who prosper'd *Noahs* vine,
   And made it bring forth grapes good store.
   But much more him I must adore,
Who of the Laws sowre juice sweet wine did make,
Ev'n God himself being pressed for my sake.

                 (ll. 22–28)

When the poem's final lines extend the boundaries of the story both backward and forward in time—pointing to the origin of the bunch of grapes in Noah's vine (Gen. 9:20), its second appearance as the "good store" of the Cluster of Eshcol (Num. 13:23), and its transformation into Christ, the fruit of the vine, in the New Testament (John 15:1 and elsewhere)— they suggest that the real sequence of events to which the speaker belongs is not the Old Testament one alone, but that longer sequence we call the history of salvation. In fact one of the important features of the poem's last stanza is its lack of interest in the problem of locating a representative story: the speaker who rewrites his story in Exodus language in stanza two surpasses that story in stanza four, but he does not look to write a "story" again. Instead, he sees himself as participant in a sequence that is at once a narrative sequence and more than that. The stress in the final lines has moved from the idea of Bible as "story" to the idea of Bible stories as lived sequences in history. Hans W. Frei has described the process this way: "Now if literal reading tends to focus on the narrative shape, implying rather than explicitly making historical references, the reverse tends to be true of figuration or typology. It tends to undertake the shift to an emphasis on the reality depicted, so that its interest in the two or more formally similar narratives . . . is really that of adjusting them to the one real, temporal sequence involved."[4] This change in stress is accomplished because the "unwritten" self of stanza one is rewritten as an Old Testament story in stanzas two and three, while the Old Testament story with which the speaker (however incompletely) identifies himself is rewritten in stanza four as a segment of the more inclusive story that both precedes and follows it in time. The typological relation thus erodes the boundaries between one account and another until the undone self with which the poem began finds himself inscribed within the widest possible setting. The boundaries between self and story, story and providential history, are broken one at a time, until self is identified with biblical story, and then with biblical history, in the final lines of the poem:

> But much more him I must adore,
> Who of the Laws sowre juice sweet wine did make,
> Ev'n God himself being pressed for my sake.

(ll. 26–28)

These successive rewritings weave the speaker's account into an ever widening field. That field is the Bible itself, understood first as narrative and then as historical account, and the speaker's identification with it provides access to representation in ways unavailable to the speakers of collapsing poems. If interpretation is subversive there—it undermines invulnerable images of the self—here interpretation is constructive—it undermines invulnerable images, but it subjects the self to rewriting before our eyes.

The alignment of biblical with personal stories provides, in other words, access to representation, though it is in the nature of such representation that it makes persons inseparable from the sequences they join. And since these sequences are at once narrative and historical ones, representation is no longer a *literary* affair alone. In "The Bunch of Grapes" the speaker is identified with a setting which extends to include nothing less than the history of salvation—an infinitely wider and more complex setting than the one in which he began.

The interpenetration of realms and the flattening of narration into history are described, in somewhat different terms, in Herbert's "The Holy Scriptures":

> Oh Book! infinite sweetnesse! let my heart
>   Suck ev'ry letter, and a hony gain,
>   Precious for any grief in any part;
> To cleare the breast, to mollifie all pain.

Thou art all health, health thriving till it make
  A full eternitie: thou art a masse
Of strange delights, where we may wish & take.
Ladies, look here; this is the thankfull glasse,
That mends the lookers eyes: this is the well
  That washes what it shows. Who can indeare
  Thy praise too much? thou art heav'ns Lidger here,
Working against the states of death and hell.
  Thou art joyes handsell: heav'n lies flat in thee,
  Subject to ev'ry mounters bended knee.

This poem is interesting because it narrows, in a variety of ways, the ordinary modes of relationship with which we are familiar. In the first quatrain the Bible is addressed directly ("Oh Book!"), but the man who addresses it does not want to "read" the book, he wants to "suck ev'ry letter." Moreover, he wants his "heart" to do the sucking, and he suggests that the outcome of the relationship he describes will be good health: the Bible "cleare[s] the breast" and "mollifie[s] all pain." These lines alter the ordinary modes of connection—or find it unnecessary to describe them—and rely instead on an unmediated relationship: heart to letter, letter to breast.

In the second stanza the Bible is portrayed not as a book at all but as a realm of plenitude: "Thou art all health, health thriving till it make / A full eternitie." Moreover, the speaker suggests that access to this realm is directly available: no expense, it seems, is incurred by the man who would avail himself of the Bible's "strange delights." This easy sense of access ("we may wish & take") suggests that commerce with biblical characters and events is a simple matter: one need not wrest oneself from the Bible, and it offers, it seems, no opposition to one's entry.

At the end of the second and the beginning of the third quatrain the Bible is described as a transforming glass "That mends the lookers eyes" and as a "well" that "washes what it shows." These lines are crucial because while earlier ones suggest an easy commerce with the biblical text, these lines suggest that persons who enter its pages are *changed*. One does not simply come and go, taking what one will. Rather one comes—and goes transformed. And yet while the process of transformation is a difficult one in other poems—speakers let go, even of defective selves, rather reluctantly—there is, here, no real resistance to change. Dark readers are transformed without expense: the glass that mends the looker's eyes makes defective selves disappear; it gives one back an *already* mended self. These lines also suggest a conflation of self and biblical other: if the Bible is a mirror in which one sees oneself mended, that is not just because one sees oneself, but because one sees others as images of the renovated self.

There is, in all of these descriptions, a common denominator: the Bible is a text that transforms persons by participating in their lives in time ("thou art heav'ns Lidger here"). So that while affiliation with the Bible provides, in the early stanzas of "The Bunch of Grapes," access to representation, and provides, in "The Holy Scriptures," a renovated image, both poems suggest, as well, that the reader's relationship to the Bible is more than that of person to representing text. The Bible does not just provide access to representation by telling the story of salvation. It transforms the very notion of representation into an active idea: by telling the story to which we belong it permits us to live, consciously, in time. The conclusion to "The Holy Scriptures" points in the same direction:

> Thou art joyes handsell: heav'n lies flat in thee,
> Subject to ev'ry mounters bended knee.

> (ll. 13–14)

These lines collapse heaven into the pages of the biblical text—flattening absolutely the distance, and difference, between the two. Furthermore, the lines conflate mounting and praying, so that one climbs this text by bending one's knees— stepping up by kneeling down. And as the book becomes heaven, so readers become mounters: one walks into the Bible as though it were not a text but a place; one walks into the Bible as into heaven. "The Holy Scriptures" eliminates, in other words, the sense of the text as "other." The distance between speaker—or mounter, or prayer—and text collapses so that one is no longer distinguishable from the next.

In the poem entitled "Aaron" a similar flattening is achieved, though here it is won at the end of a sequence of stanzas—which makes it possible to chart the path toward its accomplishment. In the first stanza of the poem the speaker describes the Old Testament figure, Aaron, who is dressed in priestly garments in Exodus 28:4ff.:

> Holinesse on the head,
> Light and perfections on the breast,
> Harmonious bells below, raising the dead
> To leade them unto life and rest:
> Thus are true Aarons drest.
>
> (ll. 1–5)

And in the second stanza he writes his own story—which is, point for point, a negative version of Aaron's:

> Profanenesse in my head,
> Defects and darknesse in my breast,
> A noise of passions ringing me for dead
> Unto a place where is no rest:
> Poore priest thus am I drest.
>
> (ll. 6–10)

These lines suggest that the speaker is already thinking in biblical terms, though the conclusion he reaches is that he and Aaron are essentially incompatible. The fact that the descriptions are paired only illustrates the speaker's emptiness. His story is the shadow of a story, its negative reflection.

In the third stanza, however, the speaker declares that he has, in addition to his own defective head, "another head / . . . another heart and breast" (ll. 11–12). This sense of access to Christ as another, better self, begins the migration of the self out of its bounded world and into a neighboring one. At this point, however, there are still two persons visible in the description: the speaker is one, and Christ is his second, his alternative self:

> Onely another head
> I have, another heart and breast,
> Another musick, making live not dead,
> Without whom I could have no rest:
> In him I am well drest.

(ll. 11–15)

This story adds a third story to the sequence—and like its predecessors it adds without changing the form of the story itself. Like the first two stanzas (and the last two) the lines of this one are bounded by the same set of end-words (head / breast / dead / rest / drest) as though to mark even more clearly the alignment, and the failure of alignment, among them.

In the fourth stanza, however, the second and third stories merge into one. Christ is no longer "another head." He is "my onely head." And the speaker's identification with him—an affiliation in stanza three, an equation in stanza four—strikes his old self, the self of stanza two, dead. This self is described as an "old man"—another, unregenerate, self—much as the rejected self at the end of "The Reprisall" is described as "The man, who once against thee fought" (l. 16). But in "The Reprisall" no new man appears, while here the death of the early self is simultaneous with its reappearance as a new man, dressed in Christ:

> Christ is my onely head,
> My alone onely heart and breast,
> My onely musick, striking me ev'n dead;
> That to the old man I may rest,
> And be in him new drest.

(ll. 16–20)

By the final stanza the identification of the self with Christ is complete. But if the fourth stanza rewrites stanza three (and therefore two), the last stanza rewrites them all—as a new version of stanza one:

So holy in my head,
Perfect and light in my deare breast,
My doctrine tun'd by Christ, (who is not dead,
But lives in me while I do rest)
Come people; Aaron's drest.

(ll. 21–25)

The self who disappears into Christ, eliminating his own, in-dependent appearance altogether, now appears not as Christ but as Aaron, and his story is virtually identical with the one that began the poem.

The speaker's identification with—and rewriting as—Aaron is illuminating, especially because Aaron is described, in the poem's first stanza, and in the Exodus chapter to which it refers (Exod. 28), as a man whose body is itself inscribed by God. Moreover the engraving on his head—which reads "Holy to the Lord"—is not a description of him. "Holy to the Lord" does not mean that Aaron is; it means that the offerings he will make to the Lord are. But even to say, simply, that the sign on his head describes something other than him is to un-derstate the case. For Aaron's priestly function demands that he "take upon himself any guilt" that attaches to the offerings he makes on behalf of his people. And so the writing on his head *must* not refer to him because it must refer to offerings, and it must not refer to him because he bears the guilt of others. The message is written on his head so that God will read it and not him.

In addition, Aaron bears the names of other persons on his breast. Light and perfections are there because Aaron "bear[s] their names before the Lord ... for remembrance" (Exod. 28:12); he insures their representation. Once again, when the Lord reads Aaron, what he sees is not Aaron's name but the names of the twelve tribes of Israel. Aaron's dressing is an elaborate undressing of Aaron the man and his redressing as a set of messages designed to be read by God. For true Aarons are not true simply because they are virtuous; they are true because they are dressed for the sake of others. Aaron's inves-titure—described in the Bible with remarkable precision—gives him a mode of presentation which is not a mode of self-

presentation at all. The manifest Aaron exists to point away
from himself; the names on his breast are not his names but
theirs. And so Aaron has an image, but the image he has is
designed to be read in his place and at his expense. Like the
speaker of the poem that bears his name, Aaron is a man who
dies to himself and reappears, rewritten, on behalf of others.
Thus are true priests dressed.

The reconstruction of the self as another is central to Herbert's "The Altar" as well; but here the defective self, who appears in stanza one of "The Bunch of Grapes" and stanza two
of "Aaron," has no existence at all. Only the regenerate
speaker appears in this poem, though what I want to suggest is
that he does not, except in fleeting glimpses, appear as a
speaker, or narrator, or articulator at all. Rather, he appears as
the ground upon which articulation proceeds:

> A broken A L T A R, Lord, thy servant reares,
> Made of a heart, and cemented with teares:
> Whose parts are as thy hand did frame;
> No workmans tool hath touch'd the same.
> A   H E A R T   alone
> Is   such   a   stone,
> As   nothing   but
> Thy pow'r doth cut.
> Wherefore each part
> Of my hard heart
> Meets in this frame,
> To praise thy name.
> That if I chance to hold my peace,
> These stones to praise thee may not cease.
> O let thy blessed S A C R I F I C E be mine,
> And sanctifie this A L T A R to be thine.

The broken altar is a work the speaking voice presents but
claims not to have made at all. He gathers the pieces into one
place and rears the altar, but says he has neither fashioned its
parts nor modified them. Nor, he insists, do they come together on their own behalf—they do not seem to have a behalf—rather they appear on behalf of another: to praise His

name. These disclaimers erode the notion of speaker as author, much as the penultimate lines separate the maker from the made thing ("That, if I chance to hold my peace, / These stones to praise thee may not cease" [ll. 13–14]).

But the crucial premise of the poem is the absolute *equation* that has been effected between the speaker's body and his verse (the stones of the altar are the pieces of his heart), crucial because it represents the complete collapse of the *distinction* between narrator and narrative work at once so powerful and so troublesome in "The Reprisall." By the time speech begins in this poem the speaker has disappeared entirely into the altar, so that the idea of narration as opposition, as a piece of work capable of stationing itself between the vulnerable speaker and his God, is inconceivable. And so is the idea of the speaker as autonomous agent, someone whose being can be stipulated apart from the things into which he is made. The disappearance of one into the other means the elimination both of the generative speaker and of the poem as his *production*.

What it certainly does not mean is the elimination of the poem. In fact, "The Altar" has greater physical presence than almost any other poem in *The Temple:* it is a stretch of language, it is a rearranged body, and it is also a fashioned object. But if its material existence is asserted with greater, not less, force, this only makes the point that the danger inherent in narrative production (a danger whose consequence, in other poems, is narrative collapse) is not a function of its materiality, but of its identification as the production of a narrator. In "The Altar" narrative work eliminates the *independent* narrator. It transforms the uneven voice of the person into the voice that fits a predetermined shape; it transforms person into icon. This is an altar because something is indeed being sacrificed—the speaking person as agent of his own appearance and maker of his own inscriptions.[5] The agent of this inscription is, of course, God. No workman's tool has touched the altar. Only God's power is great enough to move such stones as these. When the speaker suffers himself to appear as icon, to appear in the shape of something else, he has submitted to just the kind of redesign so often pointed toward, but so rarely seen in entirety, in Herbert's poems. No longer precisely a speaking man he appears before us cut, framed, rearranged, inscribed—a set of speaking stones.

"The Altar" is, like "Aaron" and "The Bunch of Grapes," a typological poem, but it eliminates the extrabiblical or unaligned appearance of the independent speaker whose collapse and reconstitution must then be enacted. Instead, what we witness in "The Altar" is a man already transformed into "the Hebrew altar which was built of unbroken stones . . . a type of the heart of man, hewn not by man's efforts but by God alone. The engraving on those stones with which 'all the words of this Law' were written 'very plainly' (Deut. xxvii. 8) was a type of the 'Epistle of Christ,' the message of salvation engraved on the Christian heart (2 Cor. iii. 3)."[6]

Barbara Lewalski has suggested that typology permits Herbert to establish a relationship with Scripture because it allows him to "personalize theology," to appropriate the biblical story and see himself as the stage upon which it is enacted: "Herbert's speaker makes these theological ideas radically personal, presenting himself as the anti-type of the Old Testament altar, his own heart as the altar which must be hewn by God, himself as the Church of the New Covenant which must be built by God, not man."[7] I have tried to suggest, instead, that a typological reading establishes the relationship of persons to Scripture by transforming entirely—not by conserving or valorizing—the idea of individual space. Typology does not "personalize theology"; it theologizes the personal, and makes unavailable the very notion of a "radically personal" account. In Herbert's typological poems persons do not appropriate and rewrite Scripture: Scripture appropriates and rewrites them.

But it is really more accurate to say that the competition between personal and scriptural stories is eliminated and that their unity is stressed in its place. Instead of merely revealing the deviant nature of the human text and *pointing* to its scriptural context, these poems present (in the case of "The Altar") or re-present (in the case of "Aaron") the text in biblical form. Moreover the speaker who makes the biblical story his own stops experiencing the distance, and the difference, between the two. In "The Bunch of Grapes" and "Aaron" the process by which two come to be understood as one is visible, but this only points to the fact that the discovery of their identity needed to be made. Of course it is made at the expense of personal stories independently conceived, and also at the expense of the idea that representation is a strictly literary matter. But in all of these poems the self's identity and continuity—with scriptural story and with salvation history—are, in the end, assured.[8]

And the fact that they are begins to suggest why typological poems can heal the doubleness that afflicts collapsing poems. In the latter, stories are always at odds with the present of the speaker who produces them: storytelling may look like an effort to represent experience in a truth-bearing way, but when the poem's end turns back upon the text it does so in an accusing fashion. Storytelling, it declares, is not an account of experience but rather a coercion, a deception, an interruption, a detour, an avoidance of experience. Furthermore, if the present is finally a "textless" one in collapsing poems, it is so because in them prior narration has been abandoned and speech in the present is unrecorded (confession in "The Reprisall"), or self-canceling ("Let me not love thee, if I love thee not" ["Affliction (I)"]), or extremely minimal ("*My Lord*" ["The Collar"]). And the story a collapsing poem tells is also problematic because it cannot contain the person whose work it is, but must, instead, be severed from him—so that the human text is, in the end, a work peculiarly empty of its author. He lives, instead, on the other side of representation—on the "margins of discourse," but not inside its boundaries.[9]

This summary description points to some central features of the human text in Herbert's collapsing poems: its alien character, its difficulty in representing persons or their experiences directly, its failure to unite storytellers and stories. But the description takes on special meaning when set against descriptions of the biblical text with which, in typological poems, human speakers align themselves. When Herbert describes the biblical text, "not as a naked Word severed from God, but as the Word of God,"[10] he points to the identity of the creator and the created thing, an identity sought, but rarely found, by human speakers—who lose control over the meanings of words, lose possession of them, cease to be represented by them. If God's "word is also his work,"[11] and if he is *in* that work, then the alienation of the maker from the made thing, a central fact in poems like "The Reprisall," is entirely absent from the biblical account with which the speakers of typological poems are affiliated. Man's work in collapsing poems is always his defective work and it *must* be severed from him. But God's work in the Bible is his *Word*.

This vision of the Bible as "the pure Word of God"[12] is tied, of course, to the dominant Protestant belief that Scripture needs no expositors. The Anglican apologist Jewel insists that the Bible is no "bare letter, uncertain, unprofitable, dumb, killing, and dead,"[13] a text whose barrenness must be filled by the living church in its intermediary role as "a lively expositor."[14] Rather, it is a *living* text whose true sense is immediately available, whose meanings are rendered vividly and directly. The elimination of official expositors is tied, in fact, to a set of interpretive principles which serves both to dislodge the Church's authority and to protect Scripture from unwarranted interpretation by its readers. The most central of these asserts that Scripture needs no interpretation because it has only one sense, and because that sense is available on the literal level. Here is William Perkins' description: "There is but one full and intire sense of every place in Scripture, and that is also the literal sense . . . To make many senses of the Scripture is to overturne all sense, and to make nothing certen."[15] And Luther put it this way: "Putting aside all human books we should steep ourselves in Scripture . . . we must recognize that Scripture is of itself most certain, simple, and open."[16]

These descriptions of the biblical text as simple, open, and clear, set it apart in essential ways from the human text as we have come to know it in Herbert's poems: despite its impulse toward transparency, the human text is persistently double, misleading, unstable, and in need of interpretation from without. For at least in collapsing poems, it either suppresses the signified or fails to have access to it altogether. The great pathos of these poems comes from the sense of powerlessness so often felt by the author who discovers, only as the poem concludes, his failure to know the meaning of the text he has created. These poems are neither open, nor clear, nor self-interpreting. In fact they demonstrate with great force the necessity, and the difficulty, of second readings. When interpreters look back upon their work they subvert the fiction that the literal meaning is the real meaning of the text—in the human story a necessary subversion—and they also suggest a realignment of meaning, redemptive in nature but unavailable to us as manifestation. Interpretation has, then, a central but a double role. It is the hero, because its work is redemptive, and it is the villain, because it collapses the fictions of clarity and sufficiency these poems are at pains to create.

When Calvin and Luther consider the problem of clarity in Scripture, in particular when they consider the arguments of those who point to Scripture's obscure or double nature, they do so only to insist, as Augustine had done before them, that the problem is essentially inauthentic: "The principles that I have described for the treatment of ambiguous pointing serve also for ambiguous constructions. For these also . . . are to be corrected according to the rule of faith, or according to the context established by the preceding and following passages; or, if neither of these is sufficient . . . whatever blameless interpretation the reader wishes may be used."[17] It is a simple matter, they declare, to establish the meaning of any passage in Scripture because the signification of all passages is *already known:*

> I admit . . . that there are many texts in the Scriptures that are obscure and abstruse, not because of the majesty of their subject matter, but because of our ignorance of their vocabulary and grammar; but these texts in no way hinder a knowledge of all the subject matter of Scripture . . . Now, when the thing signified is in the light, it does not matter if this or that sign of it is in darkness . . . Matters of the highest majesty and the profoundest mysteries are no longer hidden away, but have been brought out and are openly displayed before the very doors.[18]

In a sense what Luther suggests here is that we do not interpret Scripture in order to discover meaning—as though meaning were in question or might be missed. Instead, we read in order to bear witness to a meaning *already known in advance.* We read to see meaning made manifest before us.[19]

The notion of the Bible as a literal text makes Protestant exegesis a sort of nonexegesis—or at least it suggests that the goal of the exegete is to demonstrate the transparency of meaning, the availability of an unmediated relationship to a scriptural account that has, after all, only "one sense." It is his business, in other words, to demonstrate his own superfluity. According to the claims of the reformers, interpretation is neither an innovation nor a contribution[20]—as it is for the reader of a collapsing poem, who turns back on the text and "rereads" it in order to compensate for his own earlier failures to make sense of his experience.

Protestant exegesis also asserts that the Bible tells only one story (Christ's story; the history of salvation) in a single cumulative account all of whose events comprise a unified sequence and have a common meaning. Typological reading binds early events and figures (in the Old Testament) to later ones (in the New Testament) and reaches out to include unwritten history in the already written account. Typology demonstrates, once again, the unity and coherence of the biblical text, a coherence that depends on the fact that, as Luther suggested, "Scripture is its own interpreter, proving, judging, and illuminating everything."[21] Luther's statement describes the way that obscure portions of Scripture are illuminated by clear ones, but it also serves as a description of the way one Scripture story interprets another. The self-interpreting text (Calvin called it "self-validating")[22] is a text that glosses *itself:* one passage makes another clear; a second story illuminates and fulfills a first.

In his celebrated analysis of the figure/ fulfillment relationship Erich Auerbach suggested that "a connection is established between two events which are linked neither temporally nor causally—a connection which it is impossible to establish by reason in the horizontal dimension . . . The horizontal, that is the temporal and causal, connection of occurrences is dissolved; the here and now is no longer a mere link in an earthly chain of events, it is simultaneously something which has always been, and which will be fulfilled in the future."[23] But while Auerbach's definition insists on the historicity of the early event, his analysis, here and elsewhere, points to the subversion of chronological sequence that figuration enacts ("the temporal . . . connection of occurrences is dissolved"). It is, however, one of the extraordinary features of Protestant exegesis that it makes use of figural interpretation while asserting, at every step, that no subversion at all occurs when it is employed. In fact figuration itself becomes, for the Reformers, another way of reading on the literal level. In Luther's case, for example, to think one's way back into the pre-Advent situation is to realize that Old Testament figures are *literally* prophets of New Testament life. They give testimony to Christ's coming. As Paul Althaus suggests:

> In this Luther follows Paul who, in Romans 4, presents Abraham as the great example of true faith. And for both Luther and Paul, this faith of the fathers is not an essentially different or pre-Christian faith but, because Christ himself is already present in the Old Testament word of promise, genuine faith in Christ; it is the one and the same faith which the church today has. It is distinguished only by its "sense": that is, it differs in terms of its temporal relationship to the Christ incarnate in history. For the fathers it was faith in the promised Christ; for us it is faith in the Christ who has already appeared.   (p. 98)

And as James Preus has suggested, "For the Old Testament believer to be under the law and asking for Christ is the same as for the Christian to be in sin and asking forgiveness."[24] It is the purpose of exegesis, even (or perhaps especially) of typological exegesis, to declare that what looks like an interpretive *contribution* (a reader's discovery that Moses prefigures Christ or that Aaron prefigures him) is not really a contribution at all. Moses gives real (literal) testimony to the coming of Christ; and to understand him properly is to understand that his *literal meaning* is that he gives this testimony.

But typological interpretation does not simply connect Old Testament with New Testament events to produce a unified story: it connects contemporary history with biblical history, the unwritten with the written account. This alignment is necessary, since the idea that Scripture is the *one story* suggests, from the start, that alternative stories bear no truth: even the antithetical or uncontentious story is subject to alignment, and typology demonstrates, over and over again, the folly of imagining an exempt account. Auerbach puts the problem this way:

> The Bible's claim to truth is . . . tyrannical—it excludes all other claims. The world of the Scripture stories is not satisfied with claiming to be historically true reality—it insists that it is the only real world, is destined for autocracy. All other scenes, issues, and ordinances have no right to appear independently of it, and it is promised that all of them, the history of mankind, will be given their due place within its frame, will be subordinated to it. The Scripture stories do not . . . court our favor . . . they seek to subject us, and if we refuse to be subjected we are rebels.   (pp. 14–15)

Here, as elsewhere, the reader must establish his relationship to Scripture, but typology suggests that *relationships of difference must be overcome.* In particular, typology makes the category of the isolate human event an unnecessary one, and in its transformation of two separate accounts (the human and the divine) into one (the human under the auspices of the divine), it reduces the persistent doubleness of the human text. In typological poems there is no discrepancy between the story and the truth, for the text toward which the speaker moves and in which he finds himself represented, is the biblical text itself— so that insofar as the continuity between persons and Scripture is affirmed, self and sense find themselves, at last, united. If the speakers of collapsing poems have given up the only stories they have, the speakers of typological poems get their stories back. Instead of merely revealing the deviant nature of the human text, typological poems reinterpret that text and re-present it in biblical form. And because the alignment of

personal with biblical stories also narrows the distinction between them, it solves the problem of divided representation
with which we have been concerned.

But while persons in typological poems are no longer prevented from producing enduring stories, it is nevertheless the
case that the representation of *individual* persons never actually takes shape. In "Aaron" and "The Bunch of Grapes" the
rewriting of the self is accomplished and assured precisely because the self appears in the form of another. In "The Bunch
of Grapes" the speaker merges his journey with that of the Israelites; in "Aaron" the speaker is both dressed as another and
as one whose very body points away from the self in order to
represent others; and in "The Altar" the speaker appears in a
shape that is not his own at all. If collapsing poems make representation possible only by making it subject to recall, and
chronicles of dissolution make it possible by dismantling coherent images of the self, typological poems make representation possible by making the speaker's enduring account the
story of others rather than the story of the self.

NOTES

INTRODUCTION

1. *The English Works of George Herbert* (Boston: Houghton Mifflin, 1905), pp. xi–xii. Palmer's edition appeared in two versions—a three-volume set, and a large-paper edition in six volumes, limited to 150 copies. All citations are to the (lavish) six-volume edition.

2. "The Altar," l. 4, *The Works of George Herbert*, ed. F. E. Hutchinson (Oxford: Oxford University Press, 1941). All citations are to this edition.

3. William Empson, *Seven Types of Ambiguity* (New York: New Directions, 1966), p. 235. The first British edition appeared, as I have noted, in 1930.

4. Cf. Empson, p. 235: "But, of course, the phrase 'trying not to be ambiguous' is itself very indefinite and treacherous; it involves problems of all kinds as to what a poet can try to do, how much of his activity he is conscious of, and how much of his activity he could become conscious of if he tried."

5. Rosemond Tuve, *A Reading of George Herbert* (Chicago: University of Chicago Press, 1952), p. 23.

6. Cf. Tuve, pp. 31–32: "This is a valuable activity, and it is only too bad that it is generally accompanied by implications that this meaning is 'the meaning', and that one may praise the (original) author for it. One should praise rather the critic, who is the author of another and different poem—

and why should he not be? The more good poems in the world the better. But he should acknowledge his paternity."

7. Tuve even argues with the division of science from poetry characteristic of much New Critical thinking. "The self-defeating antipathy to 'science' among exponents of a poetic world-view is," she declares, "precisely as dangerous as its parallel, the assumption by arrogant empiricists of the completeness of their own view of reality" (p. 107).

8. Joseph Summers, *George Herbert: His Religion and Art* (Cambridge, Mass.: Harvard University Press, 1954; reprinted, 1968), p. 27.

9. Summers' sources here are H. J. C. Grierson, *Metaphysical Lyrics* (1912); George Williamson, *The Donne Tradition* (1930); and Joan Bennett, *Four Metaphysical Poets* (1934).

10. L. C. Knights' 1944 essay on Herbert, reprinted in *Explorations: Essays on Criticism Mainly on the Literature of the Seventeenth Century* (New York: New York University Press, 1964), is an example of the sort of criticism to which Summers points. Knights argues, for example, that "Herbert's poetry was for him very largely a way of working out his conflicts. But it does not, like some religious poetry, simply *express* conflict; it is consciously and steadily directed towards resolution and integration" (p. 138). Knights stresses the "positive direction" of Herbert's poems (p. 147) and speaks of the "mature 'acceptance' " (p. 144) which characterizes their endings. He suggests, furthermore, that the poems are "important human documents because they handle with honesty and insight questions that, in one form or another, we all have to meet if we wish to come to terms with life" (p. 148). In many respects Knights' position anticipates Arnold Stein's. In *George Herbert's Lyrics* (Baltimore: The Johns Hopkins University Press, 1968) Stein argues that "Herbert's lyrics are the expression of a complex and subtle mind, uniquely aware of itself and its fertile deceptions, yet trusting the depths of feeling, and trusting his own power to invent and order imaginative explorations of personal experience" (p. viii). Stein also declares that the poems "are imaginative expressions by which the poet confronts and attempts to master his own life or death" (p. 210).

11. Stanley Fish, *Self-Consuming Artifacts: The Experience of Seventeenth-Century Literature* (Los Angeles: University of California Press, 1970), pp. 157–158. Unless otherwise noted, all citations to Fish are to this work.

12. It should be noted, however, that Fish's reader is not an idiosyncratic or wildly subjective reader; indeed, he is a member of a community himself. But his community is rather unlike those imagined by his predecessors. It is neither as comprehensive as Tuve's (whose members share the Judaeo-Christian values of Western civilization) nor as uniform (and democratic) as Summers'. Fish's communities are "interpretive communities" comprised of persons who share a set of conventions for interpreting texts, and whose consolidation is at once "real" and "fragile." See "Interpreting the *Variorum*," *Critical Inquiry*, 2 (Spring 1976), 483–484.

13. Fish, pp. 383–384. Fish takes over for his own purposes the language used by W. K. Wimsatt and Monroe Beardsley in their well-known essay

"The Affective Fallacy." See *The Verbal Icon: Studies in the Meaning of Poetry* (Lexington: University of Kentucky Press, 1954), p. 21.

14. Helen Vendler, *The Poetry of George Herbert* (Cambridge, Mass.: Harvard University Press, 1975), p. 4.

15. See Richard Strier's useful analysis of Vendler's "Romantic conception of the poem as process" (p. 81) and what he calls her "expressive theory" of poetry in " 'Humanizing' Herbert," *Journal of Modern Philology*, 74 (August 1976), 78–88. Vendler's interest in the way the poem moves through stages toward the uncovering of personal truths is, indeed, central to her enterprise, and she does claim that "an expressive theory of poetry suits *The Temple* best" (p. 5). But Vendler's interest is always, at the same time, an interest in the business of aesthetic creation. Indeed, her disagreements with Arnold Stein are a function of her belief that *Stein's* is the expressive theory, and that he is more interested in Herbert's "personality" or "humanity" than in Herbert's poems. Despite the fact that both critics value Herbert's complex relation to his own materials and value his honesty in exploring them, Vendler argues that Stein's position attends to human feeling at the expense of poetic form. "When the man is the focus of attention," she argues, "his forms seem merely inheritances from his age, the sometimes regrettable accidents of a rhetoric bewitched into eccentricities" (p. 202). Stein asserts that in "poems like 'A Wreath,' 'Sinnes round,' 'The Call,' and 'Trinitie Sunday,' the expressive elements are severely limited, as the obstacles created by strict form take over the oppositions normally furnished by individual thought and feeling" (p. 154) and Vendler replies that "To think of 'strict form' as offering only 'obstacles,' to suggest that such 'obstacles' preclude 'individual thought and feeling,' to conclude that such poems must seem 'cold and thin'—this expressive theory can scarcely accommodate poets of Herbert's sort" (p. 203). It is my view that Vendler and Stein both "humanize" Herbert, for both stress the centrality to his work of certain traditionally humanistic values. But Vendler sees Herbert as a craftsman and poet working consciously toward the refinement of his own works of art, while Stein sees Herbert as "a poet in whom the desire to understand and to relate is the commanding passion" (p. 97). The obligation to openness which writing places upon poets can, Stein feels, be problematic and limiting. "All true lyric poets," he declares, "stand naked behind their enabling fictions, behind the cultivated deceptions of verbal art. They are not satisfied by the superficial discoveries of ordinary candor but search for the deeper points of personal understanding, or revelation, which will not yield themselves to direct ways of thinking or saying" (p. 210).

16. Barbara Kiefer Lewalski, *Protestant Poetics and the Seventeenth-Century Religious Lyric* (Princeton: Princeton University Press, 1979), p. ix.

17. Cf. William Empson, "George Herbert and Miss Tuve" in the "Communication" pages of *Kenyon Review*, 12 (1950), 735–738. The anecdote quoted here appears on p. 736.

18. In *The Living Temple: George Herbert and Catechizing* (Los Angeles: University of California Press, 1978) Fish again makes use of a dialectical

model, but he does not explain its relationship to the model put forward in *Self-Consuming Artifacts*. In fact, the dialectic seems to have reversed itself: the speaker believes that there is "work to be done" but discovers at the poem's end that the "work [is] already done" (chapter two). The beginning of the poem is, in other words, open and uncertain, and the end is stable and secure. This reversal of positions appears to reflect a change in Fish's theoretical stance. He continues to argue that poems are "events" in the reader's experience rather than formal objects, but he also believes that the appearance of the text is a "real" appearance because all discourse is "serious" (Cf. "How to Do Things with Austin and Searle: Speech Act Theory and Literary Criticism," *MLN*, 91 [1976], 1022). For a fuller analysis both of Fish's argument and of its relationship to his theoretical position, see my review of *The Living Temple* in *Comparative Literature*, 33 (Spring 1981), 197–202.

19. Cf. Michel Foucault, "What Is an Author?" in *Textual Strategies: Perspectives in Post-Structuralist Criticism*, ed. Josué V. Harari (Ithaca: Cornell University Press, 1979), p. 154, and Edward W. Said, *Orientalism* (New York: Vintage Books, 1979), p. 13. Foucault is interested in what he calls the "discursive practice" and the "discursive field" (p. 156) and he argues that it is "not . . . enough to repeat the empty affirmation that the author has disappeared . . . Instead, we must *locate the space* left empty by the author's disappearance" (p. 145; my italics). But although Foucault asks "where there is room for possible subjects" and "who can assume these various subject-functions," there has been, at least until quite recently, a strong sense of fatalism in his work. For "behind all these questions," he declares "we would hear hardly anything but the stirring of an indifference: 'What difference does it make who is speaking?' " (p. 160). It is for this reason that Edward Said's analysis seems to me both more satisfying and more persuasive. Said speaks of combining "the already-familiar with the fertile novelty of human work in language" (*Beginnings: Intention and Method* [New York: Basic Books, 1975]), and refers to the "interplay between the new and the customary without which . . . a beginning cannot really take place" (p. xiii). Unlike Foucault—in whose work the power of institutions renders feeble, or inaudible, the human voice ("What difference does it make who is speaking?")—Said asks, "how can we treat the cultural and historical phenomenon . . . as a kind of *willed human work* . . . in all its complexity, detail, and worth . . . ?" (*Orientalism*, p. 15). "I do believe," he continues, "in the determining imprint of individual writers upon the otherwise anonymous collective body of texts" (p. 23).

20. The term is Stephen Greenblatt's. See *Renaissance Self-Fashioning: From More to Shakespeare* (Chicago: University of Chicago Press, 1980). In his introduction Greenblatt makes a statement with which, as this chapter suggests, I fully agree: "there are always selves—a sense of personal order, a characteristic mode of address to the world, a structure of bounded desires—and always some elements of deliberate shaping in the formation and expression of identity." Greenblatt also argues that "there is in the early modern period a change in the intellectual, social, psychological, and aes-

thetic structures that govern the generation of identities. This change is difficult to characterize in our usual ways because it is not only complex but resolutely dialectical" (p. 1). Greenblatt's period is the sixteenth century, but his statement holds true for Herbert's period—and Herbert's poems—as well.

21. As I suggested earlier, Summers is also interested in the materiality of Herbert's poems, but in Summers' view monuments are sundered from their creators and they enter the world as embodiments of a nonpersonal order—as objects and emblems, but not as embodiments of the self.

1. "SO DID I WEAVE MY SELF INTO THE SENSE"

1. Whether the language of poems is conceived as "speech" or as "writing" (in Herbert's poems sometimes one, and sometimes the other, is stressed), the issue remains the same. The use of language for the purposes of self-presentation is what interests me here. (See Greenblatt, p. 9: "self-fashioning is always, though not exclusively, in language.")

2. *The Complete Poetry of John Donne*, ed. John T. Shawcross (New York: Doubleday, 1967). All citations from Donne are to this edition.

3. *The Human Condition* (Chicago: University of Chicago Press, 1958), p. 198. In general, Arendt uses this phrase to describe that which "comes into being whenever men are together in the manner of speech and action." She also distinguishes—as I do not—the space of appearance from "spaces which are the work of our hands," because the space of appearance "does not survive the actuality of the movement which brought it into being" (p. 199). But when writing is understood to be a "space of appearance" the "peculiarity" to which Arendt points must be reconsidered—for writing *does* survive its moment of generation. It conserves, however problematically, the reality that would *otherwise disappear.*

4. See Joan Webber, *The Eloquent I: Style and Self in Seventeenth-Century Prose* (Madison: University of Wisconsin Press, 1968). Although Webber draws sharp distinctions between the way poets and prose writers represent themselves (distinctions to which I do not subscribe), her analysis of the "I" of the seventeenth-century prose writer is relevant to Herbert's work. "By seventeenth-century literary self-consciousness," she declares, "I mean the writer's crucial and unremitting awareness that he is the subject of his own prose, whether or not he is literally writing autobiography" (p. 4). Her analysis of the relationship between "style and self" appears on pp. 3–14.

5. Cf. Webber, p. 12: "Given his degree of self-consciousness, [the writer] is always aware of the possibility that he is only holding the pen because he wants his words to be read, of the possibility that they will be read whether he so desires or not, of the possibility that they ought to be read (from which, or before which, arises the question of whether they are good enough to be read, or whether he ought to be engaging in this kind of activity at all). On the one hand, he claims to have no desire to publish, pretends

to be completely unaware of an audience; on the other hand, he prepares the manuscript for its readers as carefully as he can."

6. "Literary self-consciousness, then, includes consciousness of self as subject, in all the richness of the self as product and maker of his age; consciousness of self as style and thereby as a way of linking subject with object." Webber, p. 4.

7. See the complex and paradoxical analysis of this poem in the introduction to *Too Rich to Clothe the Sun: Essays on George Herbert*, ed. Claude J. Summers and Ted-Larry Pebworth (Pittsburgh: University of Pittsburgh Press, 1980), pp. xi–xii: "One of Herbert's supreme accomplishments is to make art of the very artifice he disavows, as in the numerous poems on poetry. Central to this process are his recognition of the inherent pridefulness of poetry and the deceptiveness of artifice and his juxtaposition of heavenly and earthly perspectives. In 'Jordan (II),' for example, if 'Nothing could seem too rich to clothe the sunne' (l. 11), that is because the ambitious task of describing the splendors of the Son in the artifice of language is impossible and the attempt prideful. Christ's whisper . . . rejects not only decorated language and poetic ingenuity but the pretentiousness inherent in the poet's inevitable weaving of himself 'into the sense' (l. 14)." But Summers and Pebworth continue: "Paradoxically, however, the recognition of the impossibility of clothing the sun yields art richer than the artificiality of 'quaint words, and trim invention' (l. 3), though that recognition is itself the culmination of such artifice . . . But by coupling audacious ambition to an awareness of inevitable failure, he unmasks what may in the heavenly perspective be only a poor wreath to expose what is from the earthly viewpoint truly a crown of praise."

8. Fish distinguishes the speaker of the end of Sidney's first *Astrophel and Stella* sonnet from the speaker of the end of "Jordan (II)": "one is advised to call on his own resources; the other is reminded that his resources are not his own." Fish continues: "The solution imposed (not chosen) by this poem, or by the voice that enters to preempt it, is . . . not the plain style, but no style at all and, in a way, silence. By copying out what is already there one speaks in the words of another, and therefore, to the extent that speech is an assertion of self, does not speak" (p. 199). Lewalski argues against Fish's "anti-aesthetic" this way: "plainness is not a renunciation of art but an affirmation of its divine source and its biblical standard" (p. 228). In her view the poem's final lines indicate "that God's art (already penned in the Scripture, in his heart) is the proper model to be copied, and that it affords its own poetic sweets" (p. 227). Lewalski is right to argue that the end of the poem does indeed point to a new kind of writing—but I am arguing that the writing it points to never appears in the course of the poem itself.

9. Cf. Stein, p. 21. Stein views the poems about writing poetry as expressive of Herbert's understanding that verbal art *always* deceives: "Herbert sharpened his own sense of style and language against the duplicities of thought and language; though these duplicities were known to him as a cultivated, reflective man, they were most intimately known through his expe-

rience as a practicing poet." I am suggesting, instead, that the speakers of these poems *desire language*, but that often they cannot hold on to it.

10. "The essential 'act' is that the individual should abandon the pretence that he *can* act in any way pertaining to salvation: he must experience the full realization that salvation belongs to God, that nothing he can do either by faith or works can help. The doctrine is, moreover, 'comforting,' for 'all things' are 'more ours by being his.' " Summers, p. 61.

11. Cf. Fish, pp. 175–176: "The proper response to the dilemma the poem poses is discovered to be not action, mental or physical, but humility and self-abnegation . . . The speaker of 'The Holdfast' wants nothing more than to do good, but he is frustrated in his resolve by the supererogatory goodness of God which is so extensive that it finally claims responsibility not only for the deeds that are done but for the impulse to do them." Fish's analysis is to the point—but his reading suggests that the only form of representation available to speakers is direct self-representation. I am suggesting that the indirect representation to which we are pointed in the final lines is at once problematic and saving.

12. Cf. Vendler, p. 148: "It is a crushing burden to put on oneself—to reinterpret in a personal, and personally acceptable, way every conventional liturgical and religious act: to make devotion always singular, never simply communal; to particularize, not to merge; to individuate, not to accede." But the "Good Friday" sequence, whose speaker begins by asking how he might write Christ's story, ends as that story's object—not its agent.

13. Stein values poems whose solutions pass beyond "the cultivated deceptions of verbal art" (p. 210) and he therefore values endings like this one: "It is not an answer that [like the one proposed at the end of "Jordan (II)"] can be copied, for it requires *man* to be a kind of new creator every day" (p. 24). It is indeed the case that the poem's ending requires this of the speaker, but I am here arguing that, because his activity has no representation, the ending is also a problematic one.

14. "The Dedication" to Vaughan's *Silex Scintillans*, modeled on Herbert's poem of the same name, provides clear evidence of the difference between the two writers:

> My God, thou that didst dye for me,
> These thy deaths fruits I offer thee.
> Death that to me was life, and light
> But darke, and deep pangs to thy sight.
> Some drops of thy all-quickning bloud
> Fell on my heart, these made it bud
> And put forth thus, though, Lord, before
> The ground was curs'd, and void of store.
>
> (ll. 1–7)

Vaughan's dedication is not concerned, as Herbert's is, with questions of authorship and ownership, nor with pointing to the (ultimate) division of persons from poems, and the consequent competition between the two.

Vaughan begins with the premise that his labors are all a consequence of Christ's sacrifice, and he concentrates on the positive outcome of that fact: Christ died for him; these poems are the fruits of that death; they quicken the poet and he "put[s] forth thus" (where "thus" indicates the poems on the page). Indeed the competitive spirit of Herbert's dedication poem, and the competitiveness of collapsing poems generally, distinguishes Herbert's poetry from Vaughan's. Vaughan does not first imagine an independent self (wedded to the text but separate from God) only to discover, as Herbert often must, the self's problematic implication in divine plots. Rather, Vaughan imagines a self already joined with Christ, and his poems are characterized by the absence of precisely those distinctions between self and other, inside and outside, peculiar to collapsing poems. See *The Complete Poetry of Henry Vaughan*, ed. French Fogle (New York: Doubleday, 1964). All citations are to this edition.

15. Summers cites the "Dedication" poem as evidence of the fact that "personal experience [was] of interest to the poet only in so far as [it] could be profitably used in the objective creations which were his poems." The "sharp distinction between his poems and himself" which Herbert makes in the "Dedication" "still warns the reader" (pp. 84–85). But Summers points to the separation without first pointing to the identification of persons and texts with which this poem—like so many of Herbert's—begins.

16. The phrase is Greenblatt's, p. 1.

17. The vexed nature of writing and representation toward which I here point is, in my view, central to poetry of this period. Even for a writer like Robert Southwell, known for his simple piety, the project of writing religious verse is described in unusually complex terms. In "The Author to his loving Cosen" Southwell declared: "And because the best course to let them see the errour of their workes, is to weave a new webbe in their own loome; I have heere layd a few course threds together, to invite some skillfuller wits to goe forward in the same, or to begin some finer peece, wherin it may be seene, how well verse and vertue sute together. Blame me not (good Cosen) though I send you a blame-worthy present, in which the most that can commend it, is the good will of the writer, neither Arte nor invention, giving it any credite." See *The Poems of Robert Southwell, S. J.*, ed. James H. McDonald and Nancy Pollard Brown (Oxford: Oxford University Press, Clarendon Press, 1967), pp. 1–2. All citations from Southwell are to this edition.

2. COLLAPSING PERSONAL STORIES

1. Collapsing poems are not peculiar to Herbert (though he is, I think, the most complex practitioner of the mode). Sidney's *Astrophel and Stella* sonnets (numbers 1 and 2, and number 71, for example) are clear predecessors, and, like Herbert's poems, they give us a speaker self-conscious, and critical to a fault, about the process of the poem's production. Shakespeare's *Sonnets* also provide us with numerous instances of reversal and collapse, though in Shakespeare the poem's end is sometimes a place in which restoration and

renewal occur ("For . . . / Then I scorn to change my state with kings," Sonnet 29, ll. 13–14; "all losses are restored, and sorrows end," Sonnet 30, l. 14) and sometimes a place in which reversal brings dissolution and disruption ("This thought is as a death, which cannot choose / But weep to have that which it fears to lose," Sonnet 64, ll. 13–14). See *Shakespeare's Sonnets*, ed. Stephen Booth (New Haven: Yale University Press, 1977). All citations are to this edition. Donne's love lyrics often collapse too as the speaker describes situations and relationships that cannot, he discovers, be maintained. In "Lecture upon the Shadow" his lovers stand at "the high'st degree" (l. 12) but "loves day" is declared a "short" one (l. 24) and the poem ends this way: "Love is a growing, or full constant light; / And his first minute, after noone, is night" (ll. 25–26). The final lines of "The good-morrow"—"If . . . thou and I / Love so alike, that none do slacken, none can die"—undercut, as well, the description the speaker is at pains to create. And "Womans constancy" demonstrates the fact that the very speaker who desires stability may find himself inconstant in the end. In the poems I point to here stories generally suffer collapse when the threatening world around them cannot any longer be held at bay. But in Herbert's poems what threatens the security of the self is not only knowledge of the world, it is Christian knowledge as well, so that in his poems, as in religious poetry generally, the discovery of one's proper context is at once threatening and saving. In Southwell's "The burning Babe," for example, the shivering speaker is confronted with "sodaine heate" (l. 3) in the form of a burning babe who makes "his hart to glow" (l. 4) but whose presence he does not understand. Christ speaks in the middle stanzas (three through six) and the speaker returns in stanza seven to speak in his own voice. In one sense it might be said that Christ's voice is framed by the speaker's in this poem, but the real framing device is one which does not appear until the poem's end:

> With this he vanisht out of sight,
>   And swiftly shrunk away,
> And straight I called unto my minde,
>   That it was Christmasse day.
>
> (ll. 29–32)

The poem's occasion, its mysterious occasion until the end, is Christ's birth. The shivering speaker of the beginning of the poem is cold because he has forgotten this, and his discovery both threatens our sense that he is a competent speaker and restores him to a different—and improved—kind of competence.

2. Numerous examples might be cited of poems in which speech is identified with self-construction. In Sir Thomas Wyatt's lyrics speech is often, in fact, the only sign of a speaker's value. The abandoned man of "They Flee From Me" uses speech as a means of self-preservation and self-conservation in a world which would forget him if it could. The erosion of personal identity is compensated by speech in the first stanza, and in the second stanza

speech is the means by which the speaker *resurrects* his lost past: "Thanked be fortune it hath been otherwise / Twenty times better, but once in special . . ." (ll. 8–9). (See *Sir Thomas Wyatt: The Complete Poems*, ed. R. A. Rebholz [New Haven: Yale University Press, 1978].) Donne's love lyrics are also relevant here for their identification of speech with the very creation of selves and others. "The good-morrow" suggests that, prior to relationship, the world is virtually inconceivable ("I wonder by my troth, what thou, and I / Did, till we lov'd" [ll. 1–2]) and it also suggests that speech is a way of invoking, and inscribing into the world, the valuable present ("And now good morrow to our waking soules, / Which watch not one another out of feare; / For love, all love of other sights controules; / And makes one little roome, an every where" [ll. 8–11]). Moreover in Donne's poem the eroding powers of the world outside threaten both at the start and at the finish. The final lines suggest (as I have already indicated) that the poem celebrates relationship in a world in which, as Donne's poems demonstrate throughout, relationships are notoriously unstable. In Donne and Wyatt, of course, the causes of dissolution are, as already mentioned, personal and social, while in Herbert dissolution has Christian origins. But in all of these examples— and, I would argue, in poems of this period generally—the use of speech for the purpose of generating possibilities, and of generating selves, is central, and it is central precisely because, in one form or another, the stability of selves is in question.

3. *Beginnings*, p. 24.

4. *The Sense of an Ending: Studies in the Theory of Fiction* (Oxford: Oxford University Press, 1966), p. 49.

5. I am indebted throughout this section to Edward W. Said's *Beginnings*, in particular to the second chapter, "A Meditation on Beginnings," whose insights inform my own.

6. *Poetic Closure: A Study of How Poems End* (Chicago: University of Chicago Press, 1968), p. 208.

7. Jean Starobinski, in "The Inside and the Outside," writes: "A living organism exists only by virtue of the margin . . . through which it determines, defines and opposes itself, becoming individual: limit, finiteness, individuality, the struggle waged against the outside—all these are correlative. No inside is conceivable, therefore, without the complicity of an outside on which it relies . . . No outside would be conceivable without an inside fending it off." (*Hudson Review*, 28 [1975], 342.)

8. "Ariadne's Thread: Repetition and the Narrative Line," *Critical Inquiry*, 3 (1976), 66–67.

9. *Frame Analysis: An Essay on the Organization of Experience* (New York: Harper & Row, 1974), pp. 308–309.

10. *Seventeenth-Century English Poetry: Modern Essays in Criticism*, ed. William R. Keast (Oxford: Oxford University Press, 1971), pp. 251–252.

11. "Forum," *PMLA* (October 1979), p. 946.

12. "George Herbert's 'Redemption,' " in *Essential Articles for the Study of*

George Herbert's Poetry, ed. John R. Roberts (Hamden, Conn.: Archon Books, 1979), p. 506.

13. Christ's story remains hidden until the last quatrain of the sonnet. Like the frame stories of most collapsing poems, its appearance—especially when compared to the speaker's story—is kept to a minimum.

14. Cf. Said, p. 205: "The text's preserving and obstructing and displacing functions are taken as resisting rewriting (which is what hermeneutical interpretation is at bottom), but the beginning premise of this rewriting is that the text's resistance is principally a formal matter."

15. *The Poetry of Meditation: A Study in English Religious Literature* (New Haven: Yale University Press, 1970), p. 133.

16. Fish does not actually discuss "The Collar," but his readings of poems like it suggest what his analysis might look like.

3. AUTOBIOGRAPHY AND BEYOND

1. *OED*, "Entice." The meaning of the word records both innocent and duplicitous intentions.

2. *OED*, "Crosse-bias."

3. For an interesting parallel, see Sidney's *Astrophel and Stella*, sonnet 2. In the octet the speaker describes, meticulously, the process by which he came to love Stella—intending to demonstrate to his readers that he is in complete control of himself and of his feelings. In the sextet, however, he distinguishes the present from the past and reveals his true situation:

> Now even that footstep of lost libertie
> Is gone, and now, like slave-borne *Muscovite*,
> I call it praise to suffer Tyrannie;
> And now employ the remnant of my wit,
> To make my selfe beleeve that all is well,
> While with a feeling skill I paint my hell.

Sidney's "now," like Herbert's, marks not only the discrepancy between past and present, but between two different versions of *the same* experience and two radically disjunct visions of the self. For as the final lines of the sonnet suggest, the story of lines 1–8 exists rather to "make [the] self believe that all is well" than to represent the truth—so that the "now" of line 9 (and of line 12) marks that moment when the speaker reveals not only that he is a slave, but also that he always was. See *The Poems of Sir Philip Sidney*, ed. William A. Ringler, Jr. (Oxford: Oxford University Press, Clarendon Press, 1962).

4. In *The Poetry of Meditation* Louis Martz minimizes the impact of reversing conclusions by suggesting that the speaker of a collapsing poem is "in firm control throughout" (p. 133), already "understands the situation thoroughly," and "knows from the outset how the rebellion must be, and will be, quelled" (p. 135). In Martz's view Herbert's poems are meditations

and knowledge of the end is always implicit in the beginning of a meditational sequence. The purpose of such a sequence is still, of course, didactic, but the implication is that the meditator learns some *new* lesson from his *old* experience (thereby arming himself against future occurrences), not that he is still subject to the calamity wrought by the poem's end. Following in Martz's footsteps, William Halewood, in *The Poetry of Grace: Reformation Themes and Structures in Seventeenth-Century Poetry* (New Haven: Yale University Press, 1970), described suppression of the known ending as a "device" necessitated "by the explicit plan of such a sequence," since "dramatized reconciliation can come only out of dramatized opposition" (p. 84). The purpose of the drama is, again, didactic: the speaker, already master of the experience of the past, must now become master of its lessons.

Rosemond Tuve took early exception to Martz's notion, insisting that there was "something unlike Herbert in the picture of a poet manipulating tensions to a predetermined end." "They were sins to him," she added, "keeping his Savior on the rack." Tuve was not simply reading the poems differently; she was objecting to the suggestion that Herbert's speaker is in control of his subject matter, that he has the kind of distance required to teach himself a lesson, that he has mastery. Designed to illustrate the seriousness of Herbert's method, Martz's position invented for Tuve a problem about Herbert's sincerity. She made, instead, this distinction: "truth to an experience which led to an end is not the same as driving conflicting elements with steady hand towards a known end" ("Herbert and Caritas," in *Essays by Rosemond Tuve: Spenser, Herbert, Milton,* ed. Thomas P. Roche [Princeton: Princeton University Press, 1970], p. 181, n. 9). In Tuve's mind reversal is not simply a device but a great manifestation of fidelity: the speaker who reports his experience still suffers from it; he tells the story because he has not fully overcome it.

5. "The Storyteller: Reflections on the Works of Nikolai Leskov," in *Illuminations* (New York: Schocken Books, 1973), p. 100.

6. Donne's "Good Friday, 1613. Riding Westward" provides an interesting parallel and, at the same time, an interesting counterexample, to Herbert's "Affliction (I)." In both poems speech is prior to, and in many respects incompatible with, relationship. Donne's speaker says that his "Soules forme bends toward the East" (l. 10) but of course he rides westward—away from Christ. As the final lines indicate, he imagines a time in which, corrected and cleared of deformity, his image will be restored and he will "turne [his] face" (l. 42), but that moment of face-to-face encounter with Christ is one toward which the end of the poem only points. In other words, the speaker tells his story as he turns *away from God,* and speech is both prior to relationship and identified with its absence. Moreover, the speaker of "Good Friday" appears in a "deform[ed]" state and he speaks *to* Christ only with his *back* turned toward him—so that speech is identified not simply with Christ's absence but also with the speaker's sense of himself as defective and his words as insufficiently direct. Like the speaker of "Affliction

(I)," for whom speech is possible only as long as his knowledge of God's wishes is suspended, the speaker of "Good Friday" finds that speech is possible precisely because its object is behind, rather than before, him. Of course Donne's speaker *courts* indirection—he rides westward fully conscious of the fact that it *is* Good Friday and that he is headed the wrong way, while Herbert's speaker, in "Affliction (I)" and elsewhere, tells the story he tells *in order to preserve the fiction* that he has direct access to speech. In both poets storytelling is possible when relationship with God is suspended, postponed, misplaced, or suppressed, but in Donne postponement is the occasion for indirect storytelling, in Herbert the occasion for producing *fictions* of direct accounts.

7. Geoffrey Hartman, "I. A. Richards and the Dream of Communication," in *The Fate of Reading and Other Essays* (New Haven: Yale University Press, 1975), p. 36.

8. Geoffrey Hartman, "The Voice of the Shuttle: Language from the Point of View of Literature," in *Beyond Formalism: Literary Essays 1958–1970* (New Haven: Yale University Press, 1970), p. 348.

9. "The Avoidance of Love: A Reading of *King Lear*," in *Must We Mean What We Say?: A Book of Essays* (New York: Charles Scribner's Sons, 1969), p. 284.

10. See Psalm 31 (trans. Coverdale): "I am cleane forgotten as a dead man out of mind: I am become like a broken vessel."

11. In Shakespeare's sonnets about writing sonnets a similar conflict—between the desire to write poems that embody the self (or the beloved) and the desire to relinquish such representations—is explored. The sonnets often refer to poetry's powers of conservation and preservation (Sonnets 65 and 107 are well-known examples) and they assert that in poems, rather than in "tyrants crests and tombs of brass" (Sonnet 107, l. 14), the beloved shall "find [his] monument" (l. 13). But it is also the case that what is monument in one poem is breath or spirit in another. In Sonnet 74, and again in 81, poems have the capacity to conserve persons precisely insofar as men *read* them, and in reading them "rehearse" (Sonnet 81, l. 11) the beloved's being. The conservation of persons is turned over, that is, to *readers*, who, in reciting poems, bring those represented in them back to life. If the poem is a monument, it is a "gentle" (l. 9) monument—for its immaterial nature, its character as speech rather than writing, and its changeful, dependent status are what Shakespeare finally stresses. In Part Two (chapters 4 and 5) I shall return to the idea that it is possible to speak without making monuments to the self, and without telling either coherent—or fixed—stories about the self.

12. Geoffrey Hartman, "Christopher Smart's *Magnificat:* Towards a Theory of Representation," in *The Fate of Reading*, p. 97.

13. See Robert Scholes and Robert Kellogg, *The Nature of Narrative* (Oxford: Oxford University Press, 1966), p. 215: "Inevitably, once an autobiography continues beyond the moment in which the author comes to terms

with his vocation, its interest turns outward and its form becomes open-ended." This is, of course, precisely what happens from ll. 55–66 of "Affliction (I)." While the obligation to continue beyond the natural resolution is, in Herbert, an obligation imposed by God, it bears a direct relation to the open-ended autobiography: both return to life-in-the-making, where representation is at best difficult, meanings uncertain, fictional coherence gone.

14. "Conditions et limites de l'autobiographie," in *Formen der Selbstdarstellung: Analekten zu einer Geschichte des literarischen Selbstportraits,*" ed. Günther Reichenkron and Erich Haase (Berlin: Duncker & Humblot, 1956), p. 107. Translations from the French are mine.

15. *British Autobiography in the Seventeenth Century* (London: Routledge and Kegan Paul; New York: Columbia University Press, 1969), p. 15.

16. *Design and Truth in Autobiography* (Cambridge, Mass: Harvard University Press, 1960), p. 9.

17. *Versions of the Self: Studies in English Autobiography from John Bunyan to John Stuart Mill* (New York: Basic Books, 1966), p. 11.

18. The difference between Herbert's "spiritual autobiographies" and those modeled on Augustine's *Confessions* is instructive. In Augustine, confession proceeds out of the assumption that the old, unregenerate self and the new, redeemed self are radically disjunct, and that speech is, at least in part, the celebration by a new self of the death of an old one. But if Augustine's is a conversion narrative, a story about a critical "turning around" (Book 8, chapter 7), his conversion is not the *final* moment in the story. Augustine is already converted when narration begins, and his entire account is the work of a man who knows his proper audience, knows his own history, and knows himself. Conversion, knowledge, and consciousness are the beginning points of narration, and the story comes to us already interpreted in light of the end from which it really begins. In other words, Augustine's tale is not so much written as rewritten. His infancy and boyhood, for example, are not presented as he experienced them in the past, but rather as he sees them in the redeemed present in which he writes. And so while the *Confessions* is, on the one hand, a narrative about radical change, it is also, on the other, a remarkably *unified* account. The context in which Augustine has come to live overwhelms entirely his earlier reality so that the former has, by the time his narrative begins, no independent identity at all. Instead, reality is a literary reconstruction interpreted for us by a scripturally conscious, redeemed man. Herbert shares with Augustine (as with St. Paul) a passionate interest in the conversion narrative and it appears in his work— as the poems in Part One suggest—in a variety of shapes. But in "Affliction (I)" the conversion moment is hidden from the reader, and the speaker is, moreover, incompletely converted when he begins his account. Complete conversion does not occur until the poem's final lines, but when it is achieved it does not authorize speech—it puts speech to an end. In other words, consciousness and conversion do not initiate narrative, they eclipse it. In fact in Herbert's poems confession itself is often a nonliterary activ-

ity—it takes narration apart—instead of a preeminently literary one, as it is in Augustine.

4. "NO CONTINUING CITTY"

1. The words are all, in one form or another, Donne's. See *Deaths Duell* in *John Donne: Selected Prose*, chosen by Evelyn Simpson, ed. Helen Gardner and Timothy Healy (Oxford: Oxford University Press, Clarendon Press, 1967), pp. 382–383. All citations are to this edition.

2. See Fish, p. 165: "The first three lines are replete with distinctions, distinctions of times, persons, objects, spaces, and actions. The body is distinguished from the soul and both from the heaps of dust with which they are bid take acquaintance. The words on which the syntax pivots are 'While' and 'Here,' time and place markers respectively. Even less essential words, like 'repairs' and 'betimes,' contribute to the strong impression of local identities, separable objects, discrete and specifiable monuments. Yet no sooner have these demarcations been established and assumed a kind of reality in the reader's mind, than the process of undermining them begins."

3. Cf. Fish, p. 167: "One *spells* correctly when one *discerns* the indecipherability of the text; discerning is *'sure'* only when the object of discernment dissolves; *'signes'* signify properly only when they become indistinguishable from their surroundings . . ."

4. See also Fish, p. 168. Fish suggests that the question itself "is as much the object of irony as are the markers whose dissolution it predicts; for the very basis for asking a question—for rational prediction in general—is taken away when the phenomena to which the question would direct our attention will not stay put and are, in fact, in the process of disintegrating."

5. *Sir Thomas Browne: Selected Writings*, ed. Sir Geoffrey Keynes (London: Faber and Faber, 1968), pp. 150–151. All citations are to this edition.

6. See Fish's analysis of lines 20–22 on p. 169: "As before, the referents of the relatives expand so that for the second 'which' the reader understands not only 'time,' but 'glasse,' 'flesh' . . . and even 'measures,' all of which have been crumbled into dust. With this in mind, the final gesture of the first-person voice is more than a little suspect:

Mark here below.

Mark where? and with what? and in what? 'Mark' follows immediately upon 'dust' . . . and the juxtaposition of the two words undermines the pointing motion of the imperative, leaving the reader to look at one more example of 'dustie heraldrie.' "

7. Fish argues that in this passage Donne has offered his auditor a "mnemonic device" (p. 44), a "floor plan" (p. 45) for his sermon, in order to suggest to him that he will have "a manageable experience" (p. 46). But the re-

sult, Fish argues, "is precisely the opposite of what we are here encouraged to expect: an uncomfortable and unsettling experience in the course of which the understanding is denied the satisfaction of its own operations" (p. 47). Moreover, the unsettling of expectations and "the disabling of the forms of rational thought" is Donne's goal throughout the sermon. It is his intention, Fish argues, to replace the auditor's confidence in rationality with his confidence in memory, not the "memory of places and distinctions," as we first thought, "but the memory of God's mercy, the Christian memory whose emergence into full and exclusive prominence is the shape of our experience" (p. 65). Here, as elsewhere in his analysis, Fish concentrates on the way the sermon undermines what he calls, alternatively, "our normal modes of discursive response" (p. 60), " 'the rare devices of man's brain' " (p. 58; the phrase is Milton's), and "the expository mechanisms of rational discourse" (p. 60), until the auditor loses confidence both in the sermon's ability to "organize and manage its materials," and in his own ability to do so. Fish continues: "Indeed it would not be an exaggeration to say that understanding, or the possibility of understanding, is what the sermon is finally 'about' " and Donne acknowledges this when he "enjoins us from further 'considering' " (p. 63). Fish's point is that the sermon becomes, as a Herbert poem often does, "the vehicle of its own abandonment" (p. 158). I shall argue, on the contrary, that Donne's purpose is to explore the problematics of bodily life, to demonstrate the ways of dissolution, and to assert, finally, that disembodiment is something we must both practice and perform, that it is, in fact, a mode of *being* in the world.

8. In the early pages of *Urne-Burial* Browne speaks to this problem when he suggests that cremation destroys all evidence of the shape of the human body and "leave[s] us ignorant of most personall discoveries. For since bones afford not only rectitude and stability, but figure unto the body; It is no impossible Physiognomy to conjecture at fleshly appendencies, and after what shape the muscles and carnous parts might hang in their full consistences" (p. 140). He also reminds us of the importance of conserving bodies when he suggests that, "according to learned conjecture, the bodies of men shall rise where their greatest Reliques remain" and points out that, because of this, "many are not like to erre in the Topography of their Resurrection . . ." (p. 141).

9. See Vaughan's interesting meditation on this subject in "Distraction." He first pleads with God to "Knit me, that am crumbled dust!" (l. 1), but he perceives his state as problematic because "I find my self the lesse, the more I grow" (l. 10). Unlike the speaker of Herbert's "The Temper," who begs for stability and security and wishes that he were whole, Vaughan's speaker understands that wholeness is a dangerous, if tempting, state—and he worries about all evidences of its presence:

> But now since thou didst blesse
>   So much,
> I grieve, my God! that thou hast made me such

(ll. 24–26)

because

> . . . left alone too long
>   Amidst the noise, and throng,
>   Oppressed I
> Striving to save the whole, by parcells dye.

(ll. 31–34)

Of course "striving to save the whole" is, I am arguing, the practice in which Herbert engages in collapsing poems. It is also the practice whose relinquishment is chronicled in poems about the dissolution of the body. Insofar as Herbert succeeds, his work and Vaughan's bear a resemblance to each other, for despite the claim at the end of "Distraction," Vaughan's poems rarely labor to save the whole. They are, instead, concerned to describe the dissolution of boundaries between wholes—between the self and God, the self and the biblical text, the self and its own past incarnations.

10. Browne finds it hard to imagine the being that could "unwish it self, content to be nothing, or never to have been, which was beyond the *male-content* of *Job*, who cursed not the day of his life, but his Nativity: Content to have so farre been, as to have a Title to future being; Although he had lived here but in an hidden state of life, and as it were an abortion" (p. 149).

11. I am inclined to say the same thing of Browne's *Urne-Burial*. Browne relinquishes the body in ecstasy at the end of his essay, but only after fully having imagined and explored the body's possibilities.

12. See also Vaughan's "The Lampe":

> But whensoe're I'm out, both shalbe in,
> And where thou mad'st an end, there I'le begin.

Mark Cap. 13. ver. 35

Watch you therefore, for you know not when the master of the house commeth, at Even, or at mid-night, or at the Cock-crowing, or in the morning.

13. Cf. Jeremy Taylor, *The role and exercises of holy dying* (1651), p. 5, quoted by Nancy Lee Beaty in *The Craft of Dying: The Literary Tradition of the Ars Moriendi in England* (New Haven: Yale University Press, 1979), p. 261: "and while we think a thought we die; and the clock strikes, and reckons on our portion of Eternity; we form our words with the breath of our nostrils, we have the lesse to live upon, for every word we speak."

14. Cf. Summers, p. 132: "Only three lines of the poem come to a full stop, and nine of the twenty-four lines are followed by no punctuation. Many of the semi-cadences indicated by the punctuation, moreover, prove illusory: the syntax demands no pause, and the commas serve as fairly arbitrary directions for a slight voice rest, obscuring rather than clarifying the simple 'prose' meaning." See also Fish, p. 166: "Units of meaning that seem complete in themselves are unexpectedly revealed to be only the introductory clauses in a larger utterance, an utterance whose scope finally expands to include the whole poem."

15. Herbert's poems, and Donne's sermon, are part of the tradition of "the art of dying" described by Beaty. In her discussion of Jeremy Taylor's *Holy Dying* Beaty remarks: "To begin with, the word *dying* does not refer exclusively to the death scene. Taylor . . . rejects the notion that this closing scene differs qualitatively from the others in the drama of a Christian life, and he strengthens his position with the Stoic argument that all life is a progressive dying . . . *Holy Dying* does not present man as first alive and then dead, in an abrupt dichotomy of simple analysis. Rather, Taylor's Moriens rushes precipitously to his grave, dying momently in accordance with Seneca's axiom" (p. 216). Beaty's point, here and elsewhere, is that dying is something one does in the course of one's life, that "to live well" is "really to die well" (p. 220), "to grow in spiritual strength even as [one] declines in physical vigor" (p. 223), that *"dying* is indeed synonymous with *living"* (p. 217). Dying well is a "practice" (p. 208) and since "no man can achieve perfect love and obedience through a single dramatic conversion experience, the Way of the Cross becomes a daily acknowledgment of Christ as Lord, a daily repentance before Christ as Judge, and a daily dying to sin and rising to new righteousness through trust in Christ as Redeemer" (pp. 219–220).

16. Vaughan puts before us, in "The Author's Emblem (of Himself)," a vision of the self "broken in pieces" and asks us to "Look at it . . . !": "Look, its fragments are flashing at last to heaven and to you, and my cheeks are wet with tears wrung from flint . . . By dying I have gained new life: amidst the wreckage of my worldly fortunes, I am now richer than ever" (p. 137). In the Latin original the phrase "Moriendo, *revixi"* (dying I live) makes the point succinctly. Herbert's poems are not, as Vaughan's are, ecstatic about the fact that to die well is to live truly, but they do learn this lesson and they do practice it.

17. The phrase is, of course, Vendler's. See especially chapter two of *The Poetry of George Herbert,* "Alternatives: The Reinvented Poem."

5. THE DISSOLUTION OF BODIES AND STORIES

1. I suggest that the hill toward which the speaker moves in this poem is "a mystery," and that the content of his "expectation" is as well. The reader may know that the "gladsome hill" is Mt. Zion (and that the speaker there expects his salvation), but the fact remains that the absence of a name for the hill points to a problem which is really the poem's theme: on this journey none of the conventional knowledge we bring with us is really of much use at all. Mt. Zion may be the name of the gladsome hill, but the poem opens up for question—and leaves open as question—the very meaning of getting to Zion. What, after all, is Mt. Zion? Is it the Jerusalem of this world, a geographical place to which we might go? Or the Jerusalem of the next world, a heavenly city through whose gates we will not pass in this life? Even if, at the beginning, we read "hill" and see "Zion" we will still be igno-

rant of the answers to these questions, for the speaker does not himself understand the meaning of his journey. He is barred, as the reader is, from knowledge not of sources, but of the *meaning* and *import* of sources. Since I am interested in the way speakers represent their experiences, the poem's curious (I would say mysterious) beginning, and the absence of reference to Zion in the opening lines, are indeed of importance to me—but they remain of interest precisely because the poem's subject continues to be the impossibility of having certain knowledge either of worldly or of other-worldly things. I do not ever want to suggest that readers come to poems without knowledge of sources, but I do want to continue to ask how, and in what ways, this knowledge comes into play—how it is used by speakers, how they make sense of it, when it is accessible or inaccessible to them, how they interpret it.

2. Joseph Summers calls this "the Scylla and Charybdis of the Christian life" (p. 174).

3. See William Empson's analysis of this stanza in *Seven Types*, pp. 129–131.

4. Helen Vendler argues that "the poem attempts the rhetoric of pilgrimage, but abandons entirely the ascending tone of increasing faith which normally makes allegory close with Piers becoming Christ or trumpets sounding on the other side" (p. 94). This is certainly true, and the absence in the poem of a transfiguring end is a central fact of its existence. But Vendler also speaks of "the conquering of allegorical narrative by lyric dialogue" (p. 97) in the last lines of the poem—suggesting that the expression of feeling with which the poem concludes points to the speaker's personal triumph. I agree with Vendler's first point, but not with her second. The absence of ends—there is no "ascending tone" because the speaker does not arrive at his destination—leaves the allegorical hero in difficult circumstances. He does not triumph over, but is rather the victim of, them.

5. Barbara Lewalski argues that "the death of the carnal nature is a requisite to the growth and final perfecting of the regenerate life in Christ" (p. 89), but while this poem may point to perfection it does not *portray* it.

6. In *Allegory: The Theory of a Symbolic Mode* (Ithaca: Cornell University Press, 1964), Angus Fletcher points out that "for allegorical heroes life has a segmented character, and as each event occurs a new discrete characteristic of the hero is revealed, almost as if it had no connection with prior events or with other tied-in characteristics" (p. 35). Fletcher's description is an interesting one for it points to the way in which the dissolution of self is characteristic of allegorical life. See also Gay Clifford, *The Transformations of Allegory* (London: Routledge and Kegan Paul, 1974). Clifford describes the allegorical hero as "an instrument whereby systems can be explored" (p. 23).

7. See Summers, p. 175: "The pilgrim has not reached the end of his journey at the end of the poem, for no man can describe the end except by means of a dream; but in his willingness to lose his life, we are assured that he will find it." Summers, like Vendler, points out that the poem ends with-

out causing its hero to be transfigured, but he suggests that the hero will nevertheless *be* transfigured in the future (he "will" find his life). My point is precisely that no dream is described in the poem, and that the speaker's recovered life is therefore not represented in it.

8. In "*La Cousine Bette* and Allegorical Realism," *PMLA*, 86 (1971), 241–254, Fredric Jameson points to an interesting contrast between the introspective moment—which he identifies with the novels of James and Proust, but which would serve, equally, to identify the meditative, personal lyrics of Donne and Herbert—and the allegorical moment: "Introspection . . . presupposes that consciousness, the personality, is a stable unit, comprehensible in itself; in other words that the individual life has a certain unity about it, can stand alone as a complete thing, is no longer felt as a mere part that must be seen in the light of the whole to have any meaning. The belief in the autonomy of the individual consciousness corresponds, therefore, to a moment of social development . . . in which life is felt primarily as a matter of the individual destiny, in which the private seems able to be separated from the public or social as a mode of being in itself" (252). Allegory, on the other hand, suggests that "life, rather than consciousness, is the predominant category: it focuses, therefore, not on the individual existence or personality, but on the universal, the racial, the collective; and sees the feeling of individuality as a kind of illusion, the realities of life as those of the universal genetic forces themselves" (253). Clifford points to the same thing, declaring that "the principal aims of an allegorist cannot be originality and subjectivity, though he may attain these as incidental felicities . . . If as well as being imaginative the objectives of a work are social . . . then subjectivity and originality, in the sense of the work being quite unlike anything written before, are hindrances. They prevent the general application of a particular narrative from being seen" (pp. 122–123). Allegory eliminates the notion that persons and events have original or independent life (the institutional character of meaning is the point of allegory) and specifies instead that they are features of the interpretive scheme that produces them. And so in place of a world in which lyric discourse represents a coherent self whose existence is prior to system—a notion which governs the production of accounts in autobiographical poems like "Affliction (I)" and "The Collar"—allegory proposes a world in which persons appear as aspects of systems and not as separate creations.

9. *The Pilgrim's Profession: Or a Sermon Preached at the Funerall of Mrs. Mary Gunther* (London, 1622), pp. 103–105. Cited by Lewalski, p. 94.

10. Cf. Leo Bersani, *A Future for Astyanax: Character and Desire in Literature* (Boston: Little, Brown, 1976). Bersani's texts are more recent than mine, but his questions are unusually appropriate to the poems I am examining here: "Can a psychology of fragmentary and *dis*continuous desire be reinstated? What are the strategies by which the self might once again be theatricalized? How might desire recover its original capacity for projecting non-structurable *scenes?*" (pp. 6–7). Bersani looks forward to the possibility that we might abandon the "need for preserving the intelligibility of a psychic structure"

along with the need for preserving those "continuities and coherent patterns of desire which condemn [us] to a life of repetition" (p. 4). Herbert's speakers seem, on the whole, considerably less enthusiastic about the dissolution of coherent visions of the self, but in "The Pilgrimage," and in the poems I shall examine next, limiting definitions of individuality are precisely what speakers must relinquish. See also Rosemond Tuve, "Herbert and Caritas," p. 201. Tuve points to a distinction (Augustine's) between "the love that 'uses' and the love that 'enjoys', between the good and lovely things which we pilgrims see on our journey and cannot *rest in* but rather love 'as referred to' or 'according to' or 'in' their yet lovelier author—between these, and God, whom alone we are able to take joy in as the end of our being" (italics mine). The inability to rest in what we see is characteristic of the poems I here analyze.

11. Fish refers to "The Temper," but his description serves as an analysis of "Artillerie" as well.

12. Fish quotes, on p. 158, Sir Thomas Browne's *Religio Medici*, I, 53.

13. See Vendler's extended discussion of this poem on pp. 48–54. My reading resembles Vendler's in certain respects, but I hope to make clear as I proceed the ways in which our readings differ.

14. Cf. Fish, p. 166: "Units of meaning that seem complete in themselves are unexpectedly revealed to be only the introductory clauses in a larger utterance, an utterance whose scope finally extends to include the whole poem." Fish is referring to "Church Monuments," not "The Flower," but the aptness of his statement suggests the ways in which the latter poem resembles the former.

15. For a contradictory opinion see Martz, *The Poetry of Meditation*, p. 311: "The word 'grief' . . . is erased; along with the storms and frosts which have provided the basic imagery for dozens of stanzas scattered throughout the whole preceding portion of the 'Church.' Instead, we have now the dominant image of the flourishing flower, to replace the image of the 'blasted,' 'wasted' plant which has so often dominated earlier poems . . ." I am suggesting that *no* single image finally dominates, that the poem is, in fact, *about* the impossibility of establishing with sureness any single image.

16. Arnold Stein suggests that "all of the complex human awareness of self is concentrated at one point: the difficulty of feeling oneself to be the same person in the morning of joy as in the night of grief, though both extremes derive from God" (p. 200).

17. In this respect, as in many others, Herbert's religious lyrics differ from Donne's. In the *Holy Sonnets* Donne regularly imagines two extremes: he presents, in "Batter my heart," the self armored against God—where God is he who must break down, by violent and illegal action, all resistance to relationship; and he portrays, in "Thou hast made me," the self in a state of complete dissolution, unable to "sustaine" itself for a single hour, and capable of relationship only by intervention. In both poems we are presented with a speaker as he appears prior to and in the absence of relationship, where relationship would at once save, and annihilate, the self as we know

it. Donne does not, in these poems, portray the self *in relationship* to God as Herbert does in the poems I have been analyzing in chapters five and six. Even in "Good Friday, 1613. Riding Westward," where the speaker does not find himself in an extreme or threatening situation, he is nevertheless able to speak to Jesus precisely because his back is turned upon him. See my discussion of Donne's "Good Friday" in chapter 4, note 6.

18. Fish claims that "to stop saying amiss is not only to stop distinguishing 'this' from 'that,' but to stop distinguishing oneself from God, and finally to stop, to cease to be. Learning to 'spell' in these terms is a self-diminishing action in the course of which the individual lets go, one by one, of all the ways of thinking, seeing and saying that sustain the illusion of his independence, until finally he is absorbed into the deity whose omnipresence he has acknowledged (thy word is *all*)" (p. 157). But we must be careful to note that Herbert's speaker says, "Thy word is all, *if* we could spell" (italics mine) and it seems perfectly clear that he cannot spell—though in some sense he wishes he could.

CONCLUSION

1. *The Arte of English Poesie*, ed. Gladys Doidge Willcock and Alice Walker (Cambridge: The University Press, 1936), p. 215.

2. See Ira Clark's application of Puttenham in " 'Lord, In Thee the *Beauty* Lies in The *Discovery*': 'Love Unknown' and Reading Herbert," in *Essential Articles for the Study of George Herbert's Poetry*, ed. John R. Roberts (Hamden, Conn.: Archon Books, 1979), pp. 473–493.

3. See Alan Charity, *Events and Their Afterlife: The Dialectic of Christian Typology in the Bible and Dante* (Cambridge: The University Press, 1966), p. 153.

4. *The Eclipse of Biblical Narrative: A Study in Eighteenth- and Nineteenth-Century Hermeneutics* (New Haven: Yale University Press, 1974), pp. 27–28.

5. Here I take issue with Stanley Fish, who argues that "The Altar" is a poem with a "double motion." The speaker begins, Fish says, by asserting agency and control (the poem's shape is just such an assertion) and ends by relinquishing his claims "to both the form and the effects of his art" (p. 212). While this is often what does happen in Herbert's poems it is not, I am arguing, what happens here. It is my contention that the "impression [the poem] makes as a verbal object" does not "fly in the face of Herbert's self-sacrificing aesthetic" (p. 215) at all, but rather that it is the supreme example of a self-sacrificing aesthetic. The shape is never (not even at the start) an assertion of agency. It is an illustration of what happens when agency and the *capacity to appear in one's own shape* have already been relinquished.

6. Summers, pp. 141–142.

7. "Typology and Poetry" in *Illustrious Evidence: Approaches to English Literature of the Earlier Seventeenth Century* (Los Angeles: University of California Press, 1975), p. 46.

8. Herbert's relationship to God's voice, and to biblical stories and events,

differs in important ways from that of Donne and Vaughan. As I have already suggested above, poetic speech in Donne occupies the space prior to relationship and prior to direct engagement with God's word, with his countenance, with those events which commemorate and celebrate his presence in the life of Christian persons (for example, Good Friday). Even In "Hymne to God my God, in my sicknesse," where the speaker considers his relationship to the first and the last Adam and imagines his body as a flat map on which, because "West and East / . . . are one, / . . . death doth touch the Resurrection," he describes his action in the poem as anticipation:

> I tune the Instrument here at the dore,
> And what I must do then, thinke here before.
>
> (ll. 4–5)

In death, the speaker imagines, the first and the last Adam will join—but they do not, it seems, join before that. Critics generally acknowledge that Donne's poems are not predominantly typological in orientation, but I would argue that this is because they do not portray the meeting of the personal and the divine but rather portray persons as they exist prior to such meetings. Of course if there is no possibility of encountering God directly in Donne's poems, there is no possibility of *not* encountering him in Vaughan's. Even in poems like "The Search," in which the speaker goes on a journey "to find [his] Saviour" (l. 5), the poem's structure points to *the impossibility of not finding him:* the speaker searches the Holy Land in vain, is interrupted in his thoughts by a voice that tells him to look indoors rather than out, and concludes his search with a quotation from Acts which declares not that Christ is in us but rather that we are in him. Moreover as the poem blurs the relationship between outsides and insides it also blurs the relationship between past and present, and between personal and scriptural voices. It begins in the present (" 'Tis now cleare day"), moves into the past ("I have been / As far as *Bethlem*" [ll. 5–6]), moves back into the present ("It is day" [l. 65]), declares its present retrospect ("But as I urg'd thus" [l. 67]), and is finally interrupted by an outside voice ("Leave, leave, thy gadding thoughts" [l. 75]) before even that voice is displaced by the scriptural one at the poem's end. The dissolution of boundaries between past and present, outside and inside is, in this poem, simultaneous with the dissolution of distinctions between personal and biblical texts. (Vaughan's rewriting of scriptural passages is, one suspects, a sign of the fact that he barely recognizes the Bible as "other.") In some sense, Herbert's poems might be said to mediate between the positions occupied by Donne and Vaughan. In collapsing poems speech exists prior to the speaker's encounter with God's voice, or with God's text, or with his events, though the ends of collapsing poems do indeed point (as Donne's poems often do) to their meeting. In poems about the dissolution of the body Christian knowledge is brought to the center of the discourse, but these poems concentrate on the dissolution of the personal as it meets the divine, rather than on the reconstitution of the self (or the text) in divine form. In Herbert's typological poems, however, this reconstitution is exactly what we see: in some poems we watch the personal being rewritten as a biblical story, in others we watch the biblical story displace the personal altogether.

9. The phrase is Barbara Herrnstein Smith's.

10. See "Briefe Notes on Valdesso's *Considerations,*" in Herbert's *Works,* pp. 306-307.

11. See *The Cambridge History of the Bible: The West from the Reformation to Today,* ed. S. L. Greenslade (Cambridge: The University Press, 1963), vol. 3, p. 20.

12. Horton Davies, *Worship and Theology in England: From Cranmer to Hooker, 1534-1603* (Princeton: Princeton University Press, 1970), vol. 1, p. 13. Davies reminds us that the Reformation was described as a reformation " 'according to the pure Word of God,' " and that "the 'purity' of the Word of God was always contrasted with the impurity of the traditions of men."

13. Davies, p. 16. Davies quotes from Jewel's *Apology.*

14. When John Rogers (martyred in 1555), translator of the "Matthew Bible," was interrogated by Stephen Gardiner, "Gardiner stressed the intermediary rôle of the living Church: 'No, thou canst prove nothing by Scripture, the Scripture is dead, it must have a lively expositor.' Rogers replied, 'No, the Scripture is alive.' " See A. G. Dickens, *The English Reformation* (New York: Schocken Books, 1964), p. 132.

15. "A Commentarie Upon Galatians" (Cambridge, 1604), quoted in Barbara K. Lewalski, "Typological symbolism and the 'Progress of the Soul' in Seventeenth-Century Literature," in *Literary Uses of Typology: From the Late Middle Ages to the Present,* ed. Earl Miner (Princeton: Princeton University Press, 1977) p. 81.

16. *Cambridge History,* p. 22.

17. *On Christian Doctrine,* trans. D. W. Robertson (Indianapolis: Bobbs-Merrill, 1958), Book 3, chapter 3.

18. "The Bondage of the Will," in *Luther and Erasmus: Free Will and Salvation,* ed. E. Gordon Rupp and Philip S. Watson (Philadelphia: The Westminster Press, 1969), pp. 110-111.

19. See Calvin's *Institutes of the Christian Religion,* Book 1, chapter 6, section 2: "For by his Word, God rendered faith unambiguous forever, a faith that should be superior to all opinion." See *John Calvin: Selections from His Writings,* ed. John Dillenberger (Missoula, Mont.: Scholars Press, 1975).

20. See Whitaker's *Disputations on Holy Scripture,* quoted in Lewalski, "Typological Symbolism," p. 82: "When we proceed from the sign to the thing signified we bring no new sense, but only bring out into the light what was before concealed in the sign."

21. *Cambridge History,* p. 22.

22. Paul Althaus, *The Theology of Martin Luther* (Philadelphia: Fortress Press, 1966), p. 98.

23. *Mimesis: The Representation of Reality in Western Literature*, trans. Willard R. Trask (Princeton: Princeton University Press, 1953), p. 73.

24. *From Shadow to Promise: Old Testament Interpretation from Augustine to the Young Luther* (Cambridge, Mass.: Harvard University Press, Belknap Press, 1969), p. 172.

INDEX